CommunicAsian

The rise of Asia has changed the world, now shaped by greater global connectivity, geopolitics and shifting spheres of influence. Tapping into research and decades of experience in the world's fastest-moving markets, this book makes a compelling case for a new and future-ready approach to communications planning and implementation, which the Asian Century demands.

Facing a new operating environment, policymakers and business leaders have to act quickly. This book outlines the necessary adjustments to long-established practices and value propositions in both corporate and government communications and provides a step-by-step plan for strategy development, laid out in a two-pronged approach designed to appeal to a multicultural audience.

It is an essential read for global practitioners and students in international relations and mass communications.

Oliver Stelling is an independent advisor with 25 years of experience in corporate and government communications across Asia. He served as Country Manager, Regional Director and Head of Strategy for global networks in China, Malaysia, Singapore and the United Arab Emirates. His main focus is on East–West relations, strategic communications and public diplomacy.

CommunicAsian

How Asia's Rise Is Shaping the Future of Communications, and How to Plan for It

Oliver Stelling

LONDON AND NEW YORK

Designed cover image: © Getty Images

First published 2023
by Routledge
4 Park Square, Milton Park, Abingdon, Oxon OX14 4RN

and by Routledge
605 Third Avenue, New York, NY 10158

Routledge is an imprint of the Taylor & Francis Group, an informa business

© 2023 Oliver Stelling

The right of Oliver Stelling to be identified as author of this work has been asserted in accordance with sections 77 and 78 of the Copyright, Designs and Patents Act 1988.

All rights reserved. No part of this book may be reprinted or reproduced or utilised in any form or by any electronic, mechanical, or other means, now known or hereafter invented, including photocopying and recording, or in any information storage or retrieval system, without permission in writing from the publishers.

Trademark notice: Product or corporate names may be trademarks or registered trademarks, and are used only for identification and explanation without intent to infringe.

British Library Cataloguing-in-Publication Data
A catalogue record for this book is available from the British Library

ISBN: 978-1-032-47333-8 (hbk)
ISBN: 978-1-032-47334-5 (pbk)
ISBN: 978-1-003-38562-2 (ebk)

DOI: 10.4324/9781003385622

Typeset in Bembo
by SPi Technologies India Pvt Ltd (Straive)

To Donna

Contents

Disclaimer		ix
Preface		x
Acknowledgments		xii
	Introduction	1
1	Decoding the Asian Century: How the Bet on Modernization Paid Off	4
2	Communication vs. Communications: All That Makes Us Human	20
3	Purpose and Shared Values: Communications' Best Engagement Model	32
4	Whatever We Imagine: From Aspiration to Inspiration	44
5	Looking for Polaris: How to Tackle the Global Disinformation Crisis	59
6	Public Diplomacy: Leveraging the Strong Side of Soft Power	72
7	Human Capital: Winning with New Talent Strategies	91
8	AI and Big Data: Enrolling Technocracy in Communications	103

9 Shenzhen Speed and Dubai Spirit: Engineering the
   Asianization of Communications   116

10 ACCESS and BEAT: Two Ways to Develop Future-Proof
   Strategies   128

   Epilogue   140

   Bibliography   142
   Index   145

Disclaimer

Some of the topics discussed in this book first appeared in published bylines and on my website, though never in the full context as outlined here. The majority of arguments and conclusions are original to *CommunicAsian* and all expressed opinions are mine, except for quoted contributions and attributed references to books, research pieces, surveys and news articles.

Despite its focus on Asia and communications, the book is meant to be neither some kind of travelogue nor a "PR for PR" exercise. The objective is to make the case for a new and more future-oriented approach to public relations in a fast-changing world. This cannot be done without also addressing some failed tactics plus the rise of mis- and disinformation. The sole purpose is to reveal the inherent risk of one-sided communication, not to expose the individuals behind them.

None of the references to Asians are supposed to portray billions of people as being impossible to distinguish. The term "Asian" is used to emphasize instances where the cultures in that vast region spanning 48 nations are comparable to one another yet different from Western countries in their historical, social and political context.

Since every communications strategy must be developed with a view of the particular circumstances and corporate strategy or policy goals, none of the thoughts and suggestions shared here are intended to replace deep research and analysis. Success or failure ultimately depends on the specific conditions and individual efforts to achieve all set goals. Neither the publisher nor the author shall therefore be held liable for any loss or damage allegedly arising from any guidance contained in this book.

Preface

July 2022 marked a quarter century of my work and life in Asia. Having been granted a front-row seat to the rapid rise of this vast megaregion has been a priceless experience. Observing diverse cultures and subcultures, forms of governance and business environments broadened my personal and professional outlook and made me rethink the role of communications in the wider context of geopolitics, economics, big tech and diplomacy. That is what inspired this book, while the Covid19 pandemic is what ultimately made it happen. Due to sudden border closures and prolonged flight cancellations, my wife Donna Stelling and I were forcefully separated for 24 months. It was tough, but as the saying goes, never let a crisis go to waste. As strange as it may sound, connectivity looked rather different for two years plus. But the lockdowns during Covid19 also opened new doors for more intense conversations – first on Zoom and later in the real world. As the pandemic dragged on, I chose to capture my thoughts on Asia's rise, global connectivity and its impact on communications.

CommunicAsian addresses the most sweeping transformation that communications is facing in decades. The operating environment for professionals is marked by an intensified and more global battle of narratives and shifting spheres of influence and perceptions. Yet the broader collective impact does not always seem to be fully recognized. Some practitioners appear as being devoted to a supportive role instead of pursuing full decision-making power; a mindset shift that could secure much better results. That surely isn't the case for the industry's most visionary and experienced leaders. But for those who prefer to hold on to the approach that served them well for decades, the future will be much less predictable.

When communicators head for the development of future-proof strategies, one major step is to adjust mindsets and take a deeper look at the highly complex and dynamic settings, reputational risks and gains as well as principles and values that are more likely to resonate globally. Besides, taking a stand on global issues is becoming more crucial. Mastering this with insight, foresight and flexibility requires the recognition of and adapting to greater global connectivity. Being one of the main change makers of our age, it facilitates more dialogue among cultures, which is a redeeming feature. But it also exposes the global community to worldviews many people are unfamiliar with; a fact that often causes outright rejection instead of a dedication to step up efforts to effectively manage this new state of affairs.

This book aims to dislodge routine preconceptions, calling to mind the role of purpose in communications and public diplomacy, regardless of time and place. Informed by personal experience, on-site research and countless private and public conversations, the conclusions may surprise readers. The goal has been achieved when openness to innovation inspires new thinking that leads to some soul-searching and self-questioning of long-held beliefs and idiosyncratic outlooks. If that ignites a more inclusive take on research, planning and implementation, then communications – arguably one of the most significant cultural techniques of our time – will be future-ready, and my Covid19 break will have delivered something useful. Happy reading!

Oliver Stelling
November 2022

Acknowledgments

I would like to express my deep and sincere gratitude to everyone who endorsed this project right from the start. I am particularly grateful to friends, colleagues, scholars and practitioners as well as media across Asia, Australia, Europe and the United States for sharing their opinions on the future of communications and Asia's rise. That also includes those who conveyed their private views without the intent of being quoted here. I certainly appreciate their insights too.

I also wish to thank Lucy Batrouney and Georgia Oman of Routledge/Taylor & Francis Group; Yassar Arafat of the Straive production team; and my copyeditor Matthew Van Atta for their great support and guidance in completing my book.

My special thanks go to all who contributed their comments:

Simon Anholt, independent policy advisor, author and founder of The Good Country Index, for sharing his broad and thoughtful analysis on nation branding, communications and public diplomacy.

Fares Ghneim, Partner of Dubai's analytics and technology consultancy firm AnaVizio, for his views on the future of data analytics in the PR industry.

Parag Khanna, Founder and Managing Partner of Climate Alpha and global strategic advisory firm FutureMap, for his enlightening perspectives on the future of communications and discourse power in Asia and the West. Moreover, his books have been a tremendous source of inspiration.

Imad Lahad, Managing Director of APCO Worldwide Dubai, and Mamoon Sbeih, President of the consultancy's Middle East and North Africa operations, for their deep insights about the role of AI and data analytics in communications and HR and the significance of selecting Dubai as the global hub for their Digital Lab.

Klaus Larres, Richard M. Krasno Distinguished Professor of History and International Affairs at the University of North Carolina at Chapel Hill, for all our talks, clarifying the history of US-China relations, and for inviting me to his great Krasno Global Events.

Carrington Malin, UAE-based entrepreneur and AI expert, for his information on the impact of AI on marketing and communications across the Middle East and beyond.

Scott Meyer, Instructor at Hubbard School of Journalism and Mass Communication at the University of Minnesota and former CEO of Shandwick

International, for recollecting memories about the time he introduced Reputation Management to the global PR industry and for his insights on the future of RM.

Afshin Molavi, Senior Fellow at the Foreign Policy Institute at Johns Hopkins University School of Advanced International Studies, for clarifying the meaning of globalization and the future of communications in the Emerging World.

Abdul-Rahman Risilia, Co-founder and CEO of ARC Talent in Dubai, for offering his deep and holistic views on the future of HR in communications and beyond.

Michael Webster, Director of Asia, Australia and New Zealand's leading media intelligence platform Telum Media, for his views on the current status and the trajectory of relations between comms pros and journalists.

Guido Wolf, Professor and Founder of Conex Institute in Germany, for elaborating on internal communications as a management discipline and the application of phenomenology in the social sciences.

I'd also like to extend my warmest thanks to everyone who engaged with me in conversations at recent in-person and online events:

H.E. Omar Sultan Al Olama, UAE Minister of State for AI, Digital Economy and Remote Work Applications, for our talk at Dubai's Diplomacy Lab and for laying out the UAE's take on digital diplomacy, the role of AI in leading the country's economy, and how to attract young talent.

Philipp Ivanov, CEO of Asia Society Australia, for receiving me at the Asia Briefing Live 2022 event in Melbourne; a great opportunity to engage with Australian participants and add new perspectives about the future of East–West relations.

The Dubai Chamber of Commerce and The Economist, for having me at three Global Business Forums including the inaugural GBF ASEAN hosted at Expo2020 Dubai.

Brand Finance, for inviting me to the Global Soft Power Summits and the opportunity to hear from Joseph Nye, Professor Emeritus and former Dean of Harvard's Kennedy School of Government, about the future of soft power.

Thanks to you all.

Last but not least, I am forever grateful to my beloved wife Donna for her never-ending patience, inspiration and support during our enforced long separation due to Covid19. Our future has been Asian for decades and surely will continue to be so.

Introduction

Asia's rise is shaping the future of communications, but that does not mean that the global conversation is suddenly going to be dominated by a single Asian power or entire region. Adding the Asian perspective inserts more balance, which has been long overdue. But equal attention must be paid to the practical aspects of the Asianization of communications in the information age. The stunning progress made by Asian technocracies demonstrates how vision, mission and determination can advance national development at a speed previously unseen. The more this is being adopted around the world, the less feasible it is for communicators to carry on with business as usual. Modifying long-established patterns in communications planning and execution that have not really been questioned in ages (in neither the East nor the West) helps deliver desired outcomes in an age shaped by geopolitics, increasing connectivity and the rising clout of the public voice.

Great power competition, the role of big tech and social media, and the shift to greater multipolarity command new ways to engage people in order to be understood, and to strengthen ties. Higher connectivity also calls for heightened sensitivity to the cultural and sociological aspects of human interaction and openness to different worldviews. None of that implies the need for compromising on values. On the contrary, it means defending the foundations of global dialogue and adapting to listen and be heard. For communicators, this ought to be the new so-called "license to operate." The best way to get there is the pursuit of executive authority and participation in the process of shaping business and public diplomacy strategies. Merely sticking with the old playbook of pushing self-selected messages and narratives instead of facilitating true engagement has two new outcomes: it is much easier on technical terms, yet less efficient with regard to persuasion and soft power. And that's not even half of it.

Years of declining public trust in institutions, corporations, media and government have fueled negative and enduring perceptions like "This is just PR." It's a choice of words often used to call out apparent attempts at spreading misinformation. This should prompt a serious review of the actual value proposition. But that still remains a distant goal, as shown by the casual and frequent underplaying of comms by professionals who keep asserting, "We are storytellers." While undoubtedly part of the job, this line has long ceased to represent the entirety of the practice. Instead, it further limits the chances of being granted executive authority that

DOI: 10.4324/9781003385622-1

comes with full decision-making power. That aside, it may also serve as a deliberate deflection from harsh realities.

As ironic as it may sound, communicators often fail to express the full scope and scale of their line of business. Owing to that, the progression of the practice is still relatively slow moving – in both the public eye and the real world. Even when the unexploited potential of communications is fully recognized but the pace of adjustment remains slower than the evolution of the operating environment, the gap will only widen. Needless to say, having a firm hold on innovative tools and channels is vital to the successful handling of any near-term volatility and the management of one's public view. The merits of having the capacity to persuade are in plain sight. At the same time, the repercussions from using the wrong tone of voice when communicating with foreign audiences can be rather disruptive.

With unsurpassed access to social media, messaging, video and gaming apps plus greater physical connectivity via global travel (which is seeing a return to the pre-Covid19 normal), the old adage of the "Global Village" has taken on a whole new meaning. And since younger generations place greater emphasis on trustworthiness, activism and advocacy, mastering the art of real stakeholder engagement is no longer just a clever choice for some early adopters. Instead, it is the new strategic imperative for everyone related to information sharing and relationship management.

To provide a broader view of the changes in operating environments and theoretical underpinnings of enhancing the engagement of global audiences today, this book is taking readers on a journey that places communications at the heart of various reality checks.

The assessment begins with modern history, globalization and geoeconomics and a look at discourse power and global perceptions. As legendary Japanese swordsman and philosopher Miyamoto Musashi (c. 1584–1645) was said to have proclaimed: "Perception is strong and sight weak. In strategy it is important to see distant things as if they were close and to take a distanced view of close things."[1] In communications, that should include an analysis of the theoretical grounds of human interaction. Delving into the vast but less-known body of literature about communication theory, the book lays the foundation for the redesign of international engagement models, emphasizing purpose, values and the art of stage-managing future-readiness by taking inspiration from innovation-led national development. After that it addresses the need to detect and combat propaganda, one of the greatest dangers to humanity that requires a refocus on media literacy and closer collaboration between media, researchers, legal experts and communicators. This is followed by a probe into modern Public Diplomacy, which is no longer about absolute control but about ways to gain real influence. Communications plays a major role in balancing values and principles for the sake of unlocking the full potential of soft power; a tremendous asset with comparable upsides for corporate communications. From there the book moves on to talent management as a way to weather the increasing competition now stretching around the globe and assesses HR's role in building future-ready workforces. The following chapter discusses how communicators can benefit from accumulating some kind of a digital sixth sense. By tapping into the automated analysis of published content, speeches, presentations and media appearances, they open a path to develop future-ready strategies, better protect corporate reputations and eventually secure that much-touted "Fifth Seat at the Boardroom Table." Getting nearer to the end, the book pores over some ostensibly insurmountable challenges linked to the development of strategies in less time and how to overcome them. In summarizing the book's key takeaways, the final chapter delivers a purposefully designed two-pronged approach to strategic comms development in multicultural environments.

The prospect of shaping corporate decisions and the public conversation about ventures and projects, brands, NGOs and diplomatic causes should be highly aspirational. But that does require the long-overdue transition from the self-reference as storytellers and messengers (and in some cases crowd pleasers) to analysts, positive market disruptors, strategy integrators, clout (not cloud) providers and decision makers. Communicating innovation has always been essential, as is the commitment to innovating communications.

Reference

1. "Quote by Miyamoto Musashi." *Quoteslyfe*, https://quoteslyfe.com/quote/Perception-is-strong-and-sight-weak-In-104089.

1 Decoding the Asian Century
How the Bet on Modernization Paid Off

"It's the end of the world as we know it (and I feel fine)."[1] The song released by American rock band R.E.M. in the late 1980s still resounds. Much of the Western world acted for years like they put it back on repeat play; humming along while not caring too much about the implications of the assumed end of globalization. The US–China trade war, Covid19 and Russia's invasion of Ukraine definitely altered this stance. The pandemic alone caused countless disruptions in people's lives, while the invasion created a humanitarian disaster and growing uncertainty about global energy and food security.

A number of prominent commentators have expressed concerns about the likelihood of geopolitical realignments and the fragmentation of the world economy long before the recovery from the pandemic. With more than $10 trillion in assets, Blackrock is the world's largest investment management corporation. As reported by various media including the *New York Times*, Blackrock Chairman and CEO Larry Fink is convinced that the end of globalization as we know it had already arrived.[2] It's a view not shared by emerging markets fund manager Mark Mobius, who publicly stated that he does not quite understand Fink's thinking.[3] At the time this book was finished, it was too early to conclusively assess all possible ramifications. Nevertheless, "as we know it" could just be the line that analysts and investors will eventually agree upon.

The increasing demand for self-reliance and deglobalization is noticeable, but a total retreat from the global system seems highly unlikely. Globalization is prone to survive because it is entrenched in something that will never again vanish: global connectivity or even "hyper-connectivity." Adding to this, it's not a Western-centric model of connectedness either. Afshin Molavi, Senior Fellow at the Foreign Policy Institute of the Johns Hopkins University School of Advanced International Studies, explained why: "If we define globalization as the increasing cross-border interconnection of goods, people, services, capital and ideas – and not the convergence toward Western ideas and structures, as some define it – then it remains alive and well."[4]

Just where exactly are we headed in the short and long term? And what is the impact of global challenges like climate change, Covid19, big power competition and the resulting calls for a decoupling of economies and seismic shifts in global supply chains? There were no easy answers to all these questions even before the war that Russia unleashed on Ukraine. The global energy crisis and high levels of inflation have come with serious consequences for the economic outlook of economies around the world. While being a major blow for the global recovery, change – even massive change – is a historical standard that does not end the future.

What History Teaches Us

In modern history, certain ages earned their trademark by setting the stage for the expansion of geopolitical influence and persuasive power that served geographies and nation states. In the Western hemisphere, awareness of these "branded centuries" is for the most part limited to the past few hundred years. Europe's 500 years of colonialism and the productivity gains that stemmed from the industrial revolution, which began in Britain around 1760 and soon expanded to the old continent, rebranded the 19th century as the European Century. This was then replaced by the American Century; the popular recognition of US victories and those of its liberal allies over communist, fascist and other authoritarian regimes that were further enhanced by the global appeal of America's cultural influence that skyrocketed in the post–World War II era.

The power of attraction of course existed long before it became a subject of academic research. And it was never limited to Western or non-Asian values alone. While much of the West regards world history as being rooted in the ancient civilizations of Egypt and Mesopotamia and Greco-Roman culture, Asian regions and territories dominated the world's centuries and millennia long before. British historian Peter Frankopan, author of *The Silk Roads*,[5] noted that from the beginning of time, the center of Asia was where empires were made. There is consensus among most analysts of international politics that we are once again at the dawn of a new age. While not everyone seems prepared yet to accept the arrival of the "Asian Century," the term itself has already become a household name in some quarters, long before this new era has reached its midway point. That underscores the coherence and persuasiveness of Asian accomplishments.

In the Asian Century as in every other age, opportunities don't disappear because of great power rivalry and associated uncertainties. Besides, various emerging markets are no longer, well, emerging. They have arrived, with some being better prepared for the future than developed nations. This is particularly true for Asia, the world's most populous region and home to some of the fastest-growing economies. Most are deeply connected to the global community; a fact that is already reshaping the world. This is what shapes the future of communications, as being laid out on the "Backstory" page of my website.[6]

Asia has emerged as an incubator of innovative thinking, with entrepreneurs and governments actively promoting modernization in tech, healthcare, mobility, education and effective governance structures. Hundreds of Special Economic Zones (SEZ) and accelerators have sprung up across Central, Southeast, East and West Asia. Innovation and economic growth are always at the center of all.

As a result of the 2008 financial crisis, Middle East North Africa (MENA) economies shifted their focus toward China to seek investment and trade as the United States went through a recession that the People's Republic of China (PRC) largely avoided. The closer ties also led to an alignment of some forms of policymaking. Across Asia and the Middle East, cities and entire regions are now being rebuilt in a similar fashion; driven by pragmatic and visionary leaders, executives and innovators. As a result, Asia is on track to lead global infrastructure spending.

The Middle East is in the midst of a massive construction boom, especially Egypt and the wealthy GCC states. Saudi Arabia alone is expected to spend $1.1 trillion on infrastructure projects from 2019 to 2038, a number that accounts for 1.2 percent of the global total. The United Arab Emirates (UAE), on the other hand, is reported to invest $350 billion during the same time period. Central Asia, India, China, Japan and the ASEAN nations are also pumping billions of dollars into roads and rail networks, renewable energy, AI, education and public health. Many of these investments have become engines of inclusive growth as well as regional and global integration. It's a remarkable shift from Asia's previous perception as the world's factory of cheap goods. What's more, their development model of fast, export-driven industrialization has clearly delivered on its promise. Pioneered by Japan, South Korea and Taiwan, it was later adopted and rapidly expanded by the PRC and others. As confirmed by several global organizations including the World Bank,[7] China's rise has lifted more than 800 million people out of poverty since the beginning of reforms in 1978. While its economy was slowing due to extended zero-Covid policies and the dramatic rise of infections after the abrupt re-opening, China's status as the world's second-largest superpower is not going to vanish.

Hong Kong and Singapore rose to become Asia's world cities and premier financial hubs. Hong Kong managed to retain its top-tier status for decades, but during Covid19 it saw the most serious population outflow in 60 years. More than 140,000 residents and many companies left the Special Administrative Region (SAR) in 2021 and 2022. The resulting brain drain might alter the course and change Hong Kong's position as a vibrant center of commerce. Its leaders are very much aware of that risk and chose to host the 2022 Global Financial Leaders' Investment Summit in order to change the SARs perception. But whether its comeback party will succeed is far from clear.

Singapore, once built on trade, tourism and traditional industries, was the main beneficiary of Hong Kong's drop. Having been successful at investing in developing industries such as biotech, clean energy and healthcare to stay competitive, its Monetary Authority now strives to turn the small nation into Asia's leading financial center and a global fintech hub. That would help coping with a possible plunge in growth related to recession among the world's major economies. As reported in the Global Financial Centres Index (GFCI 32), the city state overtook Hong Kong by one rating point in late 2022. Furthermore, Hong Kong's exports contracted significantly, and according to IATA, the SAR also lost its status as an international aviation hub.[8]

India has been one of just 18 outperforming emerging economies to achieve robust and consistent high growth over three decades. The nation is a leader in IT and cloud computing and has begun to open its economy. "Make in India" is a government initiative launched in 2014 to boost productivity by enhancing the domestic manufacturing sector and attracting more Foreign Direct Investment

(FDI). Long known for its absence of international brands, India then saw a spike in demand for high-quality and global luxury goods.

The ten ASEAN states now account for 3.5 percent of the global economy, making them the fifth-largest economy in the world. Indonesia remains a particularly promising future market. In 2022, FDI to the world's largest archipelagic state was on a significant upwards trend, surging 63.6 percent year-on-year to US$10.83 billion in Q3/2022. As widely reported, the country's economy is expected to see a 5.0 percent growth in 2022 and roughly 5.2 percent in 2023.

With roughly one-eighth of Indonesia's population, Malaysia stands out for its highly diversified economy and early adoption of cutting-edge technology for manufacturing. What also helped its development is the closeness to major trade routes, attraction of foreign investment and comparatively stable governance. Like Vietnam, the nation may at some point benefit from China's withdrawal from global manufacturing dominance. Besides, Malaysia has made considerable progress in the advancement of integrating digital technology on all levels of society including the national education system, all with the intent to achieve its Malaysia 5.0 goals of becoming the digital hub of ASEAN. Between 2008 and 2015, Malaysia reduced its poverty rate from 17 percent to 2.7 percent. The country also created over two million new jobs, and its GDP increased by nearly 50 percent in seven years, narrowing the gap toward the high income target from 33 percent to 19 percent. In view of the Ukraine conflict, Bank Negara (Malaysia's Central Bank) cut its economic growth forecast in late March 2022 to somewhere between 5.3 and 6.3 percent; a moderate deceleration of the recovery from Covid19.

The trajectory of multiple Asian markets is quite distinct from that of many places in Europe and the United States, where capital projects often take years to move from planning stage to execution, if they move at all. Conceived in 1996, Germany's Berlin Brandenburg Airport (BER) took another ten years for construction to begin. Yet the coming years were marred by bankruptcy, safety issues and other glitches. BER finally opened its gates in October 2020. While this case stands out for all stated reasons, endless delays due to bureaucratic procedures or political disputes are very common in Western democracies. In the United States, the so-called "Infrastructure Week" announced by former President Donald Trump never took off, despite being proclaimed several times since June 2017. Under President Joe Biden, things improved when the House of Representatives finally passed the hard-fought $1 trillion infrastructure bill in November 2021; the nation's best shot at rebuilding roads, bridges, railroads and airports and also expanding access to broadband internet. Historians described it as the closest thing to the New Deal policies of the 1930s led by President Franklin D. Roosevelt, Dwight D. Eisenhower's Interstate Highway System in 1956, and the Great Society of the 1960s, headed by Lyndon B. Johnson.

Build It and They'll Come

A key number to keep in mind is $26 trillion, or $1.7 trillion per year. According to a 2017 report by the Asian Development Bank,[9] that's the amount developing Asia will need to invest between 2016 and 2030 to battle poverty, boost economic growth and fight the climate crisis. Their young and fast-growing populations (median age: 30.7 years) need more energy, better education and healthcare and decent jobs; while aging infrastructure, built decades ago for a fraction of today's population, is in dire need of replacement. The path to be followed is very straightforward: think big.

The tallest tower, the fastest train, the largest airport – there is definitely a different mindset among Asian leaders who see outstanding accomplishments as a way to attract talent, entrepreneurs and FDI and influence global opinions about the emerging markets. What's more, the distinction between political systems in the East and the West hands power to technological elites who are chosen based on their expertise and performance in specific areas of responsibility. West Asia (the Middle East) in particular managed to come up with a unique approach that prioritizes the speedy delivery of high-quality projects and in doing so accelerates economic growth while attracting ever more investors.

The UAE placed its bets on forecasting the future and is now leading the field as a real innovation trailblazer. The small Gulf nation on the northeastern coast of the Arabian Peninsula is creating physical features and nurturing talent to sustain future growth and wealth. Dubai in particular is moving fast in defining what cities in the 21st century should offer. Its rulers had long ago concluded that the emirate's future is not in oil – there was never that much to begin with. Dubai's reserves stand at roughly 4 billion barrels, while Abu Dhabi has 92 billion barrels. Because of that, the emirate adopted the now-famous "Build it and they'll come" policy, which set the course for the nation and its smart investments in future-ready technology, infrastructure and logistics. The emirate has aspirations to become the world's logistics hub and global blockchain capital and is transforming its economy in the vein of sustainable, smart cities that keep attracting more talent from the region and all over the world.

Dubai's hosting of Expo 2020, or the "World's Greatest Show," turned out to be a key catalyst. The six-month-long event (delayed by one year due to the pandemic) was the first World's Fair to take place in the Middle East, and one that also told the story of the emirate's phenomenal success to a global audience. A total of 192 nation state pavilions presented their future-preparedness and the best their countries have to offer. In addition, several more corporate entities and international organizations showcased their accomplishments and outlook in separate pavilions. While many of the larger countries pushed technology from the moment one entered their pavilions, the ten ASEAN states plus a number of Pacific nations and African states greeted visitors with a cultural showcase. By drawing attention to the ethnic variety, arts and culture plus the wonders of their natural world before moving on to the latest achievements in tech, commodities and sustainability, these nations managed to create emotional bonds ahead of engaging the public on everything else their nations have to offer.

The question "Who needs a World Exhibition in the internet age?" was quickly rendered irrelevant. Guided by the theme "Connecting Minds, Creating the Future," the organizers over-delivered on providing answers to the great questions of our time. Visitors were able to experience how to deal with global warming, seismic societal shifts and new diseases while learning about the scientific breakthroughs and technologies that will keep us afloat.

Infrastructure investment including a mega-event like the World's Fair is an investment in the sustained wealth of an economy. Back in 2013 when the Bureau International des Expositions (BIE) granted Dubai the right to host Expo, the envisioned number of visitors (or visits, to be precise) stood at 25 million. The event was expected to add around $23 billion to the economy, equating to around 24.4 percent of Dubai's GDP between 2015 and 2021. In the end, Expo 2020 reported almost 24 million visits, a number close to its original target and a stellar success, given the impact of Covid19 on world travel. Dubai's investment in openness paid off and became the boost to tourism and hospitality that Dubai had foreseen. The Expo site was packed with crowds every single day, and Dubai quite literally became the world's new "Connectivity Capital" – the place where the world meets. It was a message put on full display by various news channels including CNN International, which happens to broadcast its flagship Middle East news program *Connect the World* live from Abu Dhabi since 2009. During the Expo, it was partly aired from Dubai; another boost to the emirate's discourse power. Expo visitors included numerous heads of states, top-level ministers, global investors, world renowned artists, actors and athletes plus millions of tourists keen to witness cultural performances and the most immersive and mind-blowing experience any Expo host has ever staged.

On a related note, visiting a place where more languages are spoken than in any other country is a rather unique experience; one that creates a special bond. Although Arabic is the UAE's mother tongue, English is the most spoken language. Visitors also encountered expatriates who converse in Farsi (Persian), Hindi, Urdu, Bengali, Tamil, Malayalam, Tagalog, Chinese and more.

The huge number of business forums, conferences and trade deals worth billions of dollars added to the list of accomplishments. That makes it "Exhibit A" in any future assessment of successful nation branding exercises: connecting minds in the world's most cosmopolitan and connected city. All this is also reflected in the official Expo 2020 theme song, titled "This Is Our Time." Furthermore, Expo 2020 comes with a legacy program that will continue for at least another decade. The 438-hectare (1083 acres) site is being repurposed into "District 2020," an integrated mixed-use and traffic-free community.

Qatar is harnessing the power of sports along similar lines and with the goal of galvanizing its national development. The Gulf state with a population of 2.96 million hosted the 15th Asian Games in 2005; a feat that set itself up for the next step: the successful bid to host the FIFA World Cup in 2022. The contribution to the economy was estimated at around $20 billion, primarily linked to civil infrastructure.

Thinking big and "Build it and they'll come" has borne fruit for many Asian states, partly because this is about more than just replacing the old. As Parag Khanna, global strategist, Founder and CEO of Climate Alpha and Founder and Managing Partner of FutureMap, writes in his seminal book *The Future Is Asian*:[10] "Many are joining in the largest-scale case of what economists call the advantage of late development, or 'second-mover advantage': leapfrogging over traditional technologies or behaviors to the newest standards."

The key to success is twofold: having a vision and connecting communities to development priorities. By getting this message across, communities can become stakeholders in progress. It's the Open Secret of Asia's Rise and an extension of the initial theme. One may even assign a new tagline, something like "Do it and they'll join."

Who Owns the Asian Century?

The Asian success stories have undoubtedly reshaped the global view of Asia's rise, which can no longer be ignored. But where and when exactly did it all start? What is the outcome? And who can assert ultimate "proprietary rights" on par with the previous linguistic ownership claims by Europe and America?

As I wrote in *Power and Persuasion in the Asian Century*, originally published March 4, 2021, by the CPD Blog through the USC Center on Public Diplomacy (CPD),[11] this new age has been forecast since the late 1980s. Singaporean scholar Kishore Mahbubani suggested that May 2020 marks its dawn: the moment Asian economies bounced back from the Coronavirus outbreak.[12] Yet the national transformation programs across this vast region did not start the day before yesterday. The sweeping modernization has been underway for decades, shifting the balance of economic power while driving the expansion of Asia's middle classes.

Still, Mahbubani made a valid point: 2020 is the year the Asian Century finally went mainstream. Thanks to 24-hour pandemic news coverage and a pervasive digital media environment, Asia's rebound whilst the United States and Europe were pondering "lockdown-lites" had thrust the accomplishments of Asian technocracies into the international spotlight. The spring of 2020 was the decisive point when momentum was clearly on Asia's side, but another reality kicked in as well: in the West, consciousness of this age is not the same as understanding. That made it an opening for media, think tanks, corporate communicators and diplomats to leverage peak awareness of Asia's rise (and Asian consciousness of that awareness) to educate Western audiences about Asian diversity and the potential to lead in matters of global importance. However, to make a lasting impact, such endeavors rely upon the championing of shared interests among Eastern and Western publics; a multifaceted task centered on policy and results-driven communications.

China, for example, framed the promotion of universal values as a Western attempt to weaken the theoretical foundations of the party's leadership.[13] This position is difficult to defend on the world stage. However, its underlying argument is also discussed by Asian scholars of various origins and academic disciplines. Their point: the term "universal values" is related to Eurocentrism and being used to interpret the world by placing an emphasis on European or Anglo-American values, intents and purposes. That said, opposing universal values is seen as rejecting the foundations of global cooperation, which is essential for scientific progress in many areas such as public health and climate change. For China, it also stands in contradiction to the stated objective of creating a "Community of Shared Future," one of China's signature concepts of forging international relations. The predictable net result is a continuous rise in public demand of a more crisis-resilient world with less confrontation and antagonism. While this looks like a stalemate that is hard to avoid, paying greater attention to semantics in international dialogue may chart a path to overcome this apparent impasse. The details are outlined in Chapters 2 and 6.

Beijing's decades of attainments and wins are certainly beyond question. The country's rapid progress in areas such as poverty alleviation, science, infrastructure, fin-tech, AI and space exploration made it a key player in the advancement of Asia's rise. But that does not turn the Asian Century into a Chinese century. While Chinese nationalists keep pushing the line "Zhōngguó shì rénlèi jìnbù, wénmíng hé zhìxù de dēngtǎ" (China is the beacon of human advancement, civilization and order), which is accepted in much of the Global South, the rest of the world sees it differently. As shown in numerous surveys, China's increasing authoritarianism has negatively impacted its international image.

The world has changed, and what no longer applies is a view of history that pits the decades-long and hence more familiar status of one dominating and now largely divided superpower against the rise of another one whose progress over the past 40 years has been dazzling. The Communist Party of China (CPC) – mostly referred to as CCP in the West – is actively promoting a set of narratives including its peaceful rise and multilateralism. That claim, however, is objected even across many parts of Asia. While hosting some 55 official ethnic groups, China is urging them to forego their culture, stop teaching their languages and create "ethnic unity." Official photographs from Chinese party congresses display very few women or minorities. Released by China's propaganda department, they leave no doubt that this is precisely what Beijing wants its domestic audience and the world to see: Chinese culture is defined by the Han majority, which makes up roughly 92 percent of the population. While female delegate numbers were slightly higher at the 20th Communist Party Congress in 2022 than at the 19th Congress in 2017, the party picked no woman for any top position. Together, all this hardly aligns with the assertion of openness, gender equality and inclusion.

The situation is quite different in parts of Southeast Asia. In Malaysia, the Muslim Malays and Bumiputra (Indigenous non-Malay like the Orang Asli of Peninsular Malaysia, and various Indigenous peoples of Malaysian Borneo including the Ibans, Murats and Kadazans) make for about 70 percent of the population. Chinese and Indians account for 22.6 percent and 6.9 percent, respectively.[14] In 2021, the newly installed Prime Minister Ismail Sabri Yakoob launched his plan to unite the nation and restore economic prosperity under the concept "Keluarga Malaysia" (the Malaysian Family). Social inclusion and the reduction of ethnic tension is also what motivated Malaysians to vote for Anwar Ibrahim in the country's 15th general election (GE15).

The world's most diverse country, both ethnically and linguistically, also happens to be Asian: Papua New Guinea. Others that manage to fit the entire world within their borders include Qatar, Pakistan, Indonesia, India, Singapore and the UAE.

To cut to the chase, no single power owns this century. What we are witnessing is the resurgence of the most heterogeneous region of the world that is home to 4.7 billion people. Many Asian nations have managed to craft enormously powerful national narratives about the upsides for all who adjust quickly. But as anticipated, not everyone buys into it.

The years-long US–China trade war has negatively impacted the US economy and slowed down China's formerly rapid growth, with Asia's emerging markets now growing even faster than China. Both nations know that continuously souring relations are not in their best economic interest. Aiming to become completely self-sufficient is not a pragmatic forward strategy. Yet the announcement in late 2022 of more export control regulations targeted at China's tech sector showed that the Biden administration won't support China's rise anymore. The move also came with the resignation of US executives and engineers working in China's semiconductor manufacturing industry.

Transparency, diversity and security of international supply chains have become a subject important enough for G20 democracies to assert that trade cannot come at the expense of its values or security. Unlike before, that is a trend even reflected in many election outcomes across Europe. Be that as it may, supply chains are generally known to be resilient, as long as there is still some willingness to compromise. While global trade growth has decelerated in the wake of trade wars, Brexit and Covid19, trade between Asian nations is on the rise. In November 2020, fifteen Asian-Pacific nations formed the world's largest trading bloc, the Regional Comprehensive Economic Partnership (RCEP), covering nearly one-third of the global economy. Ratified by 13 out of 15 countries by mid-2022, RCEP is now on track to become the world's largest export supplier and second-largest import destination. Ironically, the acronym "RCEP" is also part of the word "perception."

The Comprehensive and Progressive Agreement for Trans-Pacific Partnership (CPTPP) was signed in March 2018. It is a Free Trade Agreement (FTA) between Australia, Brunei Darussalam, Canada, Chile, Japan, Malaysia, Mexico, Peru, New Zealand, Singapore and Vietnam that came into effect in December 2018. Another major development is the African Continental Free Trade Area (AfCFTA), which covers 54 countries, making it the world's largest FTA since the formation of the World Trade Organization (WTO).

Collectively, all these trade deals spell opportunity for an accelerated global economic recovery and deepened ties among nations. What's more, there is a chance of more contact between people and businesses, and more lucky breaks – provided the world avoids more disruptive global events based on different norms, cultures and legal systems. If history is any guide, we are seeing the sustained development of global trade. Things will continue to move in the right direction. After all, Asia accounts for roughly 61 percent of the world's total population; a fact that makes it hard to imagine that the interconnectedness of cultures is not going to pick up the pace.

Power and Influence in a More Multipolar World

The old bipolarity of the Cold War era ended between 1989, when the Berlin Wall fell, and 1991, when the Soviet Union collapsed. The United States and the West in general saw this as a triumph of liberal over non-liberal states and a global peace-keeping operation that stabilized the prevailing unipolar order. The rise of Asia has redrawn the international system, now being led by more than one superpower.

Under President Trump, the United States missed out on reassuring Asia with a focus on economic statecraft oriented toward stability and peace while helping

Asian economies reduce inequality. Relations have not yet fully recovered, as the post-Trump period was focused on rebuilding America's alliance with the EU and NATO and fixing its domestic problems. NATO then began to tag China as a source of "systemic challenges" to Euro-Atlantic security. The alliance also declared the "no limits partnership" between Beijing and the Kremlin as an attempt to undercut Western values. All this adds some perspective to one critical point: the fact that prospects of a multipolar world order are still far from being universally embraced. Even when Asia's polycentric nature is tacitly accepted and Asia's support acknowledged, a vast range of concerns remain. At the top of all is the lack of faith in the stability of a world characterized by rising authoritarian states that are pushing a multipolar world based on plurality of systems of governance. It is widely seen as a way to change the balance of power in their favor and to simply create the next unipolar order. But given the complex nature of this age, that is never going to work. As mentioned before, the Asian Century is not about total ownership or control, let alone one state being capable of resolving the most pressing global challenges on its own. Influence comes with openness to collaboration.

A few years ago, former British Prime Minister Gordon Brown proposed the formation of a temporary global government taskforce to coordinate an effective response to the global economic crisis and the Coronavirus epidemic. His main point was that no single country can deal with this crisis by itself. To some extent Brown's reasoning aligns with the core idea of the Asian Century: it is indeed down to "all of us" or the global community at large. Brown's proposal generated plenty of media coverage but not enough endorsement from global leaders. The increasing competition of perceived national priorities and rationales remains one of humanity's gravest challenges. That raises the stakes for leaders who must fill the content vacuum related to a lack of real progress on matters that affect the entire planet. Making headway in bringing the world together would pay off instantly. Yet that requires a serious commitment to engage on real terms and build trust and alliances.

In *Vertrauen: Ein Mechanismus der Reduktion Sozialer Komplexität* (*Trust and Power*),[15] German sociologist Niklas Luhmann explained the correlation between relationships, politics and business. He concluded that trust is central to all communication and critical for reducing social complexity. The same applies to international relations, where complexity increases in line with connectedness. For nation states as well as businesses, only genuine trust builds resilience, an important asset under any scenario.

Every year, the international standing of nations is revealed in a number of global surveys that establish the global perception, reputation, soft power and leadership of over 100 countries across a wide range of indicators and categories.

The Anholt-Ipsos Nation Brand Index (NBI)[16] assesses information obtained from over 60,000 interviews conducted online in 20 panel countries, plus 60 measured nations across the globe. The 2021 NBI showed which nations had managed to improve their reputations from the previous year; an upshot mostly related to their containment strategies of the Covid19 pandemic. Most Western nations finally caught up with other nations, whereas only a few Asia Pacific states improved their standing; mainly because they already ranked higher. The top five ranking nations were Germany, which retained its top position for the 5th year in a row; Canada, which jumped from 3rd to 2nd place; Japan, which emerged as the frontrunner among all Asian nations, leaping from 4th to 3rd place; Italy, which rose from 6th to 4th place due to high rankings in Culture, Tourism and People; and the United Kingdom, which dropped from 2nd to 5th but maintained its overall positive reputation. The United States saw a slow recovery and progressed from 10th to 8th place. And China climbed from 35th to 31st place.

The Brand Finance Global Soft Power Index (GSPI)[17] is based on data obtained from more than 100,000 respondents in 100 countries, plus a rating of 120 nations from around the world. The main indicators are Familiarity, Reputation and Influence. Soft power is measured by rankings in Business and Trade; Governance; International Relations; Culture and Heritage; Media and Communication; Education and Science; and People and Values. In 2022 the results were mostly affected by each nation's handling of the pandemic in the year before and the performance rankings on three metrics: Economic Recovery, Healthcare and Vaccinations, and International Aid. The United States jumped from 6th to 1st place, reclaiming its top rank in soft power. It's the result of advances across all Soft Power pillars. The United Kingdom leaped from 3rd to 2nd place. Germany dropped from 1st to 3rd place, for the most part due to the resurgence of the US and the UK. China climbed from 8th to 4th place, the best ever performance. Japan fell from 2nd to 5th place. The UAE rose from 17th to 15th place, leading the Middle East and North Africa in a number of fields, especially Business and Trade, Ease of Doing Business, and Strong and Stable Economy. The nation's successful handling of the pandemic also contributed to its soft power rise, as did Expo 2020.

The difference in rankings is further underscored by a range of other surveys. Transparency International's Corruption Perceptions Index (CPI) ranks 180 countries and territories by their perceived levels of public sector corruption. The Heritage Foundation's Index of Economic Freedom measures the impact of liberty and free markets around the globe. The Human Development Report released by the United Nations is arguably the most inclusive and practical analysis of the best countries to live in. And the World Intellectual Property Organization (WIPO) is tracking the most recent global innovation trends, ranking 132 economies based on 81 different indicators. WIPO's Global Innovation Index (GII) 2021 and 2022 were carried out with a special focus on the impact of the Covid19 pandemic on innovation.

On top of that, there are the regular public opinion polls conducted by leading institutes such as Gallup and Pew Research Center. They also add a lot of detail to the perceived strengths and weaknesses of nation states, their leaders and economies. Together, all those surveys and polls provide a fairly comprehensive picture of national perceptions and actual influence. Making sense of the often-differing outcomes requires a closer examination of each individual report, an alignment of the terminology used across all studies and a comparison of their geographical reach. But scoring high across all should always be the desired outcome.

Regardless of their countries' global image, Asians tend to place much faith in their systems of governance. In China's case this view goes even one step further.

As Brian Wong wrote in a piece for *The Diplomat*, most of the Chinese population firmly believes that China's international reputation remains to be favorable.[18] This is certainly true for Africa, whose largest trading partner is China. The continent is also a major recipient of Chinese infrastructure investment and development aid. What helps Beijing is its focus on fast decision-making and quicker implementation of major infrastructure projects. Chinese FDI stocks grew from $490 million in 2003 to $43.4 billion in 2020.[19] The same applies to parts of Latin America and the Caribbean, where trade is also growing. Yet unfavorable views of China have surged among all major trading partners, including the United States, Canada, the UK, the EU, Japan, South Korea and Australia, the developed nations that enabled China's decades-long rise in the first place. This trend has been repeatedly documented by Gallup and Pew Research as well as other pollsters and research institutes. The status of China deserves continuous attention as it is the one power that challenges the United States in global influence operations. But as mentioned before, the Asian Century is not a Chinese one. It's a fact that Asians themselves may want to exploit a bit more.

Who Will Define the Asian Century?

The task of educating a broader global public on the finer points of the Asian Century's complexity is with media, analysts, business and government leaders – essentially anyone who can advance the understanding of Asia's rise through better communication. Parag Khanna expressed the well-established and deeply entrenched views that shape the prevalent perceptions in both East and West:

> From the Western perspective, most communication related to Asia is still *at Asia* rather than *within Asia*. It is more about selling than communicating or understanding. This is perhaps one of the reasons why there is still such a divergence and misperception between East and West. At the same time, Asian communications has become a rich space, but certainly not a single voice.[20]

A paradigm shift toward a more unified stance would undoubtedly strengthen Asian discourse power. For Khanna, there is already a rising but quiet confidence among Asia's well-run democratic technocracies. "It will not be measured in Western recognition but in the continued pursuit and achievement of modernization."

Asia could gain even more global influence by putting a premium on intra-Asian integration and higher connectivity. In the digital space, that might include lowering the price of broadband internet rates. Vietnam leads that space in Asia with some of the lowest rates in the world.[21] Another important factor is openness in discussing what matters most for Asia's populations while shaping the region's global perception. For years now, the central topics that dominate the public debate have been drawing on relations between China and Taiwan as well as general peace and stability in the Indo Pacific. The question "What happens if China were to invade Taiwan?" surely comes up in multiple boardroom meetings too. But such subjects are not what global or even Asian businesses with branches and staff in China are going to address publicly. While this raises the question about one's devotion to intellectual honesty, most corporate executives still prefer to keep a low profile on matters related to big power rivalry. However, such a stance is not necessarily unchangeable.

Malaysia is one of Asia's most integrated and diverse states; one that values its good relations with all neighbors. Robert Kaplan highlights the historical foundation in his book *Asia's Cauldron*,[22] in which he clarifies that the Southeast Asian nation is one of the few countries in the world where Chinese ceramics, Islamic coins, and South Indian bronze can be found at the same archeological sites. Hence, Malaysia looks like the right place to engage publics on the topic of international relations.

In April 2022, Malaysia's Institute of Strategic and International Studies (ISIS) hosted a webinar titled "War in Ukraine: What Does It Mean for Southeast Asia?"[23] In a remarkable shift from the conventional practice, all speakers called upon ASEAN to take a stance. As Rastam Mohd Isa, former Secretary-General at Malaysia's Ministry of Foreign Affairs noted: "We have missed the opportunity to strengthen ASEAN to stand up for principles that are sacred to our own existence." It's a message echoed by Thailand's former Foreign Minister Kasit Piromya: "ASEAN has not managed to coordinate its response or position. We have lost that sense of togetherness." Dino Patti Djalal, Indonesia's former Ambassador to the United States, took a similar position: "ASEAN diplomacy is punching way below its weight." Meanwhile, William Choong, Senior Fellow at the ISEAS–Yusof Ishak Institute in Singapore emphasized that "opposing the invasion is not about taking sides but about international law."

With geopolitics entering the global discourse in ways unseen before; taking a stance can no longer be discounted. The question of how to deal with all this is becoming an increasingly difficult task, as no one is keen to involuntarily create any additional havoc in already-uncertain times. But as soon as the value of discourse power is fully recognized and addressed in new business and communications strategies, the chances of finding a prominent voice on the world stage increase. That said, the broader and more inclusive public discourse on the geopolitics of Asia's rise is likely to come from leaders and commentators with full access to content from Western and Asian sources; all without having to abide by any form of self-imposed or enforced censorship. Of course, none of that dissolves Asian discourse power entirely, certainly not domestically. But in authoritarian systems, it surely limits the stories to whatever is considered politically acceptable. The outcome is predictable: Asian leaders' storytelling will always contribute to the globally established narrative of the Asian Century but won't necessarily dominate the discourse.

Parag Khanna underscores the necessary next step in Asian state-to-state communication:

> National cultures are becoming saturated with marketing and media, which has generally made for a much livelier discourse. The next frontier – I hope – will be much more intra-Asian conversation across borders despite language differences. This will help to further break down the notion of the "other" in a region that does in fact have a deeply interwoven history. [24]

Until then, the Asia-centric conversation is going to be driven by a vast and diverse group of influencers. Among them are media, lawmakers, think tanks and academics as well as global citizens, investors and visionary leaders; and of course social media users all over the world. It's a natural consequence in a world shaped by multipolarity and hence defined by numerous centers of power or influence. To put it plainly, any nation state that actively promotes a multipolar world order but then claims exclusivity and interpretative authority over the Asian Century narrative is barking up the wrong tree.

One effect of greater multipolarity is a surge in competing interpretations and repudiations of worldviews and matters of global interest. That is going to create more noise and distraction; a view shared by Afshin Molavi who is also the editor of the *Emerging World* newsletter[25] and author of the *New Silk Road Monitor* blog.[26] At the "BRI Dialogue – D12 in Conversation with Afshin Molavi," he made it abundantly clear that

> driven by the rise of China, the rise of many Emerging Markets, rapid urbanization, unprecedented connectivity, and growing middle classes, we have these middle powers rising as countries become richer and stake their claim geopolitically as well. So it's not such a simple Cold War world. It's not such a simple unipolar world. We're living in a world where many voices are grappling and trying to declare their voice to be heard. Therefore it's going to be a slightly more chaotic world.[27]

On that premise, a re-evaluation of all we think we know about how to manage cross-cultural dialogue in diplomacy and business is unavoidable. It's a crucial moment; the unequaled opportunity to advance the cause of leaders in corporate and government communications with greater purpose. This can be achieved by offering some sound advice on how to engage audiences and influence perceptions with convincing and verifiable narratives and stories that survive any form of scrutiny. The bar is unquestionably higher than it used to be, as the main focus – before diving into the specifics of any strategy – must be on the broader elements that make this new age stand out. To recap, they include but are not limited to geopolitics, diversity, inclusion and trust. Any narrative that is supposed to resonate with a wider global community must seek to integrate some if not all of these in order to make a real impact.

This also proves that the old mantra "all communications is local" is no longer valid, at least not in the way it was traditionally seen. Properly addressing local audiences is critical, but in the age of "Globalization 2.0," all local and international communications are intertwined, which calls for a master plan that aligns the main components of all messages with narratives that connect with publics in various localities. It is also essential to bear in mind that being diplomatic and sensitive is the best way to communicate with a multicultural audience. It is not just about saying the right thing, but also saying it in the right way.

I can already hear corporate communications pros insisting: "Wait, that's what we've been doing all the time." Yes, but. It is an often-stated claim behind international comms strategies and campaigns, but one that is not always implemented. With the intricacy and significance of cross-cultural dialogue on the rise, it should help to pay more attention to the superior research by thinkers and scholars from various lines of academic study who have laid the foundations of communication theory and, in doing so, contributed significantly to defining the chief tenets and main aspiration of international communications.

References

1. "R.E.M. – It's the End of the World as We Know It (and I Feel Fine)." *YouTube*, 17 Mar. 2009, https://youtube.com/watch?v=Z0GFRcFm-aY
2. Ross, Sorkin, et al. "Wall Street Warns About the End of Globalization." *New York Times*, 24 Mar. 2022, https://nytimes.com/2022/03/24/business/dealbook/globalization-fink-marks.html
3. Dunkley, Emma. "Globalisation Is NOT Dead, Insists Mark Mobius." *Mail Online*, 26 Mar. 2022, https://dailymail.co.uk/money/markets/article-10655413/Globalisation-NOT-dead-insists-Mark-Mobius.html
4. Molavi, Afshin. "Putin's Bomb and the Global Shrapnel." *Emerging World*, 10 Apr. 2022, https://eworld.substack.com/p/putins-bomb-and-the-global-shrapnel?s=r
5. Frankopan, Peter. *The Silk Roads*. New York, Bloomsbury, 2015.
6. Stelling, Oliver. "Shenzhen Speed and Dubai Spirit." *oliverstelling.com*, 7 Jul. 2021, https://oliverstelling.com/backstory
7. "The World Bank in China." *The World Bank*, 12 Apr. 2022, https://worldbank.org/en/country/china/overview#1
8. CAPA – Centre for Aviation. "Hong Kong 'Loses Its Status as an International Hub' as a Reaction to China's Zero-COVID19 Policy." *CAPA – Centre for Aviation*, 27 Sep. 2022, https://centreforaviation.com/analysis/reports/hong-kong-loses-its-status-as-an-international-hub-as-a-reaction-to-chinas-zero-Covid19-policy-623502
9. *Asian Development Bank*, Feb. 2017, https://adb.org/publications/asia-infrastructure-needs
10. Khanna, Parag. *The Future Is Asian: Global Order in the Twenty-First Century*. London, W&N, 2019.
11. Stelling, Oliver. "Power and Persuasion in the Asian Century." *USC Center on Public Diplomacy*, 4 Mar. 2021, https://uscpublicdiplomacy.org/blog/power-and-persuasion-asian-century
12. "Kishore Mahbubani Says This Is the Dawn of the Asian Century." *The Economist*, 17 Nov. 2020, https://economist.com/the-world-ahead/2020/11/17/kishore-mahbubani-says-this-is-the-dawn-of-the-asian-century
13. "Document 9: A ChinaFile Translation." *ChinaFile*, 30 Oct. 2015, https://chinafile.com/document-9-chinafile-translation
14. "Current Population Estimates, Malaysia, 2020." *Department of Statistics Malaysia Official Portal*, 15 July 2020, https://dosm.gov.my/v1/index.php?r=column/cthemeByCat&cat=155&bul_id=OVByWjg5YkQ3MWFZRTN5bDJiaEVhZz09&menu_id=L0pheU43NWJwRWVSZklWdzQ4TlhUUT09
15. Luhmann, Niklas. *Vertrauen: Ein Mechanismus der Reduktion Sozialer Komplexität (Trust and Power)* (3rd German ed.). Stuttgart, F. Enke, 1989.
16. "Anholt Ipsos Nation Brands Index 2021." *Ipsos*, 19 Oct. 2021, https://ipsos.com/en/nation-brands-index-2021
17. *Brandirectory*. https://brandirectory.com/softpower
18. Wong, Brian. "Chinese People Think China Is Popular Overseas: Americans Disagree." *The Diplomat*, 9 Nov. 2021, https://thediplomat.com/2021/11/chinese-people-think-china-is-popular-overseas-americans-disagree/
19. Fu, Yike. "The Quiet China-Africa Revolution: Chinese Investment." *The Diplomat*, 22 Nov. 2021, https://thediplomat.com/2021/11/the-quiet-china-africa-revolution-chinese-investment

20. Khanna, Parag. Conversation with author, April 2022.
21. Dharmaraj, Samaya. "Vietnam Among Countries with Most Affordable Mobile Internet." *OpenGovAsia*, 3 Mar. 2022, https://opengovasia.com/vietnam-among-countries-with-most-affordable-mobile-internet
22. Kaplan, Robert. *Asia's Cauldron: The South China Sea and the End of a Stable Pacific*. New York, Random House, 2014.
23. ISIS Malaysia. "War in Ukraine: What Does It Mean for Southeast Asia?" *YouTube*, 7 Apr. 2022, https://youtube.com/watch?v=23xLX77_j6Y
24. Khanna, Parag. Conversation with author, April 2022.
25. Molavi, Afshin. *Emerging World*. https://eworld.substack.com
26. Molavi, Afshin. *The New Silk Road Monitor*. https://newsilkroadmonitor.com/
27. Dialogues, Bri. "BRI Dialogue – D12 in Conversation with Afshin Molavi." *YouTube*, 31 Mar. 2022, https://youtube.com/watch?v=UcrqyUpA_Ms

2 Communication vs. Communications

All That Makes Us Human

Human interaction involves both verbal and nonverbal communication. A common take is that the former only conveys information, whereas the latter includes gestures, facial expressions and more. If true, it would imply that the subject at the center is a "case closed" and unworthy of any deeper inquiry. But that is wide of the mark. "Any fool can know. The point is to understand."[1] The statement, often attributed to Albert Einstein but without proof, is spot on, as understanding is indeed critical. An analysis of the vast but not so widely known body of literature about communication theory reveals some of the untapped potential of strategic communications and its relevance in intercultural communications.

Getting involved with diverse cultures, governance models and business environments will always broaden one's worldviews. Yet making sense of it all requires some deeper awareness of how person-to-person interaction works. Being rooted in philosophy, sociology, anthropology and linguistics, the academic assessment of human interaction offers a much broader view on how to connect in a modern age. The take on what defines "mutual understanding" may come as a surprise. It's a real tipping point bound to change long-held views, create demand for a more purposeful approach to communications and adjustments that meet a revived set of criteria.

Western Communication Theory

Located within the "Alte Sternwarte" (old observatory), Bonn's Institute for Communication Research and Phonetics (IKP) was quite literally the place to facilitate real discovery about human interaction. Its top lecturers, Johann G. Juchem[2] and Heinrich Walter Schmitz[3] and the head of the Institute, communication scientist, phonetician and linguist Gerold Ungeheuer,[4] spearheaded the conceptualization of a solution-centric communication theory connected to social sciences and action theory. Ungeheuer also coined the terms "communication semantics" and "individual world theory."

Juchem derived his theses from sign-theoretical and epistemological considerations and concentrated on the concepts of reflexivity and ethno-methodology. Schmitz delved deep into the ethnography of communication, first denoted by linguist, sociolinguist and anthropologist Dell Hymes in 1962. Their lectures were particularly insightful, as they used to start with an outline of their latest

DOI: 10.4324/9781003385622-3

interdisciplinary research before facilitating an open debate on their sociological and philosophical deliberations and those of the predominant thinkers in our field of study. The purpose was clear: to achieve a common understanding in the lecture hall and thus facilitate support of the very theory they outlined. As Guido Wolf, head of Conex Institute and also one of my study friends at the IKP, keeps reminding me every time we catch up: "Remember, we have seen the stars." We sure did, right there, at the old observatory. Let's telescope in on some of the brightest among them.

Heinrich von Kleist (1777–1811) was a German novelist and philosopher. A somewhat troubled and controversial figure in his day, Kleist now ranks among the most revered German playwrights of the 19th century. His work influenced famous novelist Franz Kafka and was even adapted for operas and feature films. Directly related but much lesser known than his plays and novellas are Kleist's views on the connection between clarity of thought and speech, which he expressed in a short philosophical essay titled *On the Gradual Production of Thoughts during Speech* (*Über die allmähliche Verfertigung der Gedanken beim Reden*).[5]

As I wrote a while ago,[6] this is not some prophetic take on the dangers of mindless babble and the stream of consciousness that we often see when turning on the TV. It's also not about thinking aloud or language shaping the way we think, although that is the case. Instead, Kleist clarifies the benefit of speaking to someone else with "the sensible intention of instructing yourself." The central idea: If you ever find yourself stuck in a labyrinth of unfinished thoughts and don't know how to break out and get to the point, speak to the first person you come across. The brain fog will clear up and the right words will come with ease. Two things are at play here: the mindfulness of the human intellect that someone else is listening, and "the necessity to find an end for the beginning," as he puts it. Here is what Kleist wrote back in the early 1800s:

> When I talk about it with my sister, who sits behind me and works, then I discover what I would not have been able to express by perhaps hours of brooding. Not as if she were telling me, in the true sense of the word; for she knows neither the book of law, nor … did she led me by clever questions to the point that matters, even though this last one is often the case. But because I do have some preconception, which is in some way connected with what I am looking for, I just need to begin boldly and get started. That's when the mind, obliged to find an end for the beginning, transforms my confused concept as I speak into thoughts that are perfectly clear, so that – to my surprise – the end of the sentence coincides with the desired knowledge.[7]

In short, it's not the actual feedback or alternate point of view, if there is any. What matters is the sheer presence of someone who's listening that will get us over that writer's or thinker's block. As we hang out more on social media and spend less face time with people, Kleist reminds us that thought and speech go hand in glove. The point was definitely not lost on my clients when we discussed a media or presentation skills refresher. The rationale is very much the same: it's not so much what we say, but what they hear. One can easily lose the edge in making an audience understand us, and that calls for some regular practice. I happily stepped in as coach and "Kleist's little sister," including the distractions:

> Nothing is more beneficial to me than some movement of my sister, as if she wanted to interrupt me; because my already strained mind will only be stimulated even more by this attempt from the outside to snatch from me the speech which I am in possession of.[8]

There are two reasons why quoting this 200-year-old piece in a book about the future of communications adds up. First, Kleist produced a timeless gem that combines deep insight with modern-day advice. In the context of his time, he realized the significance of that "other person in the room" who reacts and comments and in doing so helps us articulate more clearly what we want to say. It's a function that is unavailable on social media where our "first take" is instantly out there for everyone to see; the main cause behind so many "when will Twitter add an edit button" comments.

As for speaking without knowing, the rewards of taking that leap of faith are instant, because "speech is not an impediment or sort of brake on the wheel of intellect. It's more like a second wheel running parallel with it on the same axle."

To be clear, the process of explaining all this is meant to reflect the early lectures by Juchem and Schmitz and designed to get readers of this book curious about communication theory, that treasure trove of not so well known yet highly relevant scholarly research. Juchem and Schmitz used Kleist's comprehensible writings during the first semester to draw all students into the more complex and abstract academic literature that would come next. It was a thoughtful method and perfectly in line with the core subject of making communication work by adjusting to the listener. It sure worked for me and left a lasting impression about their wisdom and trustworthiness.

The *Organon Model*,[9] devised by German psychologist and linguist Karl Bühler (1879–1963), is one of the key theories that explain human interaction. The name is a reference to Plato's metaphor of language as an "organon" (Greek for "tool"). Bühler singled out three main functions of communication: *Ausdrucksfunktion* (expressive function), *Darstellungsfunktion* (representation function) and *Appellfunktion* (appellate or conative function). These were later expanded by Russian American linguist Roman Jakobson to include the poetic function, phatic or contact function and metalinguistic function.

Bühler's point was that communication goes beyond a simplistic sender–receiver model, the transmission of predetermined and fixed content from one head to the other. How a message is received depends on the way it is encoded by its sender – through verbal, paraverbal and nonverbal means – and the degree to which the recipient can decode it.

Another much-cited scholar is Paul Watzlawick (1921–2007). His famous five axioms of communication[10] were met with much curiosity outside academic circles due to their choice of popular wording and special emphasis on pragmatism while adding a whole range of new perspectives to communication. First, one cannot not communicate. That includes behavior such as facial expressions and gestures. Second, all content is determined by relationships. Third, communication always depends on cause and effect, which can affect the sequence of and reaction to statements and therefore the direction of any conversation. Fourth, all communication is based on digital (long ago used to refer to verbal communication) as well as analog communication (nonverbal actions), which can lead to distinct interpretations of spoken language depending on the simultaneous signals sent via gestures, tone, distance and position. And fifth, communication can be symmetrical or complementary, which addresses the roles or positions of power that can shape all interaction and is particularly pertinent in institutional communications across government and business.

Plenty of other academics contributed to the extensive body of literature paving the road to a more comprehensive communication theory. They include Max Weber, Georg Simmel, the aforementioned Niklas Luhmann, and Alfred Schütz, to name but a few.

Luhmann's theories on the correlation between organization and society and their connection with communication, semantics, risk and trust stand out for their ingenuity and impact on the theoretical foundation of communications as a practice. They include his concept of "communicative filters" that shape perspectives with the implicit goal of reducing complexity and creating trust, which together enables communication. In *Speaking and Being Silent (Reden und Schweigen)*,[11] Luhmann and co-author Peter Fuchs address the tautology in philosophies and redundancy in rationalities of communication, where talking and being silent are opposed and the only conceivable terms within the field of communication. One is essentially the nonappearance of the other, without an assessment of the means by which either are accomplished or forced. Luhmann questioned whether this constrained means of thought would continue to be fitting.

Alfred Schütz (1899–1959) ranks among the most influential sociologists of the 20th century. In his *Phenomenology of the Social World*,[12] he provides a solid philosophical basis for the sociological theories of Max Weber and teachings of German philosopher Edmund Husserl who conceived the concepts of phenomenology and "life world" (Lebenswelt). Schütz added some critical thoughts about motive and motivation in human interaction, described as the distinction between "because motives" (Weil-Motive) and "in-order-to motives" (Um-zu Motive). Both are worthy of special attention by communicators, as their use is critical to the shaping of perceptions and can also be a source of support or rejection. "Because motives" are more closely linked to the past ("I did this because") while in-order-to motives ("I am doing this in order to") displays one's envisioned future. The latter is more likely to resonate with audiences, as any display of future orientation makes it more encouraging for audiences to listen. Addressing the ever-present question of "What's in it for me?" is particularly significant for all positioning and messaging exercises where the foundations for vision and mission statements are being laid.

Any review of the academic work on communication theory cannot be completed without mentioning Europe's greatest political philosopher and sociologist, Jürgen Habermas (born 1929), author of *The Theory of Communicative Action*.[13] Centered on his interpretation of Edmund Husserl's concept of "life-world," Habermas describes the origin of society and the mutual attempt at making sense of the world and others. His principles of ideal verbal communication accentuate mutual understanding, truth, sincerity in expression, the right to speak and legitimacy as key factors to maintaining communication. Much of his thought was influenced by the Frankfurt School, a group of intellectuals inspired by Karl Marx but not at all convinced of his take on the influence of culture in modern capitalist society. Yet recent comments by Habermas did raise some concerns about his current interpretation of Lebenswelt. By adding his voice to the appeasers of Russian President Putin in a guest-essay for *Süddeutsche Zeitung* in which he accused Ukraine of "blackmail," his stance on truth and sincerity in expression suddenly raised doubts. Or was it just further proof that sincerity is a moral principle but no precondition for the functioning of communication? More on that in the section on truthfulness in communication, which addresses his four speech act classes.

There have been numerous other shots at establishing a widely accepted communication theory that explains how humans interact and achieve common understanding. What remains important is to acknowledge that even the general public has some kind of communication theory at their disposal. When delving into scholarly research of communication and communications, a key requirement is be open to subjective takes that add insight and context to the real life conditions of human interaction.

The provisional conclusion of all academic research is this: understanding between and among humans is not reliant on any quantifiable intake of the sender's messages (flashback to the Organon Model). The reality of how, when and why human interaction succeeds underscores what's at the heart of human nature: understanding is achieved when all participants believe they achieved it.

"Walking the talk" (putting words into action) is critical, but so is "understanding and being understood." Both are central parts of mastering the art of conveying ideas, concepts and values with a diverse audience.

Eastern Communication Theory

As stated, all scientific studies mentioned to this point refer to Western theories, which largely reflect a primarily 20th-century view of the world. Asian communication theory, on the other hand, is not based on one consistent model of scientific research in a culturally homogeneous region. Instead, it is largely founded in the classic works of Asia's great philosophies – primarily Chinese and Indian – and heavily influenced by the variety of religions, beliefs and cultural values that emerged over thousands of years in various parts of Asia. While that makes it harder to get a full overview and compare it with the Western strategies, any attempt will help understand the underlying cause of diverging worldviews, recognize their significance in the modern age and search for areas of agreement.

In *Encyclopedia of Communication Theory*,[14] the editors Stephen W. Littlejohn and Karen A. Foss present the views of Shelton A. Gunaratne. The late Sri Lankan journalist and professor of mass communications affiliated with Minnesota State University shaped much of the scientific debate, elaborating on the new perspectives Asian communication theory adds to the meanings of communication. At the heart of his academic works was the argument for de-Westernizing communication and social science research, starting with a reversal of the positivist Western view of theory and its focus on individualism, which diverges from the Asian view of reciprocal responsibility between individual and society and harmony with nature.

To add some context to this academic thought, the said distinction between Eastern and Western worldviews and ways of rationalizing communication do in fact come with consequences. The West, for example, is often painted as not respecting Asian values while showing a lack of knowledge about Eastern cultural traits. The alleged unawareness includes an understanding of hierarchy (vs. the West's more egalitarian system), the importance of face-saving, the role of collectivism (as opposed to Western individualism), as well as different speech patterns, articulation techniques and choices of nonverbal communication.

In view of all those different stances, there are obviously some significant hurdles to overcome; more than we already face in our own cultural sphere. At the same time, another question emerges: "How future-ready are the East and the West when interacting with the world in today's age?"

The various perspectives, even if misguided, cannot be dealt with if there is no dialogue. Misunderstandings and misinterpretations of Asian and Western culture demand a well-conceived strategy. At the center is one essential question: how to orchestrate consensus that mutual understanding has been achieved via cross-cultural dialogue? Since much of the discourse happens in English and takes place via global broadcast, print and online media as well as communication apps created by Western and Asian developers, the search for a common perspective is more important than ever. And if that means anyone operating in another part of the world must make a greater effort to understand the cultural background of its consumers, users, partners or clients, that's not a bad thing, either.

Applying Theory to Practice

When engaging in international communications, one must revisit the basic tenets of people-to-people communication and – as mentioned before – move on from the one-dimensional sender–receiver model. A more outcome-focused model involves pragmatics; a critical part of linguistics that takes a broader view on human interaction in order to add more clarity to its interpretation. Together with semantics, which describes the meaning of words and language, pragmatism, which is all about the social context in which conversations take place, can only improve intercultural communications. It also helps with the development of strategies that enhance content and foster enduring relationships through voluntary sharing and advocacy. The approach covers all channels of communication but is most consequential in social media, which must no longer be treated as a purely technical relationship like traditional broadcast media. The real significance lies with people-to-people connectivity and the opportunity to listen, converse and understand what motivates audiences. Dialogue and cooperation also depend on the readiness to accept the need of tolerating disagreements. Leaders must realize that the mobile technology and social media have democratized communication, which is affecting other areas of society and has therefore become a real inflection point. When anyone can publish content, then perceptions are no longer controlled by the few, but by the many. That also accelerates the interconnectedness of publics around the globe, especially in Asia, where the demographics speak for themselves.

One decade ago, Indonesia's capital Jakarta (soon to be shifted to the state of Kalimantan in Borneo under the name Nusantara) ranked as the world's social media capital. According to Paris-based social media agency Semiocast, more tweets were sent from Jakarta than from any other city in the world. For six straight years, that badge was then awarded to the Philippines, which topped the global rankings for both social media and internet usage. And that is exactly the point. The younger a population and the more access it has to technology and social media, the more urgent is the need to speak in their language. Again, there is much work to be done for PR pros.

Watzlawick primarily referred to interpersonal communication but did not exclude non-direct interaction such as written communication. Even if we don't post or tweet for a week we're still communicating. And if we add an emoji to our post or tweet, we cover the all-important nonverbal part of communications. Yes, it's far from perfect, but it's the closest thing to physical encounters and the best way to stay connected while traditional forms of individual and mass communications such as print and broadcast media are fading. It also serves the purpose of establishing and maintaining emotional bonds. The same applies to exchanges between organizations and audiences. They work best when resembling those between human beings.

As stated in Watzlawick's fifth axiom, communication can either be symmetric or complementary. Symmetry would require that organizations and their stakeholders communicate on equal terms. In any intercultural dialogue, that would require some form of commitment by all actors to remove obstacles related to the choice of language, translations and interpretations of all content and to avoid creating any imbalance between all parties. It is hard to achieve, but possible. Complementary communication, on the other hand, is distinguished by the dissimilarities between all engaged parties. That makes it more realistic in terms of the situation on the ground but not a desirable long-term guiding principle for the development of real dialogue. With Asia being the most ethnically, culturally and linguistically diverse region of the planet, striking the right balance between symmetry and complementarity is going to be critical. Our choices of staying connected with our stakeholders at home and abroad need to be factored into any corporate or public policy strategy. Communication is what makes us human. Speaking of which…

Communication vs. Communications

Given our exposure to a daily torrent of published opinions and editorial content via social and traditional media, it is normal to occasionally encounter words and phrases that we are not 100 percent familiar with. If they attract our attention, we might go that extra mile and google their actual meaning. If not, most people simply move on. Communications – the one with the "s" – is one of those words. Outside the industry, the term does not draw much public attention, except for debates on policy, diplomacy and international relations. Yet it hardly ever raises questions about its actual meaning and connotations. After all, it sounds like communication, and we all know how that works, don't we?

Communications is often seen as nothing more than a shot at whitewashing public relations and lobbying; a profession with an ironically mixed reputation. But that overlooks its real meaning and significance. As noted, communication is what defines us as human beings, as it forms the core of relationships through expressed thoughts and feelings and the emotional bonds and other forms of kinship that follow. It's a stimulus-response chain and basic human trait that is believed to have advanced in line with our evolution as Homo sapiens some 150,000 to 200,000 years ago. By contrast, communications describes how messages are delivered, including not just the use of technology but also the strategic or tactical approach to enable authentic, ongoing dialogues and express whatever we must in order to achieve our set goals and shape them in ways that resonate with the target audience.

Both are obviously interrelated but not identical and must therefore be treated differently. Blurring both would not only cause confusion and misunderstandings on our own patch but complicate intercultural dialogue; particularly with cultures whose vocabularies don't include two distinctive terms and would hence consider both as being basically synonymous.

The distinction is more consequential than it may appear on the face of it. Scholars and practitioners have been preaching for years that mastering the art and science of communications amounts to seizing the opportunity to lead with a cultural technique that secures our competitive advantage as individuals, institutions, businesses or governmental entities. This argument has historical merit as it derives its authority from the dawn of verbal and written communication all the way to the invention of the printing press, the telegraph and telephone, broadcast and the internet. Even in ancient times, having control over the tools and techniques of communications was a matter of precedence; one that rested with those privileged few who could read.

One would assume that the documented evolution of communications would be convincing enough to make the case for leaders to pay more attention to it. Regrettably, that is not always the case. While most would agree that a positive perception is no longer a "nice-to-have," not everyone seems duly concerned about how to articulate one's own story and make the case why anyone should listen. Some are more focused on repeating past successes than explaining to investors and other stakeholders what the future looks like, let alone what's in it for them. In the Middle East, a leading real estate developer was bent on its truly impressive years-long growth story. But no one articulated what the future holds for investors. This triggered a comprehensive exercise with the executive board, including a repositioning of the group and an overhaul of its entire messaging and stakeholder engagement strategy. The foundation was laid by engaging in deep conversations that explored what's at the heart of the company's value proposition, challenging assumptions and affirming truths. To say it with Schütz, it was a shift from "We did what we did because" to "We are going to do this in order to."[15]

Examples like this show the potential of strategic communications. Its importance cannot be overstated given the increasing influence of social media, the vast power and reach of communication apps and the direct encounters made possible through global travel. In the Asian Century, the measure of human success on all levels is closely linked to the capacity to talk, be heard and understood by a global audience – and to be trusted.

After Donald Trump's election win in 2016, PR pros began to publish piece after piece about what PR can learn from Trump; suggesting that he's superb at public relations. The proof points were anything from shaky to outright wrong, and the conclusions quite disturbing. None of that helped to improve the public perception of PR.

In his widely reported speech at the 77th session of the United Nations General Assembly (UNGA77) on September 20, 2022, UN Secretary-General António Guterres openly criticized the PR industry for shielding the fossil-fuel industry from scrutiny.[16] His point: the lobbying efforts resemble those by the tobacco industry some decades ago. US House Democrats then held a hearing on the role of PR agencies in helping big oil, accusing them of misleading the public on climate change.

PR surely helps with news stories, as much of what we read, listen to and watch is highly contingent on media relations. But what distinguishes it from strategic communications is the primary focus on serving client needs. Of course, many practitioners know how to balance those with public interest, but that has still not changed the public perception. The public relations industry has long been facing its own problems in the fields of moral values and professionalism. The ethics scandals of some agencies and networks whose own prestige lies in tatters surely proved this to be right.

On Truthfulness in Communication

The scientific debate about truthfulness and ethics in communication occasionally refers to Habermas's four speech act classes: Communicativa, Constativa, Representativa and Regulativa. All of them are associated with validity claims: comprehensibility, truth, authenticity and appropriateness. The validity claim of the constatives (explanations, reports, assertions, denials) is centered on "truth." Habermas places this within the broader framework of his universal pragmatics and the concept of communicative rationality, which in his view is tied to the justifiability and criticism of verbal statements. But that is not always reflected by reality.

My master's thesis was focused on lies in communication. The proposition was this: communication and understanding work regardless of whether what is being talked about is true or not. This of course was no moral or ethical judgment, but an acknowledgment of what is, unfortunately, a matter of fact. Lies and "white lies" are part of human interaction and cannot be excluded from communication theory. The main reason is that the same relationship principles apply. The liar has to align his strategy with the listener, and the listener has to get involved with the liar, aiming to understand his choice of phrasing, construct meanings and reconcile all with his experiences and individual world theory.

I remember Gerold Ungeheuer explaining that lies make a very convincing argument for the functioning of the communication process. The liar has to meet all the conditions to get the listener to accept or believe his false claims. He must achieve understanding (at this instant in the sense of compatible experiences or contents of consciousness) against his own knowledge of the "true" conditions and experiences. And then he must reach understanding and persuasion despite the listener's intuition and doubts. On the whole this shows that regardless of a lie's rating and possible consequences, the act of lying is not devoid of any fundamental communicative skills such as the ability to persuade and to make a strong and believable case.

Let's contrast that with truth. If the concept of communication were firmly linked to the pursuit of truth, the entire epistemological problem of truthfulness would put a considerable strain on any communication theory that is supposed to provide a scope for action in constantly changing environments. In essence, this would imply that there cannot be any "real" communication without it being based on truth. And there could be no successful communication if lying had infiltrated the conversation at any point. That, of course, is not how it works. Deliberate attempts to warp reality to confuse audiences are persistent in politics, in media, in business and even in science. And some of these lies are only too gladly accepted if not desired by the recipients.

Cross-cultural communication is destined to face even more of those challenges because of the geographic distance and diversity of sociocultural context. In view of that, learning to live with misinformation, disinformation and propaganda is no matter of choice, but the only option we have. In fact, divulging falsehoods and lies when they occur can become a strategic and tactical advantage. The critical part is to manage this without curtailing communication, especially in international relations. If it derails any progress in accomplishing values- or principles-based objectives, then what is the point? Wouldn't it be better to keep the conversation going? The significance of values and principles will be discussed in Chapter 6 on public diplomacy.

Achieving Mutual Understanding and Trust

To achieve mutual understanding (now defined as the shared belief between all actors that understanding has indeed been accomplished) should be a common goal and is frequently stated by scholars as one of the main objectives of public diplomacy. It appears to be vulnerable too and is frequently portrayed as being naïve and detached from reality. But its pursuit can come with a lot of discourse power; particularly when being publicly recognized as a way of standing up for honesty and genuineness.

Greater connectivity is what shapes the future of our planet. It surely prepared people from different cultural backgrounds to be more open to other worldviews and keen to create deeper ties, the foundation for intensified collaboration. But dealing with that also raises challenges posed by ethnic, religious, linguistic and political divisions. This is what Niklas Luhmann meant when making the case for trust in international relations in order to reduce complexity. The correlation between relationships, politics and business can be difficult to manage unless cross-cultural communications moves up the value chain. This is not limited to diplomacy. The main task for anyone charged with creating a sustainable and adjustable approach to the development of global strategies is evident. It is about managing multicultural communications with the objective to seek common ground and identify a greater purpose that will be acknowledged and supported by as many as possible.

This takes us to the next topic: what exactly is supposed to be that greater purpose, when values are being compromised for pragmatic reasons? It may all look like a futile task in a world dominated by national and corporate self-interest. But that would be no acceptable outcome. A more inclusive and strategic model of corporate communications, policy planning, diplomacy and conflict resolution via strategic communications should make it to the top of the agenda for multinationals, nongovernmental organizations (NGOs), think tanks, and diplomats. The point is to apply the defining principles and rules of engagement without sacrificing principal values and strategic interests. It's not an easy task, but it's one that can even boost persuasive power if managed in a way that generates trust in one's sincerity. If handled successfully, it also means that one has made a significant step toward promoting universally acceptable values. As always, the early adapters, including communicators, will greatly benefit. As simply put by Wayne D. Dyer: "Go the extra mile. It's never crowded there."[17]

References

1. Quoteresearch, Author. *Any Fool Can Know. The Point Is to Understand – Quote Investigator*. 20 Nov. 2021, https://quoteinvestigator.com/2021/11/20/fool-know
2. "Johann Georg Juchem." *Wikipedia, The Free Encyclopedia*, Wikimedia Foundation, 26 Jul. 2019, https://de.wikipedia.org/w/index.php?title=Johann_Georg_Juchem&oldid=190783808
3. "Heinrich Walter Schmitz." *Wikipedia, The Free Encyclopedia*, Wikimedia Foundation, 26 Mar. 2021, https://de.wikipedia.org/wiki/Heinrich_Walter_Schmitz
4. "Gerold Ungeheuer." *Wikipedia, The Free Encyclopedia*, Wikimedia Foundation, 29 May 2022, https://de.wikipedia.org/wiki/Gerold_Ungeheuer
5. "Über die allmähliche Verfertigung der Gedanken beim Reden." *Wikipedia, The Free Encyclopedia*, Wikimedia Foundation, 26 Jan. 2023, author's translation, https://commons.wikimedia.org/wiki/File:Ueber_die_allm%C3%A4hliche_Verfertigung_der_Gedanken_beim_Reden.pdf?page=
6. Stelling, Oliver. "On Speaking without Knowing." *LinkedIn*, 17 Jan. 2018, https://linkedin.com/pulse/go-ahead-speak-even-you-dont-know-what-youre-saying-oliver-stelling
7. "Über die allmähliche Verfertigung der Gedanken beim Reden."
8. "Über die allmähliche Verfertigung der Gedanken beim Reden."
9. Bühler, Karl. *The Theory of Language: The Representational Function of Language (Sprachtheorie)*. Donald Fraser Goodwin, Amsterdam, John Benjamin's Publishing Company, 1990.
10. Watzlawick, Paul. *Pragmatics of Human Communication*. New York, W. W. Norton and Company, 1967.
11. Luhmann, Niklas, and Peter Fuchs. *Reden und Schweigen* (German ed.), Frankfurt, Suhrkamp Verlag, 1989.
12. Schütz, Alfred. *The Phenomenology of the Social World*. Portsmouth, NH, Heinemann Educational, 1972.

13. Habermas, Jürgen, and Thomas McCarthy. *The Theory of Communicative Action: Volume 1*. Boston, MA, Beacon Press, 1985.
14. Littlejohn, Stephen, and Karen Foss. *Encyclopedia of Communication Theory*. Los Angeles, CA, SAGE Publications, 2009.
15. Schütz, *The Phenomenology of the Social World*.
16. United Nations. "Guterres Calls for 'Coalition of the World' to Overcome Divisions, Provide Hope in Place of Turmoil." *United Nations*, https://un.org/en/desa/guterres-calls-coalition-world-overcome-divisions-provide-hope-place-turmoil
17. "Wayne Dyer Quotes." *BrainyQuote*, https://brainyquote.com/quotes/wayne_dyer_380805

3 Purpose and Shared Values
Communications' Best Engagement Model

Some movies inspire people with great lines, the way characters act and the values they represent. One example is *The Towering Inferno*, the highest-grossing film in 1974.[1] Its ending scene contains a famous dialogue that sums up the moral strength of the two leading characters: the skyscraper's architect played by Paul Newman, and the fire chief played by Steve McQueen. Both are catching a breath after putting out the massive blaze that engulfed the world's tallest building. McQueen tells Newman that one day thousands might die in such firetraps unless somebody is asking him how to build them. It's a moment that comes to mind when watching officials and spokespersons trying to avoid responsibility during a crisis and deflecting from any possible fallout. Rarely would you hear a response like Newman's: "Okay. I'm asking."

All main characters are aware of the fire that broke out on a lower floor and is making its way up. They also know it was caused by cheap wiring and a resulting spark in a fuse box. But none of the hosts or VIP guests is willing to deal with distractions while the big launch party is underway on the 135th floor. Instead, the fire chief and the architect who never approved of the cheap wiring that caused the spark are the ones left to tackle the blaze. The script mimics how some – not all – leaders treat communications: "Having a plan is good for optics but let's not spoil the party." If something goes wrong, they turn to the architect (the strategist) and the fire chief (the head of crisis response) to come up with a quick fix. Meanwhile they keep going about their daily business. Given the increase in energy, finance and other crises that emerging and developing economies are facing there is no doubt that everyone needs an experienced fire chief with authoritative power to lead the crisis response. But listening to the architect is no less important as he already anticipated the risks and dangers. Advance scenario planning is the best way to avoid an accident turning into an inferno.

Quoting that almost 50-year-old movie is no random choice, as some senior leaders are more likely to remember that scene. Being the ones in power, they must realize that fence-sitting is unlikely to serve their corporate interests. Organizations with an established culture of listening before acting are on track to build reputational equity, both inside and outside. It is also a smart way to express purpose without pushing it too hard, something audiences notice when thinking about whom to put faith in.

DOI: 10.4324/9781003385622-4

Earning, Not Claiming

As Paul Watzlawick explained, humans draw on content and relationship to get their message across and pursue certain interests. Relationships determine our choice of content and how to frame it. If they are close-knit, as with friends and family, we can make our case in various ways without the risk of being misunderstood. If we are at the early stages of a new relationship or address an international audience, we need to find ways to convey purpose in order to build confidence, the foundation of understanding.

The reason seems straightforward, as it represents our core belief and who we are —with regard to either our competence, our cultural values or causes we consider important. In public relations, purpose serves as an answer to stakeholder questions about the "why": the essential objective and "license to operate." The latter is a phrase widely used among PR pros who seek to assist clients in defining "purpose beyond making profit." And it obviously applies to PR, too. Yet to use it in written or spoken communication would be the equivalent of continuously repeating vision and mission statements. Some actors rely on that, but that doesn't always deliver the desired results. However, it remains common to push a cause-based purpose as part of the core messaging and narrative. It may work now and then, but the inherent risk of weakening trust in whatever argument the speaker makes should be unacceptable. By raising doubts about the real purpose, it becomes an own goal – in a league of its own.

This is one of the main points made by Robert Phillips in his 2015 book *Trust Me, PR Is Dead*.[2] What he noted is the end of spin in the age of individual empowerment, showing how the PR industry has abused and exhausted trust. "Trust is not a function of PR. It is an outcome, not a message," he wrote, adding that it is also deeply behavioral, complex, fragile and hard-won every day by actions, not words. He even warned about PR firms that suggest otherwise.

The same applies to marketers who adopt slogans like "Delivering Happiness," a phrase that has seen a spike in recent years. Companies are using it across all available marcom platforms. Yet, unsurprisingly, such acts are often seen as attempts to distract from reality, such as known and well-documented track records of underdelivering. It is perhaps the most in-your-face and clumsy effort to steer the narrative in the preferred direction. Like trust, happiness is not a message, but an outcome that has to be earned. Purpose, on the other hand, can deliver the goods if it is authentically defined, well-integrated in daily operations and the organizational culture and there for everyone to see.

In practically all settings, it is vital to figure out how to cover purpose without bringing it up at every turn. Of course, any visible and helpful action would make the case in no time. But even when action matters more than words, the rationale behind it needs to be well articulated. This is where the paraverbal and nonverbal elements of communication come into play. It can also be integrated "between the lines," as part of the proof points that support sub-messages. The delivery requires some practice and training, but once mastered it can be a key factor in getting listeners, viewers and readers to buy into the overall messaging.

So how does this work when understanding is possible even in the absence of good faith as described earlier? The main point deserves to be repeated, as the conclusion must sound uncommon: mutual understanding and all desired outcomes are not subject to the transmission of information alone. The essence of it is the shared belief between all actors that understanding has indeed been achieved. Just who is leading that effort? The marketers who came up with happiness and then pushed PRs to create a credible story around it? Perhaps not. Ideally, it's those leaders who bring in related experience and stick to the truth. Once that has become the accepted reality, the self-representation by communicators must be revisited.

Industry observers have heard this a million times: "PR is facing multiple challenges and needs to adapt quickly in order to stay competitive and remain relevant." It's a simple and worn-out cliché but still worthy of reflection. Yes, PR, by definition, needs to adapt steadily. The value of being a media advisor falls and rises with the ability to shape opinions while reconciling changing public with private interests. And these changes are fast and profound. But there is some confusion here about the terms.

As described in the opening part of this chapter, the way communications works is not always plain and simple. When the fire breaks out, the finger-pointing starts, and real expertise is needed to handle the internal and external fallout. And even when there is no looming towering inferno, it sure helps to have a plan in place that covers all possible scenarios and earns trust in the preparedness to protect organizational reputations. That underscores a basic fact: making your mark in communications goes beyond knowledge of the core function of public relations as an isolated practice. In real life, making an impact is always closely linked to a comprehensive understanding of the internal expectations and complexities of all sociocultural, political, economic and technological shifts that shape the operating environment.

"Everything a company does is PR. That makes PR a management function, not a communications function." That line was used at a Middle East PR industry gathering a few years ago, and it fits in well with the old mantra, "Advertising is for visibility and PR is for credibility." The implicit message, of course, is that PR should always lead. For many in the PR community, this is nonnegotiable. PR, with its unique blend of insight, creativity, content and media leverage, belongs at the top of the marcom food chain. It certainly helps to think that way if you crave the same budgets that advertisers secure.

What aided this view to persist over decades is the client preference for integrated solutions rather than a discipline-specific approach. Yet classic PR, the traditional go-to guys for strategy, saw its mojo decline a bit when advertising and digital agencies began to make huge strides with innovative engagement strategies, personalized ads as well as e-commerce apps and other tech solutions that connect with audiences in a smooth and optimized manner. Neither CX (customer experience) nor digital marketing nor content marketing nor influencer marketing could ever be considered classic PR campaign territory. PR is also the usual first victim of marcom cost-cutting. To consider PR, and presumably only PR, as a management function because "everything a company does is PR" therefore points at cognitive bias. It's like that old saying "To a man with a hammer, everything looks like a nail."

To be sure, everything a company does is not PR. Everything a company does is communication, with or without tactical or strategic intent – just like humans who cannot not communicate. Accordingly, the process of safeguarding an organization's reputation cannot be handled by one side alone. As mentioned in Chapter 2, strategies that can foster enduring relationships help to amplify the content and its reach through voluntary sharing and advocacy. Like advertising or marketing, PR makes for a great tool in a pretty big toolbox to build ties and get closer to achieving all set goals. But how these tools are being used needs to be reviewed.

According to a survey by Muck Rack,[3] the credibility of US corporate PR professionals and CEOs among journalists dropped significantly in 2021. For Michael Webster, Director at Telum Media, Asia Pacific's leading media intelligence platform, this can be overcome. "There has always been a tension between the media and the communications industry. I'd see some tension as healthy. Our role at Telum is to help both sides communicate and understand each other more effectively."[4] This certainly helps both sides as it sets the stage for better relations and trust as an outcome, not a message. It is also a decisive step toward PR's progression to strategic communications. To place it at the top of the agenda should always be a management imperative, as it enables the development of integrated strategies and the coordination of all the actions with a clear view of direction and purpose. This could be to educate, inform or create consciousness; to influence behavior; to nurture and protect a good name and high standing; or just to make a difference.

The full-scale integration of some or all marcom functions, though, is never predetermined. The upside of leveraging their individual strengths across paid, shared and earned content always depends on the situational context. But once a plan exists that articulates the desired outcomes together with a roadmap that includes all forms of stakeholder engagement and relationship building, things are moving in the right direction. What is important to remember is that brands are built from the inside out, while reputations are earned from the outside in. This is about not just consumer goods, but also corporate and nation brands. Hence, the process deserves the utmost attention and must be managed very carefully.

The Progression from Storytelling

The talent pool to tap into when filling the role of communications strategists exists. There are pending changes in job specs, especially with regards to being tech-savvy, but the best choice is still to assemble teams with experienced PR pros. There is just one problem: many PR pros are still at ease calling themselves "storytellers." I made this point as early as 2017:

> It seems like a good catchphrase that sums up the real meaning of the profession. After all, stories shape their workday. With more content generated and consumed than ever before, the old art of storytelling is a great way to cut through the clutter. In today's attention economy, knowing how to craft and pitch a story that connects with stakeholders such as strategic partners, investors, employees as well as constituents, prospects and vendors is worth its weight in gold. But that's only half of the … umm, story.[5]

Outside the industry, all that storytelling is still widely perceived as a soft skill and an afterthought; the kind of exercise that comes after the "real work" is done. In addition, there seems to be some degree of uncertainty within the industry about its own future. PR practitioners don't talk about the consulting part of their work as much as they should – at least there is no catchphrase yet. For consultancies, this now constitutes a challenge, as clients are taking a closer look at the external consulting model, fee structures, digital prowess and value generation; triggering some serious soul-searching among PR pros.

What's more, for years now media watchers noticed a surge in articles and commentaries on two similar-sounding subjects: "The Future of the Agency" and "The Agency of the Future." For an industry that is all about projection, influence and reputation, such navel-gazing makes it look rather unconfident. Here is why. Do law firms have a future? And heart surgeons? And do lawyers and heart surgeons spend sleepless nights worrying about their future or that of their profession? No, they don't. Such loss of control over their perception does not make the storytellers look like the strategists they often claim to be.

What worries the industry is the recognition that the traditional holding model of international marcom agencies is under intense pressure. Some clients are questioning the perceived value of external counsel, while others move to bring the creative and strategic functions inhouse. That does not come as a surprise, as the purpose of integrated services is not always to serve clients better. Instead, the premise of "all under one roof" makes it harder to walk away from a contract when so many creative disciplines are affected. Clients have also been wondering why they should accept that lack of focus and attention by senior executives who were all over the place during the pitch but disappeared as soon as the contract was signed. And of course, cost optimization does not make you a better PR firm, either. The larger marcom holding companies have already seen the ramifications of that trend when clients started building up in-house capacity. They should be least surprised, though. As soon as there is a temporary drop in revenues, some of the bigger players are quick to impose hiring freezes that affect all subsidiaries, irrespective of the impact on their clients' business. The better agencies have global heads of client servicing to ensure client satisfaction during all kinds of change.

Kicking the can down the road is no longer viable. According to the Campaign In-Housing Summit,[6] arranged and hosted in late 2021, roughly 70 percent of brands are in the process of setting up an in-house agency or at least ponder the idea. Brands are more ready than ever to invest in corporate and marketing communications, digital, internal, and issues-based communications designed to build and protect a reputation.

Client scrutiny over PR value is not a bad thing. It should be considered an advantage, as it helps to refocus on core competencies. The final verdict may not be out yet, but solid counsel, based on experience and a firm grip on facts, data and audience sentiment, remains a very valuable proposition. Let's contrast that with journalism, which is also facing an increasing number of challenges.

More and more people are getting their news via social media. The option of bypassing subscription fees has further accelerated the decline in demand for print. Even when readers visit news media online, the reduced ad spend and proliferation of ad blockers is coming with significant financial losses. In addition, there are allegations of spreading fake news. Some of the most celebrated journalists had to counter fake allegations of made-up stories and repeat their commitment to the highest professional standards and work ethics. Meanwhile, propagandists adopted the fake news battle cry. The world would have known much less about the disruption caused to democracy by Trumpism and the GOP's shift to right-wing extremism if it wasn't for reporters being relentlessly engaged in fact checks and digging out the truth. Under mounting pressure, journalism emerged stronger than ever. In fact, as other commentators have also noted, this could well be the golden age of journalism. If any further proof was needed, awarding the 2021 Nobel Peace Prize to two journalists should make that case. Maria Ressa and Dmitry Andreyevich Muratov earned this highest recognition for their fight for free speech as a precondition for democracy and lasting peace. Less than a year later, both called for a world in which technology is built in service of humanity and where our global public square protects human rights above profits.[7] Now it's time for comms pros to pursue their own golden age.

Looking at both communications and independent media, it is hard to miss the overlapping interests and concerns. As professionals, there is a shared interest in authenticity. What also unites both is the growing concern over the accelerating global erosion of faith in politics, corporations and institutions, described by some as an implosion, which it has been for years.

For communications pros, shifting the self-reference from the convenient storytelling to the analytical and strategic aspects of their work would help in demystifying what they do without oversimplifying it. If managed well, it could make them instantly more credible and bolster their case, because strategic counsel is no echo chamber. It's not about telling clients what they want to hear, but about what they must hear. And based on the discussions that follow, the next step is the creation of compelling narratives that are truth-based and verifiable.

The old spin-based PR model is assigned to the dustbin of history. Unethical behavior is officially outlawed. The downfall of Bell-Pottinger and the Public Relations and Communications Association's (PRCA) role in promoting the industry's professional standards prove that. Some large networks are already moving fast to resign questionable assignments. But not everyone is taking such an unambiguous position. And spin as such is far from dead. According to the Asia-Pacific Communication Monitor (APCM) 2020–2021 survey,[8] ethical challenges and concerns remain a cause of concern. Some 56 percent of the 1,155 communications professionals who participated did face such issues recently, and many felt they lacked the resources to handle that kind of situations.

The changes in public discourse and daily threats to the foundations of trust are striking and make strategic counsel invaluable. Being serious about building and protecting reputations commands a commitment to business ethics and an interdepartmental effort to ensure the alignment of public, corporate and government interests. In short, coordinated action, not just top-down statements of intent.

This is what's at the center of ESG, the Environmental, Social, and (Corporate) Governance movement. The concept has been criticized for being a recipe for "greenwashing."[9] However, creating value for humanity is how ESG can bear fruit. Since it is more specific about its principles and objectives it is also more likely to connect with younger generations (see Chapter 7 on human capital, which deals with Gen Z's empathy for social justice and activism). It might even mark the progression from Corporate Social Responsibility (CSR), the concept of self-regulation, which had transformed corporations with its stated aim of better balancing economic, environmental and social imperatives (the so-called "Triple-Bottom-Line-Approach"). CSR itself replaced US economist Milton Friedman's decades-old argument that social responsibility of businesses was to increase profits. But the exact definition and implementation of CSR still remains subject to the interpretation of each company that is looking for greater purpose. Managing it in silos and being marginally linked to core business activities is no solution. Self-regulation with the goal of building accountability is going to stay and may even see an increase in public demand as stakeholders expect businesses to force consistent impact through all parts of their operations.

The same applies to "Purpose and Shared Values." The concept became more popular when fake news rose from its existence on the fringes to occupy a major focus area by certain media and commentators. It may just be the wakeup call that was needed. Trustworthiness can be restored and communicators can contribute by becoming strategists and truth-seekers first and storytellers second. That also includes crisis situations.

In the corporate world, the traditional focus is on business strategy, legal, finance and HR as well as public trust. For some unknown reason, not all senior executives seem to be convinced that strategic communications – the professional caretaker of their name and enabler of trust – deserves the same attention. By continuing to view communications as something that doesn't require as much thought and hard work, they miss out on accumulating serious competitive gains in a key area of influence. In contrast to that stance, leading management consulting firms including the "Big Three" – McKinsey & Company, Boston Consulting Group and Bain & Company, also known as MBB – have long realized that marketing and reputation management must become part of their own service portfolio, just like data analytics and digital transformation. But they also soon figured out that their strength is to address high-level strategy needs, not to come up with creative solutions. Because of that, top consultancies have spent years expanding their offer by hiring the best creative talent and acquiring creative agencies that are qualified to deliver on user experiences, digital marketing, design, web and mobile services, all under their own brand. But nurturing reputations still demands a more comprehensive approach. That involves securing access to top decision makers and leveraging experience in aligning the principles behind Purpose and Shared Values – both inside and outside communications.

Seeking That Higher Purpose

"Can you help us out with Allawi's campaign? You know he is running for President, right?" It was an unexpected call, but being aware of Iraq's upcoming 2010 national election and Dr. Ayad Allawi's inclusive and nonsectarian approach to governance, I was all in. Allawi was a staunch opponent of Saddam Hussein's brutal regime and had served as the interim Prime Minister of Iraq from 2004 to 2005 and President of the Governing Council of Iraq (38th Prime Minister of Iraq) in 2003. He led a largely Sunni-backed bloc, the Iraqi National Movement (INM), aka the al-Iraqiya List; raising concerns that Sunni Arabs might not vote for him, a Shiite Arab.

After four weeks of preparation I found myself in Amman, Jordan, a much safer place than Baghdad. Roughly a dozen heavily armed bodyguards secured the hotel suite where my colleagues and I caught up with Allawi and his campaign team. It was a stark reminder that comms is grounded in real-life situations with a real-life impact; not just on a domestic electorate but on Iraq's global perception. The session went well, and the foundation was laid for all his messaging and voter engagement. Not long after the workshop, the election got postponed. But when it finally took place a few months later, Allawi beat out the incumbent Nouri al-Maliki's State of Law Coalition by two seats. Nonetheless, after several months of brinkmanship and bargaining, al-Maliki managed to form a coalition bloc, securing his re-election. That said, Allawi later served as Vice President of Iraq from 2014 to 2015 and from 2016 to 2018.

There are moments when the significance of communications can even hit a comms pro. It was clear from the start what was at stake: the safety and quality of life of all Iraqis. When receiving a brief, communicators are trained to look for purpose in any situation and environment as it portends the strategic concept. The question, however, is what defines the ultimate goal. It can't just be about the best way to push client messages and receive coverage. As said, it is always about real engagement of all concerned parties. In practical terms, this calls for the "higher purpose," an aspirational goal, which does not imply that the recipient or benefactor must be a high-profile entity or individual. In fact, it works in all scenarios and settings and may be the most fitting way to deliver results across industries, business models, geographies and cultures.

There is ample evidence that leaders who made great strides in elevating Purpose and Shared Values to the executive board level are most likely to benefit from an early ROI. The advantages stretch across tangible reputational gains and higher returns plus public approval, third-party endorsement and advocacy. As long as this adjustment has not been made across the board, there will be an imbalance in communications with domestic and global audiences. In intercultural dialogue, that comes with the risk of misunderstandings and possible conflicts. Since none of these developments are comparable to any other great power shifts in recent history, the way to tackle them must begin from scratch. Practitioners and scholars as well as diplomats must act now, analyze, adapt and adjust. But can communicators live up to that challenge? Yes they can, provided there is a belief in the positive effect of the changes we witness.

The traditional concept of PR has been challenged for some years. Robert Phillips highlighted that the revolutionary times in which we live means that there will never be a return to "old trust." His conclusion was crystal clear: "New strategies are needed that speak to the world of tomorrow, not the world of yesterday."[10]

For years, agencies have spent time and money on remodeling the consulting offer to get the same access to the C-Suite that management consultants seem to occupy with ease. Looking at how they succeeded in upselling and placing themselves as trusted advisors to the board, some agencies began to change their company names or designations to reflect that altered strategic focus. But rebranding comes with risks, too. If made against the backdrop of accelerated political, societal and economic change, PR ethics scandals and eroding public trust in institutions, it may come across like an effort to distract. A better option would be to tackle the many image problems of PR head on, adopt a 100 percent focus on stakeholder needs and deliver (and talk about) high-quality outcomes.

Investing in strategic communications, crisis preparedness and new models for data analysis and measurement is a promising way to earn that trust with those calling the shots. That could also be the answer to the growing competition with management consultants who may compete in marcom but not so much on strategic communications counsel. In the end, however, we must remind ourselves that things are moving fast. The old titles and designations are on their way out, according to Martin Sorrell, Founder of venture-capital fund S4 Capital and former head of WPP, the world's largest advertising and PR group. Years ago, when speaking on the future of PR at PRovoke18,[11] he pointed out the importance of content, data and media planning and buying, all under the roof of some new kind of agency. His point was straightforward: it doesn't matter what's on the label but what's in the package. If that package contains future-oriented strategies, then communications is on track to finally fulfill its ultimate purpose of fostering actual engagement that leads to better understanding and real action.

With Transparency Comes Authority

As laid out in the previous chapters, tolerance, equity and inclusion are among the key drivers behind Asia's stellar rise. Diversity is an Asian feature, as is future preparedness, which is dealt with in the next chapter. Being able to adapt keeps all strategic and tactical avenues open for the creation of opportunity and prosperity. A major component of that is to invest in capacity-building and the gathering of insights into culture and cognition, the different perspectives they shape and how to bridge them.

East–West relations would undoubtedly benefit if the social structures and sense of self that are characteristic of Easterners and Westerners and their respective belief systems and cognitive processes are better understood. To achieve that objective, communications departments in both the East and the West need to identify more talent with comprehensive cross-cultural experience. It's an investment that truly pays for itself. Likewise, the boards of directors at multinational companies and top echelons of diplomacy must accept that even when mutual understanding is given preference, some challenges will always persist. American social psychologist Richard E. Nisbett described the sociocultural context in his book *The Geography of Thought: How Asians and Westerners Think Differently ... and Why*.[12] His main argument is that different worldviews and cognitive processes are not just an outcome of diverse environments, teachings and principles, but the result of different tools to understand the world. He concluded that if true, then efforts to improve international understanding may be less likely to pay off than one might hope. Even so, there is no known alternative to trying to improve international understanding. The final reckoning remains uncertain unless we open up to those diverse stances whilst replacing the "cheap wiring" (eminent misinformation and disinformation) that could cause a real inferno. Only then can the party go on.

The central question is what might constitute the basis for mutual understanding when different standpoints and cognitive processes determine not only how we see ourselves and others, but also how we deal with these differences. The best answer is one that provides ways to avoid situations where pointing out what is obviously wrong can be portrayed by the other side as a lack of tolerance and openness. Here is the offramp: transparency. Because of its strong association with honesty and genuineness and therefore being stripped of all cultural counterweights, it would be hard to reject or frame the concept itself as being ideologically biased toward one particular culture; whether the East or the West. It should also resonate with general publics, no matter where in the world. Once it becomes the widely accepted conduct of business that consumers, users and constituents expect and demand, then anyone who tries to deflect and distract is at risk of being debunked for ignoring facts and might quickly lose the ability to persuade. Of course, there are still more obstacles to overcome, as propaganda won't simply disappear (see Chapter 5 for more details).

Go Get Your Paul Newman

In social sciences, having agency is defined as the capacity of individuals to act independently and to plan and carry out actions, or to make an informed and voluntary decision based on their knowledge and intentions. Having agency is therefore not necessarily something that can be objectively measured or quantified. It is a way to gauge the degree of influence in one's internal and external world, and as such is subjective by definition. The best bet, therefore, is to attract talent with agency but not necessarily from an agency: your very own architect or "Paul Newman." As a genuine listener, he or she won't be shy to ask all the right questions while acknowledging prevalent issues as soon as they emerge. This is likely to induce strategies that come with a quick and deep response (not just a reaction) to the best and worst mid- and long-term outcomes.

This evolution of management consultancies marks another watershed moment for PR. Geopolitical and economic trends and their impact on corporate decisions must be taken into account by strategic communications, too. Some global agencies have already acted on that. Edelman's acquisition of Basilinna created a new boutique advisory firm that is closely linked to The Paulson Institute, a think tank focused on the US–China relationship. APCO Worldwide appointed CNN International's former Emerging Markets Editor John Defterios as a senior advisor and International Advisory Council member. Brunswick Group named the President of the Paris Peace Forum and former Director General of the World Trade Organization (WTO) Pascal Lamy as Chair of Europe. Brunswick also appointed Andreas Nick, the former VP of the Parliamentary Assembly of the Council of Europe (PACE) and member of Germany's Bundestag, as partner to shore up its capability in public affairs.

In recent years a new kind of strategic advisory firm emerged. Their focus is on helping business leaders navigate today's complex and volatile international landscape. One of them is WestExec Advisors.[13] Run by former national security advisors with deep geopolitical and policy expertise, they offer something rather unique: "Bringing the situation room to the board room." John Brennan, who served as the Director of the CIA and as Deputy National Security Advisor for Homeland Security and Counterterrorism, joined the firm as Principal.

To wrap it up, adding purpose to corporate communications, policy planning, diplomacy and conflict resolution is accomplished when the authenticity of the speaker or official is being recognized. As said, none of that should become part of the core messaging but should be seen as an outcome that is achieved once audiences notice the independence, free thought and highly regarded beliefs and actions of those who drive these efforts. Navigating this complex set of challenges surely is no easy task. But executives with hope and ambition, publicly displayed as Purpose and Shared Values, are more likely to become real agents of change. This puts them in a position to overcome the many obstacles caused by deeply entrenched internal structures and the complex and interrelated social forces and relationships of organizations that shape the thought and behavior as well as the purpose and intent of those with executive power. To handle this effectively in communications, it is crucial to move from a supportive function to that of influencing strategic decisions instead of having to weigh options after all business decisions have been made.

In *The Towering Inferno*, the architect accepted responsibility despite having done all in his power to avoid such a disaster. This resembles what you get by handing executive power to experienced communicators. Securing those with a high degree of agency and values-based aspiration is a way of safeguarding organizational success. Along with that it also protects the executive board from any loss of reputational equity. Besides, using individual aspiration is a way to inspire others.

References

1. *The Towering Inferno*. Motion Picture. Directed by John Guillermin; produced by Irwin Allen; performances by Paul Newman, Steve McQueen, Fred Astaire et al. US, Warner Bros. & Twentieth Century-Fox. 1974. Robinson, Frank and Scortia, Thomas N. *The Glass Inferno*. 1st ed., Doubleday, 1974. Stern, Richard Martin. *The Tower*. David McKay Co., 1973.
2. Phillips, Robert. *Trust Me, PR Is Dead*. London, UK, Unbound, 2015.
3. "New Muck Rack Survey: The State of Journalism 2022" [New York City, US]. *Muck Rack Blog*, 15 Mar. 2022, https://muckrack.com/blog/2022/03/15/state-of-journalism-2022
4. Webster, Michael. Conversation with author. November 2022.
5. Stelling, Oliver. "It's Not Just Storytelling. It's Also About Truth-telling." *LinkedIn*, https://linkedin.com/pulse/its-just-storytelling-also-truth-telling-oliver-stelling
6. CampaignUK. "Campaign In-Housing Summit | 19 October 2021" [London, UK]. *Campaign*, 20 Aug. 2021, https://campaignlive.co.uk/article/campaigns-in-housing-summit-19-october-2021/1721519
7. APHR. "A 10-point Plan to Address Our Information Crisis." *ASEAN Parliamentarians for Human Rights*, 5 Sep. 2022, https://aseanmp.org/2022/09/05/a-10-point-plan-to-address-our-information-crisis

8. "Asia-Pacific Communication Monitor (APCM) 2020/21 Survey." *Asia-Pacific Communications Monitor*, Mar. 2021, https://communicationmonitor.asia
9. Moran, Michael. "Can Global Regulators Save the ESG Movement from Itself?" *Foreign Policy*, 10 Jan. 2022, https://foreignpolicy.com/2022/01/10/sustainablility-esg-investing-sec-gensler-greenwashing
10. Phillips, *Trust Me, PR Is Dead*.
11. Sorrell, Martin. "PRovoke18 Coverage." *PRovoke Media*, 29 Oct. 2018, https://provokemedia.com/latest/article/video-sir-martin-sorrell-on-the-future-of-pr
12. Nisbett, Richard. *The Geography of Thought: How Asians and Westerners Think Differently… and Why*. Reprint, New York, US, Free Press (imprint of Simon and Schuster), 2004.
13. "WestExec Advisors." *WestExec Advisors – Strategic Advisory Firm in DC*, https://westexec.com

4 Whatever We Imagine

From Aspiration to Inspiration

A deep understanding of how to achieve mutual understanding is a sine qua non of future-proof communications strategies. Purpose and Shared Values help to motivate and shape authentic and sustainable engagement with multicultural audiences. And thinking big plus placing a premium on the alignment of all communications with policies and business strategies is a ticket to success. But none of that shall be limited to external communications alone. What's equally important is to craft a master plan for internal communications.

When commencing with change and transition programs, it is common to move right on to crafting the external narrative of one's imagined future. Why? Because, in the words of Pablo Picasso, "Everything you can imagine is real."[1] In any event, it is no less important to preempt possible disruptions to vital workflows by accepting the possibility of staff concerns and leaving no doubt about the upsides for all. The future is determined by optimists. Gathering internal approval and active support therefore makes the early development of a solid change management strategy one of the most mission-critical tasks.

According to Guido Wolf of the Conex Institute, internal communication is best characterized as a management discipline, which requires a professional and holistic approach linked to the goals, principles, procedures and further standards of an organization. No less important is a focus on "informal communication," the reaction or "swing" led by staffers without any official impulse. It captures the actual organizational culture and main attitudes of all employees. "If the culture is characterized by mistrust against the management, it is nearly impossible to gain quick success by planned communication," Wolf affirmed.[2]

The best way to manage informal communications is to draw attention to sources of inspiration; including people who can become a motivational force in various areas. The course of action is to start with a clear expression of shared values and culture, why change is needed now and how the organization is going to manage the process. That can be accomplished by appointing a designated team whose role is to structure an inclusive, coordinated and collaborative transition based on a robust risk assessment, including predictable roadblocks. It is also critical to cultivate a two-way dialogue and prepare for a response to resistance or just general criticism. If managed well, this will boost staff morale and productivity and foster a sense of inclusiveness, especially in vastly diverse and global environments where the workforce spreads across multiple locations.

DOI: 10.4324/9781003385622-5

Once the process of securing internal support is underway, the obvious next question is what kind of external content can and should be shared, and how. By definition this should include narratives packed with ideas that shape aspiration, namely the ambition to achieve future goals. But that's not all. Having achieved the aspired future can also become a source of inspiration, primarily for external audiences. The individual steps depend on the situational context and professional environment. But when the focus is on the main beneficiaries and the public's best interest, not just short-term corporate or political gains, the ground is laid for an engagement model that serves as the ultimate "great unifier," a strategy that also comes with a longer shelf life.

The standard method to narrow this down would begin with stakeholder mapping, audience segmentation and targeted messaging. But when the audience is truly diverse and global, it is also key to reiterate whatever we imagine as our envisioned future, how it is being articulated and by whom, and whether or not that is likely to resonate with all stakeholders. It works best when official spokespersons, including those with insights into local publics, prioritize tapping into their audiences' ambitions. The technical aspects will be addressed in Chapter 8 on AI and big data. Furthermore, there is an upside in exhibiting a roadmap of events and action points that back up all claims, demonstrate the step-by-step progress made in delivering on promises made while emphasizing how one's imagined future is serving a greater purpose such as the public good.

When Omar Ghobash, the UAE's Assistant Minister for Culture and Public Diplomacy, declared that in the UAE, tolerance is more than just a word, it is a way of life,[3] he expressed what's at the heart of the nation's power of attraction. With over 200 nationalities accounting for roughly 8.92 million, or 90 percent of the country's population of 10.08 million, the evidence is observable in every emirate. Indians and Pakistanis alone account for more than 40 percent of all UAE residents. Due to its commitment to diversity, the nation keeps accelerating its ascent. This did not start with Expo 2020 although the World's Fair stands out for its global impact. Other international events include ADIPEC, the world's most influential gathering for energy industry professionals; the Abu Dhabi Grand Prix; the World Government Summit in Dubai; the International Government Communication Forum held in Sharjah; the Dubai Rugby Sevens; and the Climate Summit COP28. The country was also elected to a two-year term at the United Nations Security Council that began in January 2022. Inspiration occupies a central position, and that propelled the nation's persuasive power all over the world.

There is a largely untold backstory, though, which ought to get more attention and, frankly, media coverage. Any nation that actively contributes to change for the better deserves its place on the podium and the nonexclusive right to claim that badge. It's a case strongly made by Simon Anholt, independent policy advisor to heads of state and CEOs and founder of the Good Country Index: "Being what I call a 'good country' is, to put it simply, balancing your domestic and international responsibilities." He further clarified: "It's doing the right thing for your own citizens and your own territory whilst doing no harm – and preferably benefiting – the citizens and territories of other countries."[4]

Benefiting the whole of humanity and the world as well as one's own people certainly goes beyond telling a country's story. It's a clear-cut strategy to strengthen a nation brand by identifying the commonalities among publics all over the world and what they see as proof of benign intentions and contributions to do good to humanity. These shared values do exist without being affected by cultural and political differences. Getting it right can lead to quick wins. It just requires imagination, flexibility, a values-based model of governance and a commitment to real and tangible results. To step up efforts is entirely reasonable as it aligns with the global community's desire to finally see real progress in tackling all the big challenges that keep piling up.

The 2005 United Nations World Summit called on countries to prepare national development strategies in line with the UN's international development goals. By 2018, some 134 countries had adhered to it and delivered their own plans, bringing the global population that lives in a country with such strategy to a staggering 80 percent.[5] It's a trend that could even accelerate the progress in achieving the Agenda 2030 for Sustainable Development, adopted by all UN member states in 2015. Creating facts on the ground such as hyper-modern infrastructure has already changed the equation in favor of Asia's fastest-moving economies. It's a story that tells itself by drawing the world's attention to the actual and visible progress made. The key components, though, demand constant attention, as perceptions can shift quickly.

Lessons from Belt and Road

In 2013, China's president Xi Jinping launched the Belt and Road Initiative (BRI); his grand design for unrivaled connectedness, increase in trade and strategic influence. The world paid attention as the $1 trillion initiative that aimed to connect over two-thirds of the world's population via overland corridors, also called the "Silk Road Economic Belt" and the "21st century Maritime Silk Road," seemed to know only winners and no losers. Even the name "Belt and Road Initiative" was an excellent choice.

For developing economies in the Middle East, Africa and Asia, the BRI looked like a big ticket to economic growth, modern infrastructure and plenty of jobs that would lift millions out of poverty. For Beijing, it opened new corridors to leverage overcapacity of state-owned enterprises, develop its Western region and gain access to new markets for Chinese brands; all while strengthening its political influence in far-flung places. Evoking imagery of the ancient Silk Road played well with a domestic audience keen to see China's historical greatness restored and further legitimize the CPC's rule. In the meantime, the West saw opportunity and got what it wanted: China's reassurance of upholding global trade and multilateralism while putting their money where the mouth is. What could be wrong with that? It was an inflection point for China's perception, as it convinced many world leaders that Beijing was ready to rebuild the global economy after the global financial crisis.

As time went by, the BRI made some remarkable progress in Africa, Central and Southeast Asia as well as parts of the Western Balkans, providing financing and labor for ports, roads and rail networks, creating thousands of jobs and new trade links. For true believers, the initiative resembled a "Mini United Nations": an exclusive club with a shared vision and agenda for world development, peace and prosperity, and always open to welcoming new members.

To link it back to the first section of this chapter, the BRI's perceived objective was to engage people in ways that serve as the ultimate "great unifier," an inspiration based on China's aspiration. However, despite the untainted appeal of Belt and Road in much of the Global South and the return of infrastructure projects in Southeast Asia, the glory days of BRI excitement seem to be over, at least for now. Global opinion shifted when waves of critical reports emerged and countries like Sri Lanka and Pakistan were facing debt distress; putting a spotlight on alleged fiscal mismanagement, political interference, economic coercion and "debt-trap diplomacy." Creating liabilities for recipients via loans that are hard to pay off undermines claims of offering aid. The European Commission responded with its "Global Gateway" initiative focused on aid and development. However, it had not made much progress in its first year.

The concerns about BRI were not limited to the West only. As early as 2018, Malaysia's then Prime Minister Mahathir Mohamad called out China's "new form of colonialism" and criticized its militarization of disputed territory in the South China Sea, a hot topic across all littoral states in Asia.[6] Mahathir also cancelled three China-backed infrastructure projects, including the East Coast Rail Link (ECRL), that were seen as being price hiked. Just before resigning from his post in 2020, he renegotiated them. The ECRL is on track for completion in 2027. Yet even some of the most fervent supporters have stopped pushing the original BRI story. While briefly being mentioned by Xi Jinping at the CPC's 20th National Congress, his main focus was clearly on the newer Global Development Initiative and Global Security Initiative. This follows the preceding emergence of another narrative that portrays Belt and Road as an engine for the integration of sustainable development, particularly environmental sustainability, and for digitalization. The references to this eminent change in direction are not disputed but perceptions diverge. As critics argued, there are no environmental guidelines for Chinese banks financing BRI projects in line with the protection of biodiversity. And as noted in several reviews and comments about Jonathan Hillman's book *The Digital Silk Road: China's Quest to Wire the World and Win the Future*,[7] China is planning for digital dominance or a world in which all routers lead to Beijing.

Belt and Road has evidently turned into a tale of two worldviews and is now dividing stakeholders along geographic and ideological lines. For some analysts, the initiative is also becoming much less tangible than it was before, creating complications in how to trace its progress. The original goal of land and maritime links is not going to vanish, but the BRI's mid- and long-term prospects for physical connectedness are somewhat uncertain. Besides, Beijing's "no-limits" partnership and "pro-Russia neutrality" provoked greater anti-China sentiment across Europe, including Eastern European nations that represent vital rail nodes for Belt and Road. The long-term consequences are yet to be seen, but adding more geopolitics to the debate over already-fragile supply chains and trade routes between China and Europe is not a win-win.

Regardless of one's position on all these postures, concerns and allegations, the host of issues China is facing are helping neither the BRI nor Beijing's ambition to create a "Community of Shared Future" or its tales of future-preparedness and benign quest for multilateral collaboration. That is not in the world's interest, either, as achieving that goal in line with global standards would have served as a major milestone in bringing the world together. China is aware of that and keeps pushing the shared future, first pronounced by former CPC general secretary Hu Jintao. "Together for a Shared Future" was also the official motto for the Beijing 2022 Winter Olympics. But critics see it as nothing but an effort to enhance the influence of authoritarian principles in the global governance system.

A Community of Shared Future is a valid cause in theory, one that would enhance views of the Asian Century and deserve global support. But a shared future without shared values or principles is impossible to accomplish. As discussed in Chapter 1, opposing universal values is seen as rejecting the foundations of global cooperation. And when the whole world is watching, there is simply no way to compartmentalize narratives. For an aspiring global superpower, everything that is said and done is being recognized as part of the overall stance on matters related to global progress. Moreover, the G7's newly established Partnership for Global Infrastructure and Investment (PGII) might offer an alternative to China's BRI. It remains unclear whether the preference for clean energy solutions, health security and digital connectivity can compete with China's previous focus on infrastructure. But even if the PGII does not attract the same number of countries, there is a real upside for Asia's developing nations. Balancing engagement with the West and with China has always been a top choice but might now also lead to a better negotiating position.

Shifting to Co-Ownership

The escalating tensions between the United States and China had already caused much disruption in trade and bilateral collaboration. When the European Union imposed sanctions on Chinese state officials involved in the oppression of the Uyghurs in Xinjiang, China responded with sanctions against members of the European Parliament and the German think tank MERICS. The EU instantly suspended the ratification of the "Comprehensive Agreement on Investment" (CAI), the China–EU trade deal, which had been seven years in the making. And when China and the EU held a virtual summit one year later in which China refused to talk about Ukraine, human rights and other issues, relations took another dive. For the EU's Foreign Policy Chief Josep Borrell, this was closer to a dialogue of the deaf; one where they could not talk about Ukraine a lot and did not even manage to agree on anything else. For an ambitious nation like China, overcoming this alienation of its preferred trading partners should be a top priority. To get there, its entire narrative needs an overhaul, as only a few of its claims resonate with Western audiences.

This break between aspiration and inspiration is no political statement but a fact supported by the previously mentioned international polls and surveys as well as published opinions by China experts like Jörg Wuttke, President of the EU

Chamber of Commerce in China. Yet Belt and Road can still serve as an offramp of sorts. Despite all stated issues surrounding it, a prolonged impasse is not a foregone conclusion. Asia's most ambitious transformational project can be revived to achieve its goal and become a symbol of global connectivity and a blueprint for resolving the ideological conflicts that prevent the world from tackling the most pressing issues.

As outlined before, the New Silk Roads are not just about the movement of goods. They also offer communication lines, the potential of stronger people-to-people bonds, academic exchange and closer cooperation in research, including food security, climate change and public health. Telling the BRI story in say, Kenya is therefore unlike doing the same in Kazakhstan or Poland. On this account, it is clear that the Belt and Road Initiative cannot be promoted like a domestic mega-project under the executive control of the CPC. As I had written in 2018,[8] communicating Belt and Road will always have to be a multi-stakeholder exercise because it means different things to different people. The only viable path forward is an open yet coordinated approach. Welcoming other nations, enterprises or institutions to not only ship goods via Belt and Road but also contribute to BRI communications would lay proof to China's claim of promoting multilateralism. It's a strategy that has worked before.

When serving as head of Malaysia for the New York–led PR team supporting Beijing's bid for the 2008 Olympic Games, I got a firsthand look at the shifting global opinion of China as a potential host. What sparked this change in China's perception was Beijing's willingness to open up and engage the world on "their terms." As a result China's image had never been better. Much credit goes to the Organizing Committee (BOCOG) Secretary General Wang Wei. Flash forward to 2008: China hosted what was widely regarded as the best Games ever. It was a major win for China and the world.

The BRI and the Olympics are similar in that they are globally recognized and in a wider sense highly inspirational ventures with seemingly limitless potential; synonymous with human progress and achievement. Both are potential sources of sympathy and goodwill – no one wants to see the Games fail. And both were also more than just Chinese initiatives. The Olympics are owned by the world community and brought together by the hosting nation. Looking at the BRI in a similar way – as a global initiative, led or hosted by China but supported and therefore co-owned by multiple parties, nation states and corporations – reveals its full potential. As mentioned before, investing in global infrastructure is a reliable path to success. But it still needs coordination and an alignment of words and action to correct the trajectory that has seen a decline in trust and credibility.

The Winter Olympics are known to attract less global attention than the Summer Olympics. Yet the 2022 Beijing Winter Games, hosted without spectators due to Covid19, saw a decline in international viewers that went well beyond all expectations. The International Olympic Committee (IOC) announced that nearly 40 percent of the Chinese population had watched the Games on TV in China. Yet in most of the West, viewership numbers hit record lows, an unacceptable outcome for a nation with aspirations to lead the world.

Even before China's border closures, extended lockdowns and lengthy quarantines as a result of its Zero Covid19 Strategy, China was experiencing a contracting number of expats. European companies in particular became more and more concerned about China's unpredictable "on-off economy."[9] The fallout is in full view: together with growing anti-Western sentiment, particularly among the Chinese youth, China's isolation is accelerating. Economically, China may survive this period of decoupling. But it is unclear how long the majority of Chinese people will tolerate the gradual separation from the rest of the world. Opening up again will be critical for securing China's economic progress and rebuilding its global image. The decision to ease zero Covid rules could indicate a commitment to adjust. Yet placing greater emphasis on overcoming the ideological divide might be the only way forward.

Co-Creation, Self-Restraint and Mutual Trust

As Parag Khanna wrote in *Bridges to Everywhere – Connectivity as Paradigm*:

> Historical models of order have been built on spheres of influence, but a stable global society today must be based on co-creation across civilizations. Such a balanced system is what Chinese scholar Zhang Weiwei describes as symmetrical rather than hierarchical. It is one in which maintaining stability requires self-restraint and mutual trust among diverse powers.[10]

Part of this is a call for the West to show respect and accept China's rise. Chinese intellectuals have long insisted that the past 200 years were an anomaly and that China only reclaims its rightful place on the world stage. While this may sound revisionist, China's rise over the last 40 years has without doubt been striking. Even though its economy is now slowing, the People's Republic has become a global actor. However, it is still lagging behind in global discourse power. Belt and Road was supposed to change that. This is of particular significance when considering the shortfall in global infrastructure financing, which amounts to between $15 trillion and $18 trillion by the year 2040. Thus, collaboration is clearly in the global interest.

The differences in value systems and politics are likely to prevail for many years to come. Yet Zhang might have staked out a valuable path forward, as there is no apparent long-term alternative to an inclusive, coordinated and participatory approach among the world leading powers. What stands out is the correlation of his thoughts with Europe's amended designation of China as a partner, competitor and strategic rival; something I covered in my guest essay *#BeltandRoadInitiative – Time for some European Realpolitik*.[11]

Co-Creation

In the years following Xi's announcement in 2013, the BRI was seen as ambitious and visionary but also loosely defined and ever expanding. China addressed that lack of a cohesive policy by creating a large number of think tanks dedicated to the study of Belt and Road. Beijing also invited global academics, commentators and policymakers to fill the amorphous construct of the BRI with content. This is where the idea of co-creation takes root. At the national level, the concept is firmly embedded in the daily administration of the BRI, which has no formal institutionalized body but one overseeing authority that operates under the National Development and Reform Commission (NDRC). A number of governmental agencies and ministries are in charge of guiding, coordinating and implementing all work, and almost all provinces in China have their own BRI implementation plans. Belt and Road is not about absolute control, but about guidance and shared responsibilities, which might serve as a blueprint for co-creation "across civilizations."

Self-Restraint

China's shift to greater assertiveness has been a matter of a sharply polarized debate for years. Whether Beijing is going to realize the need to respect other positions and be tolerant enough to accept criticism in order to win hearts and minds remains to be seen. Yet despite all differences, "the West" and China, and literally all nations, must find ways to work together in coping with global challenges. As C. Raja Mohan, Senior Fellow with the Asia Society Policy Institute in Delhi told attendees at the Asia Briefing Live 2022 hosted by Asia Society Australia: "We must engage with Russia and China. The question is on what terms."[12] For former Australian Prime Minister and China expert Kevin Rudd, the competition between both powers can follow two paths, either unmanaged or managed strategic competition under mutually agreed rules.[13]

Regardless of the endless clashes, Europe might take the lead in fomenting the managed competition by bringing all parties together. For China this is of particular importance, as the ongoing tit-for-tat could further erode its declining international image. Former President and architect of modern China Deng Xiaoping foresaw the backlash. His advice for China was to lie low as it grows economically. "Hide your strength, bide your time, never take the lead," Deng famously said. To put it another way: embrace self-restraint.

Mutual Trust

Co-creation and self-restraint are trust-building measures in themselves, but it takes more: the rejection of propaganda and assurance of fact-based, open and transparent communication. Zhang Weiwei provided the academic foundation, and Europeans have charted the political course.

The resemblance is striking: co-creation is the product of collaboration in the spirit of true partnership. Self-restraint is the favored conduct among competitors who pursue common goals. Both are within reach and rely on openness as a precondition for progress. Only mutual trust proves to be harder than ever to accomplish among strategic rivals. Since China repeatedly states that it wishes to improve global governance and practice true multilateralism, it would help to swiftly walk away from its voluntary ideological self-isolation. Beijing already stressed the importance of consultation and collaboration for shared benefits. That implies that Beijing must eventually move on from a centralized model and redefine Belt and Road as a multi-stakeholder exercise. As mentioned before, the BRI means different things to different people. Establishing the bases of trust can speed up international cooperation. However, it won't work without compliance with globally accepted norms and standards. Critics may call this naïve and a faint possibility. They have a point here, but any effort to engage is better than to disengage (or constant belt-tightening).

The Art of Stage-Managing Future-Readiness

Multilateral engagement is always about hard work and a measure of tolerance, open dialogue and political pragmatism that separates the wheat from the chaff. Countries that are blessed with enlightened leaders who have a vision that resonates with global audiences have seen a spectacular rise of their influence. Future-preparedness is an investment not just in domestic improvement but also in diplomacy, as it creates positive perceptions and connects a nation with the world.

Developing nations with established national development strategies are already seeing returns on their investments as the global community is taking note of their striking progress. Being a true innovator, the UAE managed to become the world's 11th strongest nation brand in just a matter of years. The year 2021 marked the country's Golden Jubilee: 50 years of independence and statehood. But this is not a nation that ever looks back, let alone rests on its laurels. The federation of seven emirates remains fully committed to its future-readiness and ways to expand the growing ties with the world. As Sheikh Mohammed bin Rashid Al Maktoum, Vice President and Prime Minister of the UAE and Ruler of Dubai, wrote in his highly inspirational book *Flashes of Thought*: "The future starts today, not tomorrow."[14]

To underscore its commitment to shape the nation's future along a set of clearly proclaimed objectives, the country released the "10 Principles for the Next 50 Years,"[15] a set of core guidelines for all institutions to make the union even stronger, build a sustainable economy and harness all possible resources to create a more prosperous society. The long-term goal has also been explicitly stated: over the next half century, the UAE aims for no less than becoming the best country in the world. It proves to be on the right trajectory as it continues to attract ever more people who wish to live together in harmony and tolerance.

This distinctive way of thinking has already been incorporated into the national story. In holding the "Great Narrative Meeting" in partnership with the World Economic Forum (WEF) in Dubai, the UAE's leadership and some of the most future-oriented thought leaders drilled down on how to shape the desired future over the next half century. The conference covered interactive sessions and expert workshops focused on vital areas of governance such as science, space, youth, technology and AI solutions and also fresh ideas that spark greater collaboration and advance progress on the critical global challenges.[16] In promoting its commitment to the development and building of a better future for humanity, the UAE managed to create yet another story that was noticed around the world. While this may appear to run counter to my previously stated point that purpose must not be pushed verbally all the time, this case is distinct. Trust must be earned, but having an expertly crafted national narrative that is in line with a distinguished and decades-long success story amplifies what is already in plain sight. And by always backing up ambitions with proof that it can actually deliver on them, the UAE leaders add evidence to their claims. In doing so, the country once again elevates its status as a true world leader.

What Innovation-Led Development Holds for Communications

As described earlier, when entering the process of crafting narratives and stories with a greater purpose, it is critical to obtain internal support. Equally essential is the establishment of internal consensus that all the ways of connecting with people and all storytelling must reflect the ultimate intent to persuade influencers to retell the story. That demands proactive, open and transparent communications, accountability and a willingness to listen. With better insights on the perceptions, attitudes and beliefs of core interest groups, the development of targeted campaigns that work across a variety of platforms is within reach.

Positively disruptive and creative campaigns come with a clear purpose: education and enlightenment. They must also deal with the imminent and long-term aspects of change. I touched on this in an op-ed for *Gulf News*: "Whether it is the outlook of better transportation, reduced commute times, cleaner air, greener and quieter neighborhoods, or lower energy bills: the bigger picture can seem distant and hard to grasp."[17] It is the responsibility of cities, governments and their commercial partners to secure the support from those in whose names these places are being rebuilt. Everyone will also appreciate to hear what is being done to minimize disruption while work is underway that enhances the quality of life for all. It's the lesser-known but the biggest benefit of real engagement. The feedback prompts new ideas, meaning that the chances of ever running out of relevant content and topics will diminish. What one needs to consider, though, is this: with heightened attention comes heightened pressure to always meet expectations. This elevates the central part of one's story. Successfully managing perceptions depends on an unwavering dedication to remain focused on producing quality content that doesn't plunge when the world around you changes.

For emerging markets in Asia and elsewhere, there's an analogy that might help shape the thought process behind the stories that deliver the desired results. It's the idea of presenting oneself as the nation-state equivalent of corporate start-ups. They are the companies that people love and admire and are more likely to follow because of their innovative and pioneering solutions to eminent problems or unique take on existing industry content. The commonalities are hard work and commitment. Besides, for the recipients of these messages there is always the possibility of spotting opportunities before others do. If played well, leveraging this "new kid on the block" standing can in fact turn out to be a chief advantage. It is the popular version and manifestation of a strategy that has proven to work: putting innovation at the center. And of course, it also attracts more businesses. The UAE already reports the highest number of unicorn companies in the region as well as the highest growth in corporate startups.

Among the most successful nation states in the developed and developing world, there is a lot of optimism about the future and a general consensus to constantly rethink and reinvent; even though that comes with the need to adapt all the time. The discerning factor is to make innovation the centerpiece of inclusive national strategies based on open dialogue and far-reaching consultations. Progress can also accelerate via the synchronization of regulatory policies. These typically include education and scientific research, IT and AI commoditization, intellectual property, trade and taxation, and government procurement. Yet according to the Global Innovation Index (GII) 2021 published by WIPO, the global innovation landscape is still changing too slowly:

> The GII has been warning of this for several years now, as high-income economies, notably from Northern America and Europe, continue to lead the GII ranks and have the strongest and most balanced innovation systems. There is an urgent need for this to change, particularly in the context of the Covid19 crisis. Confronted with an unprecedented crisis, it is important to fully leverage the power of innovation to collectively build a cohesive, dynamic and sustainable recovery. The short-term and longer term impacts of the pandemic on science and innovation systems have to be monitored and findings acted upon.[18]

It's a point made by all future-ready players: leveraging the power of innovation is the main driver behind long-term economic growth and advancements in the material prosperity of societies. Some of Asia's most pioneering economies have prioritized this by placing a premium on innovation in their national development strategies, even before the previously mentioned 2005 United Nations World Summit. As noted in the WIPO GII 2022: "This year, Indonesia, Uzbekistan and Pakistan entered the group of Innovation Achievers for the first time by performing above expectation on innovation for their level of economic development."[19] Meanwhile, Singapore climbed from the 8th to the 7th spot in all of Southeast Asia, East Asia and Oceania. The UAE ranked 31st globally, ascending from 33rd in 2021, while taking the 2nd spot (after Israel) among all Northern African and West Asian nations.

For more than three decades, the UAE and Singapore have benefited from a close partnership. The UAE's capital, Abu Dhabi, chose Singapore as the benchmark nation for its Strategic Vision 2030. It was an excellent choice, as Singapore continues to lead in innovation and economic development. According to the third annual IMD-SUTD Smart City Index (SCI), Singapore ranks as the world's top investor in smart city technologies.[20] The UAE's innovation-driven development has stretched across all sectors of governance and fueled many new initiatives and procedures in areas such as public-private partnerships, AI, the Internet of Things, robotic innovation, blockchain and 3D printing. One highly ambitious project is Abu Dhabi's StarLab Oasis, which is pursuing the development of organisms and products in the fields of AgriTech, climate science and more in space. The UAE also entered talks with India, Indonesia, Israel, Turkey, Britain, South Korea, Ethiopia and Kenya with the objective to form Common Economic

Partnership Agreements (CEPAs), another stride in boosting its global trade to prepare the small but increasingly influential nation for the next 50 years.

Dubai, on the other hand, is renowned for its "Can do" spirit; a strategic move that encourages a commitment to openness and tolerance in a predominantly conservative region. In 2005, Singapore's founding Prime Minister Lee Kuan Yew spoke at Citibank's Legacies of Leadership Series in Dubai. I won't forget his words: "Singapore used to be the master and Dubai the student. When I look at Dubai today, I am not so sure that is still the case." In the years after Lee Kuan Yew's visit, the transformation of the emirate into a global innovation hub accelerated even further. Known as the Middle East's "Alpha City," Dubai is leading the Arab world in the latest Innovation Index, jointly developed by the Dubai Chamber and PricewaterhouseCoopers (PwC). The emirate ranked 20th globally, ahead of global cities such as Beijing, Shanghai and Sao Paulo. It scored particularly high in the categories of infrastructure, government and society. Such rankings are not just numbers. They reflect a journey as much as a road map to achieve its ambitious goal of becoming a global trade, financial and cultural powerhouse.[21] Dubai has already seen the inauguration of the world's first 3D-printed office building. The "Office of the Future" was built in just 17 days. In 2020, the emirate became the first place in the Arab world to set off a Mars exploration probe. Dubai also launched its own Silk Road Strategy to complement the BRI and secure its place as a trade and logistics hub for Europe, Africa and Asia. Afshin Molavi hit the spot when he described Dubai as being "purpose-built for Belt and Road." Dubai's Roads and Transport Authority (RTA) is also piloting self-driving flying taxis, skypods and buses; a natural progression from the fully automated and driverless Dubai Metro, which was inaugurated in 2009. The emirate ran the first public test of flying taxis built by China's electric vehicle manufacturer XPeng in late 2022. The plan is to convert 25 percent of total mobility journeys to smart driverless ones by 2030. If more proof was needed, this is it: the Alpha City has re-imagined the blueprint for investment and capability development.

The historical evidence is undeniable: the future is with those who are open to embrace change and invest in innovation. History has also shown that no country can truly prosper and innovate all by itself. In ancient as in modern times, the free travel of people, ideas and goods is what inspires people and amounts to having an edge in key areas such as education, technology, mobility and trade. The shift from aspiration to inspiration also brings greater clarity to the process of communications planning. Aspiration is about dreams, hopes and ambitions to achieve national or life goals. Inspiration is about the stimulation of doing something. That explains why the path to global influence and power depends on a clearly articulated vision about one's aspired future. And once that future has been achieved, it can become an instant source of inspiration for others. That is why aspiration is key to orchestrating the power of attraction. And communications is as important as policy in making this happen.

None of these factors is linked to any geography. Yet overall discourse power is still largely held by the West. The point was already made in Chapter 1, which explored the geopolitics of Asia's rise: the dominating topic of the "Asian story." The clout of Western global media empires, the fact that English is the most spoken language in the world and the advantage of freedom of expression are the distinguishing factors. But aspiration is mounting all over Asia, and is becoming hugely inspiring for much of the world.

Given Asia's rapid modernization, Asian influence is definitely growing, especially in democratic technocracies. As Parag Khanna observes: "There is a standard retort that the lessons of small countries cannot be applied to large ones. But today some of the largest and most populous countries on earth are trying to make themselves into big Singapores."[22] And soon into Dubais, one might add. They are perhaps the best examples of how to fast-track the development process and therefore should be studied more closely by communicators, too.

The ambitious nation-building stories of Singapore and the UAE are without doubt exceptions that stand out for all stated reasons. But their fact-based and outcome-driven approach is wholly adaptable. For Khanna, that captures the core elements of their winning formula:

> Nothing succeeds like success. Respectability and positive image are no longer about succeeding according to a Western or historical archetype, but succeeding on one's own path. In that sense, success is about good governance, diversity, and talent attraction. Places that are doing these things are successful and gain in visibility.[23]

This delineates the path to innovation-led communications, which includes pretty much the same: good management, diversity, and talent attraction.

For Afshin Molavi, there is a new discourse emerging in Asia and the broader developing world, "one that transcends the tired binaries of democracy vs. authoritarianism." As he detailed:

> It is a discourse that values government effectiveness in creating opportunity in every sense of the word: educational, professional, social mobility, physical connectivity, and access to good healthcare and digital infrastructure. When governments deliver on these, they create the opportunity for a decent life for citizens and residents.[24]

Like Khanna, Molavi also emphasized the model promoted by Southeast Asia's city-state: "People end up voting with their feet, flocking to places like Singapore or the UAE, while fleeing places that might be categorized as democracies, but deliver very little for their citizens and residents." Public recognition of such nonconformist but demonstrably successful approach pays off in several ways. It's like those aforementioned start-ups that develop strikingly new ideas to resolve common issues and suddenly become the talk of the town. What people are looking for are signs of self-confidence and a well-stated vision that relates to them. And once there is proof that the promises are being kept and deliver benefits for all, many will feel inspired to retell the central story in line with all stated values and principles.

This is what's at the heart of innovation-led communications: acting like a start-up with a clear strategy and rollout plan, driven by authenticity and openness to some new thinking. For governments as well as businesses it is the quickest way to unlock their intrinsic persuasive power and shape narratives that resonate across cultures. But because it works so well it also draws the attention of those who seek to change the story in their favor through manipulation and the deliberate spreading of mis- and disinformation. While truth should always prevail as its core arguments are stronger, propaganda soars on connectedness and certain human traits. George Orwell predicted that future in his essay *Politics and the English Language*: "If thought corrupts language, language can also corrupt thought."[25]

References

1. *Pablo Picasso Quotes*. (n.d.). *BrainyQuote*. https://brainyquote.com/quotes/pablo_picasso_107497
2. Wolf, Guido. Conversation with author. April 2022.
3. WAM. "Tolerance Is a Way of Life in the UAE: Omar Ghobash." *Wam*, Emirates News Agency - WAM, 14 Feb. 2022, https://wam.ae/en/details/1395302993188
4. Anholt, Simon. Conversation with author. April 2022.
5. Chimhowua, Admos O. Chilhowee, et al. "The 'New' National Development Planning and Global Development Goals: Processes and Partnerships." *ScienceDirect*, Elsevier, Aug. 2019, doi.org/10.1016/j.worlddev.2019.03.013
6. Martin, Peter, and Anuradha Raghu. "Mahathir Warns Against New 'Colonialism' During Visit to China." *Bloomberg News*, 20 Aug. 2018, https://bloomberg.com/news/articles/2018-08-20/mahathir-warns-against-new-colonialism-during-visit-to-china
7. Hillman, Jonathan E. *The Digital Silk Road: China's Quest to Wire the World and Win the Future*. New York, Harper Business (imprint of HarperCollins), 2021.
8. Stelling, Oliver. "Belt and Road Deserves a World Class Brand." *LinkedIn*, 15 Sep. 2018, https://linkedin.com/pulse/belt-road-deserves-world-class-brand-oliver-stelling
9. Tang, Frank. "China's European Firms Warn 'On-off Economy,' Covid Lockdowns Cloud Business Outlook." *South China Morning Post*, 6 Apr. 2022, https://scmp.com/economy/china-economy/article/3173287/chinas-european-firms-warn-economy-covid-lockdowns-cloud
10. Khanna, Parag. "Bridges to Everywhere – Connectivity as Paradigm" [Belgrade, Serbia]. *CIRSD*, 2018, https://cirsd.org/en/horizons/horizons-summer-2018-issue-no-12/bridges-to-everywhere
11. Stelling, Oliver. "#BeltAndRoadInitiative – Time for Some European Realpolitik." *EU Reporter*, 5 May 2020, https://eureporter.co/world/china-2/2020/05/05/beltandroadinitiative-time-for-some-european-realpolitik-2
12. Mohan, C. Raja. "Asia Briefing Live 2022." *Asia Society Australia*, 18 Oct. 2022, https://bbgevent.app/asiabriefinglive
13. "Foreign Policy Magazine: Managed Strategic Competition." *Kevin Rudd*, 25 Jan. 2022, https://kevinrudd.com/archive/2021-07-09-foreign-policy-magazine-managed-strategic-competition
14. Maktoum, Rashid Mohammed Al. *Flashes of Thought*. Dubai/UAE, Motivate Publishing Ltd., 2013.
15. "The Principles of the 50." *The United Arab Emirates Government Portal*, Jul. 2022, https://u.ae/en/about-the-uae/initiatives-of-the-next-50/the-principles-of-the-50
16. "Al Gergawi, Schwab Call for United Global Action to Secure Better Future for Next Generations." *United Arab Emirates Ministry of Cabinet Affairs*, 12 Nov. 2021, https://moca.gov.ae/en/media/news/al-gergawi-schwab-call-for-united-global-action-to-secure-better-future-for-next-generations
17. Stelling, Oliver. "Connecting Communities to Development Priorities." *Analysis – Gulf News*, 11 Sep. 2013, https://gulfnews.com/business/analysis/connecting-communities-to-development-priorities-1.1226065

18. "Global Innovation Index 2021 (14th Edition), pg 56." *WIPO*, 2021, https://wipo.int/edocs/pubdocs/en/wipo_pub_gii_2021.pdf
19. "GII 2022 Results." *WIPO*, 29 Sep. 2022, https://wipo.int/edocs/pubdocs/en/wipo-pub-2000-2022-section3-en-gii-2022-results-global-innovation-index-2022-15th-edition.pdf
20. Editorial Staff. "Singapore Ranked Top of Smart City Index for Third Year." *IOT NETWORK NEWS*, 16 Nov. 2021, https://iot-nn.com/2021/11/16/singapore-ranked-top-of-smart-city-index-for-third-year
21. Sharma, Alkesh. "Dubai Ranks First in Arab World on Latest Innovation Index." *The National*, 25 Nov. 2021, https://thenationalnews.com/business/technology/2021/11/24/dubai-ranks-first-in-arab-world-on-latest-innovation-index
22. Khanna, Parag. *The Future Is Asian: Global Order in the Twenty-first Century*. London, W&N, 2019.
23. Khanna, Parag. Conversation with author. April 2022
24. Molavi, Afshin. Conversation with author. April 2022
25. Orwell, George. *Politics and the English Language*. Long Beach, CA, Sahara Publisher Books, 1946.

5 Looking for Polaris

How to Tackle the Global Disinformation Crisis

In the mid-2000s, banks and big oil ranked among the world's largest corporations, measured by market capitalization. At the time, Microsoft was the only outlier. Some 15 years later, seven out of ten were all information-based, including the top two, Apple and Microsoft, as well as Google's parent company Alphabet, Amazon, Facebook (now Meta), Berkshire Hathaway and China's Tencent. Saudi Aramco overtook Apple again in 2022 when the tech company's shares fell more than 5 percent. The stock market value also dropped for other big tech companies, leading to layoffs of tens of thousands of workers. But big tech still rules.

More than five billion people around the world are now using the internet. That's 63 percent of the world's population being online.[1] Facebook, YouTube, WhatsApp, Instagram, Weixin (WeChat) and TikTok are the most popular social media networks. Published rankings are not entirely reliable, as some platforms don't revise user data on a regular basis or release different sets of audience statistics. Yet all six are known to have at least one billion monthly active users (MAU). Facebook stands out among all, with close to three billion. WeChat has around 1.2 billion. Two other platforms are also highly influential although their user numbers are lower.

LinkedIn has roughly 106 million MAU, and Twitter used to have between 317 million and 400 million before its takeover by Elon Musk (the numbers vary depending on the source of published data). While alternative microblogging sites like Hive, Post News and Mastodon saw a spike in popularity, most users still prefer Twitter.

Digital platforms connect the world in ways never seen before, but some did not only become primary news sources and places to share personal updates. They also evolved into involuntary or deliberate traders of hate speech, propaganda and fake news. Being easily affected by various kinds of user-generated and shared content should always prompt a desire to distinguish diverse yet acceptable views from outright disinformation. LinkedIn, originally designed for professional connections, business updates and job search but now a news site too, responded by assisting users in verifying the authenticity of other accounts. Offering such help is critical. Yet it often looks like we are amusing ourselves to death, to use the famous line coined by US media critic Neil Postman. His son Andrew seemed to agree when he remembered his dad predicting Trump in 1985: "It's not George Orwell, he warned, it's *Brave New World*."[2] Of course, the elder Postman was not referring

DOI: 10.4324/9781003385622-6

to social media and Web 3.0. He spoke about the rising popularity of private TV channels in the 1980s. Yet "amusing ourselves to death" is still applicable today, as the fast spread of misinformation and disinformation on online platforms, news channels and the dark web hauls significant social, economic and political consequences yet does not necessarily get the attention it deserves.

With Artificial Intelligence affecting our lives in ever more ways, the promise it holds for the economy and society at large is enormous. AI takes over tasks that are too time-consuming and energy demanding and already enhances manufacturing and mobility as well as access to healthcare, education and banking. Once AI-based translation of spoken language has improved, humankind can connect in ways never seen before. Generative AI, though, is raising concerns about the pending surge of fake content and AI's role in accelerating the spread of disinformation.

Carrington Malin, a UAE-based entrepreneur, marketer and consultant focused on emerging technologies, is convinced that we have barely seen the tip of the iceberg yet:

> The extensive use of fake accounts, fake news and bots on social media over the past ten years has typically required any bad actor to have multi-disciplined teams to create campaigns that are big enough to have a significant impact.[3]

He argues that even so, many attempts at using digital communications to misinform are quite crude and easy to spot. But the risk remains high. "The threats posed by new AI-powered technologies to mislead the public, governments, stock markets and other audiences are considerable," he said.

This view is broadly shared by Imad Lahad, Managing Director of APCO Worldwide's Dubai operation, the consultancy that pioneered AI-driven solutions to build and protect reputations (see Chapter 8 for more details):

> This threat is still in its infancy. But with deep fakes becoming more seamless, AI misinformation campaigns will be harder to identify and counter. As such, the volume of misinformation will increase exponentially. And as a natural consequence reputation management will become more complex and even more important than it is today.[4]

Finding That North Star

The spread of misinformation (accidentally or involuntarily disseminated false content) and disinformation (intentionally created for personal, political or ideological gain) constitutes a global communication crisis. Those who ignore or downplay it only aggravate the situation. Holding fake account owners and disinformation peddlers to a lower standard increases the threat to societies and independent media as a public good. Making things worse, it also encourages new players to enter the game. In view of that, indifference and inaction are no longer an option.

In a widely reported speech at Stanford University, former US President Barack Obama called for greater social responsibility and regulatory oversight of social media giants. His main argument was as clear as it gets: "These companies need to have some other North Star than just making money and increasing profit shares."[5] It's a sensible appeal for sure, and in line with new measures by nations like Canada, Germany and Japan to protect citizens from bias or discrimination. But assigning responsibility solely to federal watchdogs and the companies at the center of it all won't guarantee authenticity, safety and privacy protection. Instead, everyone needs some kind of North Star for orientation.

Professional journalists and editors have been at the forefront of that mission for a long time, using credible reporting to debunk false stories from right- and left-wing media and hold to account businesses as well as elected and unelected officials who propagate alternative facts, bigotry and conspiracy theories. But despite the rise in investigative reporting, public awareness is still largely confined to the most conspicuous cases of untruths and quickly fades as the news cycle moves on. In the meantime, the spin doctors are getting better at what they're doing. The Great Information War is happening on all fronts and across all platforms and needs to be dealt with in a similar fashion: on all fronts and platforms. The previous two chapters made the case for what's in the public's best interest: fact-based and more meaningful engagement – the "great unifier" across societies and cultures. It works when the attention is shifting away from politics to objective facts while helping to make the internet a safer place for everyone. To achieve this goal, or at the very least begin to move in that direction, a more synchronized effort is needed to help people detect bogus information.

Big tech and social media must play their part in assisting that effort, as they are indispensable in getting the truth out – at the same speed and with the same reach. But even though most people have a pretty good idea where the North is, Polaris (the North Star, or True North) is not the brightest star in the sky. That's where citizen activism comes into play. Aiding others with "compass reading" can sensitize the public about the various forms of manipulated content that are infiltrating our lives. And by harnessing the combined knowledge and influence of business professionals, educators and media, the chance of making a real impact should increase. The important thing here is that no anti-propaganda effort must ever look like propaganda itself or make it easy to be framed as such by the real perpetrators. That reduces the options to a commitment to exhibit unbiased, unprejudiced and verifiable facts that members of the public will find convincing enough to repeat and share.

The Obscure Allure of Fake News

The term "fake news" has shaped the public debate for years. This is not about misinformation or that murky gray area between truth and fiction. Fake news is hard propaganda: the fabrication and intentional amplification of rumors, outright lies and other falsehoods, all being aimed at hiding the truth of what is actually happening. And then there are "alternative facts" – the in-your-face rejection of honest reporting that doesn't match one's worldview or agenda.

As noted in my LinkedIn article "Battling Fake News,"[6] scarcely any of this should survive more than five minutes in broad daylight. This is the 21st century, and there is no lack of genuine information or access to it. Why, then, do so many people fall for it and don't even reject it when proven wrong? Gordon Pennycook and David Rand addressed that question in a *New York Times* guest essay.[7] The authors, both psychologists, examined two schools of thought. One is arguing that we tend to rationalize our convictions, essentially trying to convince ourselves that what we've always believed or wanted to be true is in fact true. The other one is conceding that we simply fail to exercise our critical faculties. It's almost certainly a combination of both and that makes it so toxic.

Fake news has brazenly moved on from mere dishonesty and fabrication to entire ecosystems of lies and falsehoods set up to manipulate and distort the truth, often citing fake witness accounts and invented backup stories while using deceptive appeals to emotion and personal belief. And since enragement means engagement, some social media networks seem quite happy with people clashing over the most egregiously false content. This is why many subscribers to Trump's new "Truth Social" platform lost interest shortly after its launch. The number of active users now stands at roughly two million, but that is less than 1 percent of Twitter users. The absence of real outrage among a fairly homogeneous audience drove many back to Twitter where they can tap into the sources of anger they live for. Things are only going to get more complex with the release of software that alters videos, audio and images to make people look like they say and do things they never did – the "deep fakes" we hear so much about.

As far as "alleged fake news" (authentic reporting, actually) is concerned, people tend to look for information that matches what they want to hear from people who look and talk like them; their own communities, digital tribes and echo chambers. That's not to say that fake news succeeds only because reason is somehow locked in by who we are and how we see the world. People are obviously capable of changing their minds. But when laziness, political ideologies or partisan convictions obstruct the forming of accurate beliefs, the impact is far broader today than it was in the 2010s. Social media amplifies any message, especially when it comes from friends and followers. And constant repetition advances the prospect of broader acceptance; a point worth sharing, especially on social media.

The Social Network's Role

In another LinkedIn article,[8] I discussed Facebook's power to influence public opinion. The quintessential social network is a great connector of people, and of course not the only digital platform being used to spread disinformation. But in recent years, it did get quoted a lot in that context, which created plenty of regulatory woes. As revealed in multiple media reports about the Cambridge Analytica (CA) scandal, Facebook harvested personal data from 87 million user profiles to be used for CA's micro-targeting of US voters during the run-up to the 2016 US presidential election that ended with Trump's win. Facebook was also accused of capturing and using biometric data without properly obtaining informed consent. Moreover, it had been condemned for allowing extremism to spread across its platform, including by those who planned the 2021 riots at the US Capitol.

The platform's troubles were not limited to the United States and other Western countries alone. Amnesty International claims that Facebook had underperformed in preventing users from inciting offline violence by amplifying harmful anti-Rohingya hate speech in Myanmar during the Rohingya "clearance operations" in 2016 and 2017.[9] In the Middle East and Africa, the platform's fastest-growing regions for years, Facebook also underwent a popularity crisis. Approval rates and ad sales plunged to new lows when the network was seen as silencing pro-Palestinian voices during the Israel–Hamas conflict in 2021.

In late 2021, Facebook – the parent company – was renamed and rebranded as "Meta," shifting the focus to a host of shared virtual worlds and experiences. The timing was widely perceived as an attempt to distract from the testimony by whistleblower Frances Haugen. The former staffer spoke out about the inner workings of Facebook and its main focus on protecting "astronomical profits."[10] As she stated in one of the hearings: "Safety is a cost center, not a growth center." The network is facing increasing competition from TikTok and a rise in costs and expenses. In early 2022 the Facebook app lost roughly one million daily active users. Later that year, its CEO, Mark Zuckerberg announced massive layoffs affecting thousands of employees in response to a dramatic decline in sales and drop in operating income. The challenges it faces won't disappear overnight but may trigger a review of corporate communications. If Meta or Facebook were seen as being at the forefront of battling against false narratives, the reputational gains can be significant and lead to financial gains as well.

Investing in the metaverse as such remains a smart and future-ready move. But highly immersive virtual worlds come with new high risks; a reminder that safety matters more than ever. Chris Cox, Meta's chief product officer, stressed the importance of international standards and rating systems at Davos.[11] The rationale is entirely clear: there won't be a single metaverse, but many. The compounded annual growth rate (CAGR) of the global metaverse is close to 40 percent. This means the market could reach as much as several hundred billion dollars by 2030.

Uncovering the Truth – Publicly

The writings of German novelist and philosopher Heinrich von Kleist were not just centered on the benefits of speaking to another person with the intent of adding clarity to thought and speech. His work also touches upon rhetoric and error in written and spoken language. Like Immanuel Kant in his *Critique of Pure Reason*, Kleist was convinced that human perception is not completely reliable and that the human intellect is basically unable to discern truth. He wrote about it extensively, denouncing the injustice caused by misspeaking, misunderstanding and mistaken identities. Although times have changed, some aspects of his argument continue to be valid because they are founded on human nature. As the psychologists Pennycook and Rand explained, not all people who should or could know the truth are ready for it. This raises the specter for a continued and even faster and wider spread of disinformation.

Grappling with propaganda is still largely reactive rather than proactive. Questioning and verifying sources of quoted content and the trustworthiness of the individuals or organizations behind them (especially those we don't follow) may have become a daily routine for some social media users. For others it may seem excessively tiring. As a result, chances are high that the truth is mostly discovered by users who already distrust certain sources. People who are not checking them regularly may one day fall prey to fraud; either because they basically don't care enough, or because they just take everything at face value.

"Truth is by nature self-evident. As soon as you remove the cobwebs of ignorance that surround it, it shines clear."[12] These words by India's Mahatma Gandhi are still holding up well. It's all about helping people to detect lies and thwarting obfuscation by removing the cobwebs. A good way to get started is to disentangle some of the most common propaganda tactics and to make it harder for propagandists to get off scot-free. Aside from the dangers posed to society by hard propaganda, there is already a considerable risk for nefarious actors who are habitually circulating falsehoods. Creating public records of misleading tweets or propaganda articles may please their loyalists. But it can also quickly wipe out whatever credibility is left with critical thinkers at home and abroad. The occasional backlash has already prompted many to abandon their official social media accounts, hide behind anonymous ones and manipulate minds by wielding the emotional power of hidden and subliminal messages. The rationale for playing that card is to pass the buck by claiming plausible deniability. But those who think they can protect themselves by switching to more cunning tactics may actually miscalculate. Most verbal acrobatics are easy to spot as they follow familiar patterns that reveal the hidden motives. When looking for the North Star or Polaris, the "where" and "how" are as important as the "who" and "what."

Some of the hard and soft propaganda tactics below share a few characteristics. But that's just the nature of the game.

Denial and Deflection

Denial and deflection is a common way of trying to paint false talking points as truth and facts. The fundamental aim is to avoid having to deal with real and factual evidence, the kind of which would be impossible to disprove, by raising doubt about the legitimacy of the accusation or accuser.

What to look out for:

- *Blame-shifting, finger-pointing and scapegoating*. When confronted with evidence of dishonesty, some actors instantly claim victimhood and start blaming the opponent or political adversary for what they themselves are being accused of. "It's just a smear campaign" is an often-used phrase by propaganda departments that charge the opponents with slander when confronted with truisms they cannot invalidate.
- *Non sequitur*. The Latin term refers to any disconnect between thoughts and conclusions. This can be unintentional but is also frequently used for propaganda purposes.
- *Whataboutism*. The immediate twist to unrelated and in most cases stronger counter-accusations; an attempt to deflect from the original subject while refusing to address it.
- *Rhetorical deflection*. The attempt by propagandists to shift attention away with continuous rhetorical questions.

- *Reframing.* The endeavor to redefine the meaning of words and phrases. That's when annexation becomes reunification, liberation or denazification, and peaceful protesters are being labeled as rioters or foreign agents.
- *Blocking academic freedom.* While being instrumental for making progress and gaining influence abroad, some actors that claim to promote science are also limiting critical thinking and social debates, as they see it as a threat to their power claims.

Gaslighting

Some propagandists use psychological manipulation to make people doubt their own judgment, sanity or even what they have seen with their own eyes. It works particularly well in scenarios that lack people-to-people connection and real communication.

What to look out for:

- *Clouding people's views.* The attempt to question an individual's memories, observations or feelings with the ultimate intent to make them follow their manipulated reality.
- *Pushing false impressions.* The constant repetition of the same lies and spurious narratives based on the conviction that they can become the truth if only repeated often enough.
- *Using false analogies.* The intentional use of improper comparisons that aim to offset known discrepancies in any argument by linking them to similarities that are commonly accepted.
- *Citing questionable sources.* Many people who have spent all their lives in echo chambers have lost touch with reality and don't seem to care whose voices matter and which ones are discredited. When spotting quotes from dubious sources, none of the content shall be trusted.
- *Astroturfing.* The coordinated approach to create misconceptions of broad grassroots support for opinions, policies or corporations and individuals even when there is no such endorsement.
- *"Incorrect perceptions."* It's an often used term in public statements by those who push total control over all narratives without dealing with the facts.
- *Saying the quiet part loud.* When public exposure of propaganda lies becomes overwhelming, some propagandists place a greater emphasis on instantly striking back than on coherence in their narratives.

Flooding the Zone

Not all propaganda is meant to win over the opponent's mind. Some schemes are deployed to drown out critical narratives, sow doubt and suspicion and create political chaos. This has become more popular since social media and chat groups helped flooding the zone and as a result weakened the uncensored media landscape. To anyone who can see through it all, this tactic also signals something else: a lack of real discourse power.

What to look out for:

- *The disinformation blitzkrieg*. When the amount of rumors and alleged news stories from ideologically aligned sources – all with a single take on highly disputed topics – seems overwhelming, chances are that receivers switch off. This is exactly what was intended: creating exhaustion and confusion with the goal of people disengaging.
- *Warped reality*. With no regard for truth, the messaging dispersed by those who just want to sow doubt might be the most bizarre their audience will ever hear. When spotting such offbeat accusations, obfuscations and cases of intentional vagueness, a closer look at the source may lift one out of that deliberate chaos.
- *Bullhorn tactics*. When none of the prior tactics worked, the final ploy is to display outrage (e.g. smears, name calling and ad hominem attacks), which are supposed to trigger the same degree of anger among the general public. As previously said, enragement means engagement. Its worst form is dehumanizing or subjecting political opponents or different ethnic groups to hostility and hatred. Yet the more spine-chilling the rhetoric, the more likely the propaganda house of cards is about to collapse or has already buckled.

Critical Thinking and Media Literacy

"Forewarned is Forearmed" is the translation of the Latin saying "Praemonitus, Praemunitus"; a fitting phrase for any labors of countering propaganda. The aforementioned lists are far from complete but do describe some widely used techniques. When previously unwitting audiences realize the extent to which propaganda is infiltrating public discourse and how it can affect them and those they care about, they might find a purpose in sharing these tactics.

What started with news stories and investigative journalism is now expanding to government initiatives, think tank projects and measures by nonprofits and volunteers aimed at debunking and defunding online disinformation. Plenty of independent fact-checks help in effectively countering confirmation bias, implicit bias and other patterns of deviation from norm and rationality in judgment.

In 2019, Avaaz, the world's largest online activist network, proposed the "Correct the Record" plan. The objective was to curb fake news by requiring social media companies to direct all users who have been susceptible to demonstrably false information on their pages and sites toward fact-checks.[13] One year later, an academic study conducted by George Washington University and Ohio State University proved that Correct the Record did in fact deliver on its promise. Providing social media users who have seen misleading information with corrections from fact-checkers can decrease belief in disinformation by about one half (49.4 percent).

The *Washington Post* Fact Checker began as a provisional venture during the 2008 presidential campaign and gained popularity with its "Pinocchio" rating scale for misleading claims. In Singapore, the government embarked on a so-called "whole-of-society approach" to counter misinformation in four steps: (1) the promotion of trusted local news media companies;(2) legislation such as the Protection from Online Falsehoods and Manipulation Act (POFMA);(3) nurturing an "Informed Public"; and (4) building a robust fact-checking ecosystem. According to Tan Kiat How, Minister of State for Communications and Information, the Singaporean government realized that it cannot do this alone and therefore welcomed participation of the private and people sectors.[14] It's a perfect case for turning anti-propaganda efforts into a story that people recognize.

Many more endeavors are underway to effectively fight info wars using education and social media to undo the damage done. Reporting and sharing insights gathered from several initiatives that investigate disinformation and information operations is important in addressing cognitive bias. Here are some examples from the US, Europe and Asia:

- Reporters Without Borders (RSF)[15] promotes and defends press freedom. Based in Paris, it runs nine international offices and has more than 150 correspondents in all five continents.
- The Dispatch Fact Check[16] looks at claims from elected US officials, reports from the media, and disinformation on social media to help people understand what's true and what's not.
- The Lincoln Project[17] is a political action committee dedicated to the preservation, protection, and defense of US democracy. The highly popular movement has some 2.6 million Twitter followers and releases regular podcasts, videos and news updates.
- EUvsDisinfo[18] is an initiative by the European External Action Service's East StratCom Task Force. Its objective is to raise public awareness of Russian disinformation operations and to help EU governments and citizens to develop resistance to digital media manipulation.
- The European Parliament's "Special Committee on Foreign Interference in all Democratic Processes in the EU, including Disinformation" (INGE 2)[19] pushes for a common strategy to counter propaganda by shoring up coordination between all EU countries.
- Correctiv[20] is a donation-funded German research center in support of investigative journalism and the promotion of media competence.
- Doublethink Lab[21] operates at the intersection of the internet, public discourse, civil society, and democratic governance. The Taiwanese civil society organization's main objective is to research modern threats to democracy and devise strategies to counter them.

All these initiatives help cultivate critical thinking and media literacy, often referenced as the "21st Century Survival Skill." As expected, some are facing occasional setbacks and partisan criticisms about their real intent. To counter that, it makes sense to offer as much context as possible. A new trend has emerged that addresses this point by providing access to original source material and even translations to make foreign language content available for the global public.

- Interpret: China[22] is an open source project by the Center for Strategic and International Studies (CSIS). Its stated objective is to contextualize and interpret the significance of select translated documents to facilitate a more nuanced, comprehensive understanding of China's aims and ambitions by policymakers and the public.
- The Great Translation Movement[23] is a volunteer anti-war initiative launched during the Russian invasion of Ukraine. Its Twitter account gathered more than 160,000 followers in less than three months.[24] The screenshots and translations of publicly available Chinese articles and social media posts gave Western audiences a rare glimpse at the officially sanctioned narratives and pro-Russian, anti-American, anti-Japanese, anti-Semitic and anti-Western sentiment circulating online in China.

On US mainstream media, several programs are committed to shed light on propaganda tactics by Republicans and hyper-partisan media. In a much-disputed move, CNN cancelled Brian Stelter's show *Reliable Sources* after 30 years on air. One that still stands out though is MSNBC's *The ReidOut* with Joy Reid. Similar endeavors are underway on European media. *The Cube* on Euronews comprises of a team of specialist social media journalists who find, verify and debunk the biggest misinformation in real time.

Moreover, some journalists have started to reveal the truth on their own social media channels. One of the most dedicated ones is Julia Davis, columnist at *The Daily Beast* and creator of the Russian Media Monitor. With more than 437,000 followers on Twitter, her posts about Russian propaganda are seen all over the world. Another trend is the expanding number of parody Twitter accounts that engage publics by highlighting propaganda. Despite being an obvious satire account, the extremely popular @DPRK_News was locked by Twitter in 2021 for impersonating North Korea's communist government. An even more popular one is @DarthPutinKGB. Over half a million followers seek out the truth behind Putin's unprovoked aggression toward Ukraine and his claim of remaining a "master strategist."

Helping to decode media messages makes a difference because it is not about better shielding ourselves from fake news, but about being more aware of how it influences our beliefs and behaviors. We are better off if we start to declutter our day and free up time to think so that we can spot and reject false information. Managing the information overload has already prompted users to filter their news sources. In the future, more AI solutions will aid in that effort. Social media and tech companies also took note and caught up with human or automatic fact-checkers, user restrictions and screening apps. The rollout of verification technologies such as NewsGuard and various other apps, add-ons and extensions for safer browsing may be convenient, but no one should consider the core issue resolved by downloading some software. Once we start leaving fact-checks to third parties, we are doomed because we unlearn how to use our heads.

Anjana Susarla, Associate Professor of Information Systems at Michigan State University, looked into information explosion and the proliferation of digital devices and stressed that the divide is no longer just about access. Her point: the savviest users are navigating away from devices and recognize how algorithms affect their lives. Meanwhile the rest relies even more on algorithms to guide their decisions.[25] The better informed we are, the less likely we will allow algorithms to take over and guide our opinions by playing to our cast of mind or self-esteem in ways that affect our understanding, actions and decisions. What we need to regain is our mental freedom and greater self-control: "Thinking More, Like Never Before."

Life in the Post-Truth World

As the old saying goes, you are either part of the solution or part of the problem. Edward Bernays, the self-professed "Father of Public Relations," was unambiguous in promoting the manipulation of public opinion. Close to 100 years ago, he argued that intelligent men must realize that propaganda is the modern instrument by which they can fight for productive ends and help bring order out of chaos.[26] His name still comes up occasionally, but his justification for the use of state propaganda to "engineer consent" sounds rather outdated. His take was part of the problem, as propaganda creates more, not less chaos; back then as well as in the internet age.

In late 2016, Oxford Dictionaries picked "post-truth" as the word of the year – the obvious result of the UK's deeply divisive Brexit vote and the MAGA messaging dispersed during the Trump campaign. The term captures the new reality that shapes public life and affirms that learning to cope with misinformation and disinformation has become essential. Around the world, the tide may be turning against the most glaring forms of disingenuousness. But the potential of exposing hypocrisy as well as hard and soft propaganda is still far from being fulfilled. For communications pros there are several openings here to deliver on Purpose and Shared Values – not by acting like self-styled legal experts, but by seeking collaboration with subject matter experts as keen as they are to reveal the truth.

Given the fact that literally all professionals in the information space have to find new ways to deal with the intense surge of falsehoods and manipulations, the willingness to team up with others to convey the tactics behind and damage caused by propaganda might in fact be seen as a welcome move. It signals a commitment to continued education or 'decoupling' PR from propaganda; a move that would help rebuilding trust and discourse power. First in line should be news media, investigative journalists and educators such as mass communications scholars. Collaboration can even be expanded by partnering with legal advisors, analysts, ethics experts and policymakers. Some think tanks are already researching and partnering with other relevant stakeholders to boost literacy and achieve actual change. Communicators can support all this by engaging their contacts, by contributing to research pieces and media articles and by citing the various strands of online and offline disinformation they encounter and how they interweave to create distortion. Beyond that they can secure support from clients who see a clear upside for their operating environment and the greater public good. Furthermore, they can use insight gained from global conversations to enlighten audiences about different worldviews and how they affect dialogues.

In the end, things will come to light. The active promotion of informed civic activism might even accelerate the advancement from that indistinct self-characterization as storytellers to that of real thinkers and doers with a mission. It just needs to follow a stringent set of rules that places transparency at the top. What should really make the difference is that this action plan delivers a modern-age "license to operate." On top of that, it signals acceptance of the end of old-school PR.

As the struggle against untruths is accelerating, it is equally important to establish some ground rules and consensus about what defines the red lines between diverging opinions, freedom of speech and the intentional distortion of truth. Since most propaganda is covert, either intentionally or unintentionally, its disclosure must be overt: telling it like it is. At the same time one has to go to great lengths to avert intolerance, a rise in paranoia and descent into racism, vitriol, chauvinism and xenophobia. The openness to other worldviews remains critical. Much of that falls into the hands of diplomacy, above all Public Diplomacy.

References

1. "Digital Around the World." *DataReportal*, Apr. 2022, https://datareportal.com/global-digital-overview
2. "My Dad Predicted Trump in 1985 – It's Not Orwell, He Warned, It's Brave New World." *The Guardian*, 20 Apr. 2018, https://theguardian.com/media/2017/feb/02/amusing-ourselves-to-death-neil-postman-trump-orwell-huxley
3. Malin, Carrington. Conversation with author. May 2022.
4. Lahad, Imad. Interview with author. April 2022.
5. Reclaim the Net. "Transcript of President Barack Obama's Speech at Stanford, April 21, 2022." *Reclaim the Net*, 23 Apr. 2022, https://reclaimthenet.org/transcript-of-president-barack-obamas-speech-at-stanford-april-21-2022
6. Stelling, Oliver. "Battling Fake News: Don't Rely on Others to Think for You." *LinkedIn*, 30 Apr. 2019, https://linkedin.com/pulse/battling-fake-news-dont-rely-others-think-you-oliver-stelling
7. Pennycook, Gordon, and David Rand. "Opinion | Why Do People Fall for Fake News?" *The New York Times*, 23 Jan. 2019, https://nytimes.com/2019/01/19/opinion/sunday/fake-news.html?smtyp=cur&smid=tw-nytopinion
8. Stelling, Oliver. "Facebook's PR Crisis Deepens." *oliverstelling.com*, 30 Oct. 2021, https://oliverstelling.com/blog/facebook-s-pr-crisis-deepens
9. Amnesty International. "Myanmar: Facebook's Systems Promoted Violence Against Rohingya; Meta Owes Reparations – New Report." *Amnesty International*, 29 Sep. 2022, https://amnesty.org/en/latest/news/2022/09/myanmar-facebooks-systems-promoted-violence-against-rohingya-meta-owes-reparations-new-report
10. Brown, Abram. "Facebook 'Puts Astronomical Profits Over People,' Whistle-Blower Tells Congress." *Forbes*, 5 Oct. 2021, https://forbes.com/sites/abrambrown/2021/10/05/facebook-will-likely-resume-work-on-instagram-for-kids-whistleblower-tells-congress/?sh=7f6f29cc4cda
11. Shead, Sam. "Serious Crime in the Metaverse Should Be Outlawed by the U.N., UAE Minister Says." *CNBC*, 25 May 2022, https://2022/05/25/metaverse-murders-need-to-be-policed-says-uae-tech-minister.html
12. "Mahatma Gandhi Quotes." (n.d.). *BrainyQuote*. Retrieved 3 Nov. 2022, from https://brainyquote.com/quotes/mahatma_gandhi_135180
13. Perrigo, Billy. "How This Radical New Proposal Could Curb Fake News on Social Media." *Time*, 28 Feb. 2019, https://time.com/5540995/correct-the-record-polling-fake-news

14. Leo, Lakeisha. "Singapore Takes a 'Whole-of-Society' Approach to Combat Misinformation: Tan Kiat How." *CNA*, 29 Apr. 2022, https://channelnewsasia.com/singapore/tan-kiat-how-approach-combat-misinformation-local-news-2656731
15. "Homepage." *RSF*, 23 Sep. 2022, https://rsf.org/en
16. *The Dispatch Fact Check*. https://factcheck.thedispatch.com
17. *The Lincoln Project*. https://lincolnproject.us
18. *EU vs Disinfo*. https://euvsdisinfo.eu
19. *Foreign Interference Committee Resumes Its Work | News | European Parliament*. 12 May 2022, https://europarl.europa.eu/news/en/press-room/20220509IPR29109/foreign-interference-committee-resumes-its-work
20. CORRECTIV – Recherchen für die Gesellschaft. *correctiv.org*, 10 Jun. 2022, https://correctiv.org
21. *Doublethink Lab*. https://doublethinklab.org
22. *Interpret: China*. https://interpret.csis.org
23. *The Great Translation Movement*. https://twitter.com/tgtm_official
24. McCarthy, Simone. "Twitter Users Are Exposing Pro-Russian Sentiment in China, and Beijing Is Not Happy." *CNN*, 13 Apr. 2022, https://2022/04/13/china/china-ukraine-great-translation-movement-intl-hnk-mic/index.html
25. Susarla, Anjana. "The New Digital Divide Is Between People Who Opt Out of Algorithms and People Who Don't." *The Conversation*, 17 Apr. 2019, https://theconversation.com/the-new-digital-divide-is-between-people-who-opt-out-of-algorithms-and-people-who-dont-114719
26. Bernays, Edward, and Di Stefano Lorenzo. *Propaganda: With a New Foreword*. Independently published, 2022.

6 Public Diplomacy
Leveraging the Strong Side of Soft Power

"The words 'politics' and 'communication' are nearly synonymous."[1] The words by historian and financial theorist William J. Bernstein ring even truer as geopolitics is increasingly infiltrating debates on international relations, trade, supply chains and even education. Politics is indeed very much communication applied in the service of power. By definition, this also relies heavily on diplomacy.

Foreign policy is shaped by strategies designed to manage global relations and protect a state's international and domestic interests. The audience predominantly consists of heads of state, foreign diplomats and militaries. By contrast, media analyses and commentaries determine what everyone else learns about a nation's position on world politics. While most states prioritize traditional diplomacy as the foundation of foreign policy, others see advantages in coercive diplomacy and the exertion of economic pressure and military force. The new ideological struggle and sharp competition between great powers has once again developed into a regular feature of bilateral relations. It's a point made by a number of authors in various books and research pieces. For example, Michael McFaul, the former US Ambassador to Russia, laid it out in his book *From Cold War to Hot Peace*.[2]

The fragmentation of diplomacy into new subcategories is another trend. Health, mask, vaccine, ping pong, Twitter, diaspora and subnational diplomacy emerged as the most recent prime movers of public perception, reshaping Public Diplomacy (PD), one of the most critical elements of a country's statecraft abroad. Since the desired long-term outcome relies on the ability to forge productive relationships and convince foreign publics of a government's responsibility, benign intents and actions, trust matters the most. When people have faith in a nation's commitment to collaboration, peaceful coexistence and a broader understanding via stronger people-to-people ties, the obvious primary aim of advancing national interests won't be seen as counterpart.

Each nation must choose its own path to achieve that goal, but sticking to old ways usually fails to assure success. The world has become aware of covert tactics and now expects more openness and transparency. It's therefore no longer about image but reputation, which can't be claimed but must be earned. In PD, a lasting positive reputation is deeply reliant on two factors: shared content and the actors behind it. Successful PD relies on the continuous and active promotion of core

DOI: 10.4324/9781003385622-7

values such as the advancement of the common good; be it global peace, prosperity or sustainable development. Just as important are more specific interests such as attracting foreign direct investment, trade, tourism and more. This is its primary function: shaping positive public views that foster trust-based engagement while protecting national reputations.

For years on end, the related content was a byproduct of standard diplomacy, extracted from official statements, communiqués and public announcements. In the Asian Century, PD has expanded to involve a broader range of actors beyond government levels; a shift that comes with legacies. When non-state actors engage in various forms of cultural and citizen-diplomacy, there can be no total control over the narrative. This is by no means a purely modernist view. A famous quote of Lao Tzu (Laozi), the ancient Chinese philosopher and founder of Taoism, laid bare his thoughts from over 2,000 years ago: "Governing a great nation is like cooking a small fish – too much handling will spoil it"[3]

While perceived as a risk by some diplomats, it should be seen as a welcome evolution and ultimate advantage. After all, it never helps to be control-sick in any dynamic operating environment. The new imperative is to maximize influence, not control. Not adapting to it would be on par with "discounted diplomacy" – a barrage of missed opportunities. More advantageous is the development of a national PD strategy that identifies and aligns a nation's desired global perception with ways of exploiting and endorsing community participation by amplifying the core narrative via a host of actors.

For Simon Anholt, founder of the Good Country Index, this is essential: "If you exclude non-state actors you give the impression that culture is the property and remit of the state and of course it's under those precise conditions that culture dies. And, eventually, democracy too."[4]

There are historic precedents that prove the value of spotting opportunities and turning them into diplomatic advantages. A rather consequential moment that underscores that very point dates back several decades. In 1971, when the United States and China had not yet established bilateral ties, an unplanned encounter between American table tennis player Glenn Cowen and the Chinese tennis team at the World Table Tennis Championship in Nagoya (Japan) resulted in an unexpected but highly positive legacy. Cowen had accidentally boarded the Chinese team's bus. He was first greeted with awkward silence, but then Chinese player Zhuang Zedong reached out and presented Cowen with a silkscreen portrait of the Huangshan Mountains. This gesture of friendship is widely quoted as an ice-breaking moment in US–China relations.

I spoke with Klaus Larres, Richard M. Krasno Distinguished Professor of History and International Affairs at UNC in Chapel Hill, to get his opinion. Larres, the author of *Uncertain Allies: Nixon, Kissinger, and the Threat of a United Europe*,[5] sees Zhuang's move as one that may indeed have led to the US team being invited to visit China, paving the way for two official ice-breakers: Henry Kissinger's secret mission in 1971 and Richard Nixon's official trip in 1972. However, it would never have happened without a pre-existing desire by Washington and Beijing to improve relations:

During that time, the US and China had already signaled interest in a more friendly relationship as both sides were keen to gain advantages over the Soviet Union. Ping pong diplomacy was then used as the first guinea pig to test how serious the other side was.[6]

US–China ambassadorial talks had in fact been underway since 1955 but had made little progress. Larres said:

> Nixon believed it might be advantageous to approach China. His objective was to outmaneuver Moscow in the context of the East-West conflict and obtain Chinese help to put pressure on the North Vietnamese, with whom they had good relations, to overcome the Vietnam War.

He added, "Ping pong diplomacy did not lead to a decisive breakthrough in US-Chinese relations, but Washington and Beijing used this unusual diplomatic vehicle to exploit the situation. The ping pong players were instrumentalized, but without them knowing it."[7]

Opportunities to engage in such ways can emerge at any time and at every level. If handled well, this can significantly improve a nation's standing with global audiences. Some career diplomats may feel that giving up control over the messaging is way too risky, considering that not everyone is aware of the bigger picture. But that is missing the point. International relations have moved on from total control or asserting simplistic national-power narratives. What matters today are flexibility and readiness to acknowledge global connectivity and the multifaceted nature of each nation's story, none of which can be captured by one actor and be dispersed in single encounters anyway. Effectively managing the national positioning requires close synergy between all government agencies plus a preconceived master narrative that can be shared and personalized by multiple actors such as artists, athletes and so-called "brand ambassadors" – all without having to engineer every single content detail. The upside of broadening diplomacy and preparing for planned and unplanned encounters in new settings, both physical and digital, is more than evident and does outweigh all perceived risks.

Diplomacy in the Digital Age

Technology and social media have significantly altered public diplomacy over the past ten years as foreign offices, embassies, consulates and NGOs as well as individuals have grown more and more accustomed to take to Facebook, Twitter, Instagram and the like. Millennials (aka Generation Y, born between 1981 and 1996) and Gen Z (aka Zoomers, born between 1997 and 2012) are making it come to life. Diplomats from these two generations grew up with these platforms but still need to build credibility and check their own critical thinking as tweeting is not automatically linked to clear messaging. The underlying idea of "techplomacy" or "twiplomacy" is that tech can increase the effectiveness of connecting with foreign audiences. But as mentioned, there still needs to be a strategy how to engage over the course of time; for example, via specialized messaging services in local languages that provide user-centric information. This might include travel updates, expanded consular services and Covid19-related health advice or high-level chatbots (not the common ones) that mirror conversations with humans based on sophisticated machine learning.

Before Covid19 struck the world, such channels and tools were only one way to conduct diplomatic practices. During the pandemic, most communications in diplomacy moved to the virtual realm. Virtual encounters are easier and less time-consuming to conduct. But as with everything tech, digital platforms are also constantly evolving. Users always remain on the lookout for the latest and coolest app. On top of that there is "social media fatigue"; the effect of having to manage the connection with too many friends and followers. This may ultimately promote consciousness of the advantages of digital engagement vis-à-vis digital storytelling in diplomacy. Some Ministries of Foreign Affairs are now organizing capacity-building sessions that aim to familiarize diplomats with the emerging digital media landscape as a modern and strategic communication tool.[8]

Speaking at the USC Center on Public Diplomacy's webinar *Public Diplomacy 3.0: Mapping the Next Stages of Tech Disruption* on January 20, 2022, Corneliu Bjola, Associate Professor in Diplomatic Studies at the University of Oxford, expressed that social media has peaked: "In 2012, people spent 90 minutes a day on it; in 2018: 142 minutes; in 2021 the same, no growth. And in 2022? Users say they are going to spend less time on it than last year."[9] What he refers to is what can be categorized as "traditional social media." Those more familiar platforms are seeing a change in user behavior, as more are logging in for information only, not for posting as much own content. As Bjola explains, many have also come to feel the dark side of these platforms, such as the hazards of trolling and other forms of emotional abuse. There is just one exception: TikTok, the world's increasingly popular go-to place for mobile videos. The nature of this video-focused social networking service is of special interest, as it points at a bigger shift away from news-centered platforms and toward entertainment. China is already leading that space with so-called role-playing games (RPG) such as "Showa American Story" by NEKCOM Games and "Genshin Impact" by Chinese developer miHoYo. TikTok is also pushing for new gaming features with an initial focus on wider expansion across Southeast Asia. The same is true for Tencent Games, which sees Southeast Asia, the Middle East and Latin America as its fastest-growing markets. Other major tech players like Sony and Netflix are following that same path, planning to incorporate more games on their platforms. Another top investor is Saudi Arabia's Savvy Gaming Group, a government-funded business reportedly aiming to spend over $37 billion on gaming start-ups and company acquisitions.[10]

It may seem implausible at first, but the evidence is at hand: online or mobile gaming in particular advances winning hearts and minds as users engage more with these apps. Capitalizing on this trend is a great way to connect with people. And while social media is here to stay, one cannot rely on it alone. Looking beyond and exploring the potential contributions and precedent-setting implications of the next generation of digital technologies is vital. Governments are already paying attention, and some are even developing their own games to shape perceptions.

For instance, China is now urging major developers to integrate traditional Chinese culture with the objective to tell the Chinese story well. At a forum hosted in late 2021 by the China Audio-Video and Digital Publishing Association (CADPA), leading gaming producers such as Tencent and Yoka Games discussed this, as reported by the China Media Project.[11]

The main purpose is to create micro-communities; the way to promote and harness active user participation. Others pursue that same objective via messaging apps; not WhatsApp but Telegram, the instant messaging service that has some 500 million users. According to Bjola, countries like Singapore and Somalia even have their own public diplomacy channel on Telegram.

Diplomacy is first and foremost about bringing people together, and these new platforms deliver on that. Yet it still remains important to maintain a significant measure of personal diplomacy. Online encounters cannot represent all benefits, as they minimize the nonverbal aspect of communication. Personal dialogue is essential for building trust and to detect the general mood of an audience in a particular setting and to act accordingly. The future of public diplomacy will therefore be hybrid, using both digital resources and in-person diplomacy.

What matters now is to set the stage for a successful management of this process in a continuously changing environment and throughout its various stages and available channels. Apart from that, the rules ensuring cybersecurity must be written and widely shared to protect users from hackers and other illicit actors that could compromise personal data. The top priority is to keep intact the essence of diplomacy without retreating to old pre-social media standards or disassociating it from foreign policy. This includes monitoring of all social media channels in order to identify topics that dominate public discussions among domestic and global publics, including those who may not be directly affected but are still observing and who use social media platforms as their own megaphone. Next comes the assurance of adequate and timely responses. The reaction to such public responses must then be recorded and analyzed. This is best done via a predetermined set of quantitative and qualitative performance indicators that measure the effectiveness of diplomatic action and make it easier to discover any deficits in making an impact.

Finally, a rather familiar question comes up again: what is the most efficient way to gain influence with international audiences from various cultural, linguistic and political backgrounds? The first thing is to garner the best possible understanding of who exactly these audiences are, where they live and what they must or would want to hear. The next step is to self-reflect on the purpose of diplomatic communications in any given scenario: is it meant to inform, to persuade or to achieve something else? The answer would then steer the approach toward the desired outcome of either conveying knowledge with the intent to achieve general acceptance by the audience, or motivating them to engage with some kind of action. In the digital space, this may look like a clear-cut transaction: do whatever increases the number of likes and followers. But that would be a misconception of what defines real influence based on the engagement model of "traditional social media." As the increasing popularity of games and messaging apps has shown, a more reliable indicator is the level of actual participation; be it via online mentions, comments and dialogue, the sharing of or engaging in webinars or games, and advocacy in the real world. The difference may look negligible, but each of these factors requires more than just an internet army of paid or unpaid multipliers. One of the drivers behind the rise of the so-called "think tank diplomacy" is the pushing of national narratives within a scholarly setting; a presumed way to gain more discourse power. But the reality is that using these platforms to repeat the same stories over and over again, without real engagement of speakers and audiences with different views, amounts to preaching to the converted.

In 2022, Ukraine's President Volodymr Zelensky emerged as a global leader in the digital diplomacy space. His continued presence at virtual and physical events and the empathy of his speeches at UN and G7 meetings created a global follower base, securing active support and compassion for his war-torn country. Like Zelensky, senior ambassadors also know how to connect these dots and take the lead. But the strategic design of digital diplomacy still requires a deal of adaptive thinking and appreciation of data analysis to recognize online behavior patterns and prepare for effective message projection and appropriate reactions to online events in real time.

Avoiding the "Diplomessy Trap"

Rivalry and competition between the United States and China are disquieting. Yet despite all conflicting interests across a range of issues, the two nations have long maintained a delicate balance of competitive and cooperative dynamics to jointly address global challenges. It all changed with Trump's trade and tech wars and the surge of Beijing's wolf warrior diplomacy, which led to more complex power dynamics and a clash of self-proclaimed exceptionalism. The resulting lack of conversation and established communication channels could lead to a direct confrontation between two nuclear powers – a geopolitical doomsday scenario.

When Joe Biden became US President, much of the world expected a quick resumption of bilateral relations. But China's more bellicose stance on Taiwan and stated intent to work with Moscow to promote "real democracy" promptly changed that outlook. Biden's repeated remarks about America's intent to defend Taiwan in case of an invasion enraged the Chinese leadership, raising suspicions about Washington abandoning its policy of "strategic ambiguity." When US Defense Secretary Lloyd Austin and his Chinese counterpart Wei Fenghe met in Singapore in 2022 they agreed that communication is crucial in order to rebuild fraught relations and reduce the risk of simmering tensions. Yet they did not settle on a shared vision for a secure and more prosperous Indo-Pacific region. Worries spiked again when House Speaker Nancy Pelosi visited Taiwan. China reacted with extensive military exercises in the Taiwan Strait and announced the end of climate talks with the United States, a de facto punishment not just of "US" but of "us," the world at large, including China itself. Shortly afterwards, US Secretary of State Anthony Blinken and China's Foreign Minister Wang Yi spoke on the sidelines of UNGA77 and again addressed the need to maintain open lines of communication. Joe Biden and Xi Jinping repeated that line right after China's 20th Party Congress and during the G20 meeting in Bali.

All these are positive signs, but simply returning to the status quo ante won't be enough. Keeping the conversation going reduces the risk of miscalculation, but the focus must shift from "just talk" to a more balanced, civil and substantive dialogue. Together this adds up to making real progress in persuasive diplomacy, the combination of "Push and Pull" as communications pros put it. Effectively balancing these components has become the order of the day for those actively involved in foreign policy and public diplomacy. Instead of placing domestic politics above all else, engaging foreign publics in ways that are ideology-free and designed to improve a nation's international standing is the best way to ensure positive outcomes. Closer attention to cultural sensitivity, purpose, realism and nuance would not only infuse the discourse with balance and symmetry, but also make diplomacy more relatable and less transactional, laying the foundation for sustained international support and the advancement of cross-cultural relations.

For now, though, the rhetoric remains tense, as the value systems seem for the most part incompatible. Pushing the narrative of mutual trust and understanding as the new standard has become a frequent claim but is often exposed as a mere distraction from reality. Washington and Beijing have to work on that as a complete diplomatic and economic disentanglement comes with no advantages. India's Minister of External Affairs S Jaishankar took a similar stance when he stressed the need to reduce cross-border tensions with China in the Himalayas by maintaining communication with Beijing.[12]

For China, the challenge ahead is to overcome the built-in conflict of nonaligned domestic and foreign messaging. The downsides of any observable disconnect between words and action in foreign policy and PD – the "Diplomessy Trap," as I call it – are obvious. Confucius (Kong Fuzi), the most prominent Chinese philosopher for thousands of years, got it right: "The object of the superior man is truth."[13]

When aggravated by a confrontational tone, global public sentiment can sway in a split second. Any inconsistencies are likely to be spotted right away, picked up by traditional and social media and further analyzed by influential think tanks and globally recognized publications such as *Foreign Policy* or *Foreign Affairs*, to name just two with close to or even more than one million followers. That should be a strong enough case to take these matters seriously.

When earning active public support at home and abroad is being recognized as a highly valuable asset, the road ahead is clear. Mastering the art of pairing national self-interest with that of the global community does come with multiple upsides. If it includes the pledge to learn from other disciplines, the chances of achieving any set objectives could increase significantly while also expanding discourse power, trust and public support. In some cases that will require an investment in capacity building and novel ways of gathering insights into culture and cognition, the different outlooks they shape and how to cover them. In practical terms, it also depends on personnel choices.

To recap, the rationale for seeing beyond the horizon has more to do with worldwide connectedness than the traditional focus by political leaders. To make it all work, an important factor is to realize (and then spread the word) that public diplomacy and traditional diplomacy are subsets of communications. The earliest known diplomatic records are the Egyptian Amarna letters that date back to the 14th century BCE.[14] Communications as defined today has existed for much longer and also serves a broader set of purposes. This clarifies that nation and place branding, two practices that are often linked to public diplomacy, must be led and guided by strategic communications.

Weighing Values and Principles

Diplomatic actions are more likely to be perceived via social or traditional media rather than physical encounters. With the intention of avoiding the "Diplomessy Trap" and its possible fallout, some state actors have followed the corporate sector in seeking help from public relations firms to develop the messaging and narratives and help with their distribution in key markets. The question is whether these firms are ready to invest beyond the usual study of RFPs (Request for Proposals) and PR briefs and reject propaganda while advocating more transparent communications.

As long as agencies put strategic thinkers in place that are empowered to guide or at least assist top diplomats on how to explain national strategies and course correct when needed, these assignments are acceptable and can help avoid major missteps. But any attempt to optimize the spread of misinformation must be rejected by the global community. As previously mentioned, appointing external subject matter experts is not uncommon, not even among PR firms. Think tanks are key contributors to policymaking based on deep research and analysis. If communicators enter that same realm with a greater emphasis on reputation research and analysis plus impact-oriented communications strategy and campaign design, their value proposition would improve significantly.

Of course, such expansion of communications in diplomacy goes well beyond the crafting of official messages for spokespersons of national authorities and assisting in their delivery to relevant stakeholders. Information must flow continuously, as any information vacuum raises concerns about possible covert motives. But again, communicators should see themselves as more than just narrators. While a focus on producing new content is never wrong, it is neither the first nor the only step. It is vital to start with a research-led analysis of all existing content and the way it is expressed. To make things work, that would have to include an assessment of online and offline collaterals, branding and communications from a perspective of short-, mid- and long-term operational and reputational gains or damages. If done with a deeper understanding of what makes this century Asian and what can be learned from communication theory, the chances of an improved outreach are much higher. If the next stride includes the pledge to incorporate Purpose and Shared Values and the demands of local and foreign audiences, plus a review of a nation's envisioned future and how to articulate it to publics with supposedly opposing views, real and lasting reputational gains are obtainable. Furthermore, vowing to prevent diplomats from willingly or unwillingly using forms of nuanced propaganda also foils reputational damage. Think tanks and research institutes might well turn out to be most valuable partners for communicators in that effort. Once the relationship is established, it would also ease the much-needed continuous dialogue between both and advance their power of persuasion.

All of this starts with listening before talking. This clears the way for greater tolerance and acceptance of differences in worldviews; a favorable outcome in any environment where the expansion of public diplomacy toward a more global mandate is being seriously considered. That is by no means an argument to accept "different truths." The notion of a global community won't work without a shared commitment to transparency, clarity and rejection of conspiracy theories and propaganda.

The EU's Foreign Policy Chief Josep Borrell stated that there is no contradiction between playing power politics and promoting EU values. "On the contrary, showing that you will not abandon your principles is a sign of strength."[15] If managed successfully, this works not only for diplomacy but also for organizations, institutions and brands in markets where taking a stance comes with real challenges. Experienced diplomats (and corporate leaders) know how to play this game and gain ground by being frank about their values and ethical principles. Being open to listen to and accept other opinions can become an act of public engagement in itself and even incline loyalty. Last but not least, it provides deeper insights into forms of public objection and thereby helps with the development of more efficient messaging, narratives, policy explainers and proof points that promote national interests and defend all that underpins a state's foreign policy.

While the promotion of universal values amounts to the gold standard of any form of constructive international collaboration, insisting that others must always side with it is no future-proof strategy. As mentioned in the section "Who Owns the Asian Century?" in Chapter 1, the inconsistencies of rejecting shared values seem obvious and don't help bringing the world closer together. It's another standoff that can be resolved by focusing more on communications and particularly semantics in international dialogue. Borrell affirmed that when he stressed the power of "principles." While he most likely referred to values and principles as being interchangeable, there is an opening here. Values are linked to deep-rooted cultural beliefs and political systems that shape national identities and are therefore less likely to be overturned. Principles, on the other hand, are more closely aligned with internationally agreed norms and standards that facilitate dialogue and negotiations in the process of policymaking while protecting national interests.

International law is the case in point, as it can never be imposed by one power alone. It is based on globally accepted treaties and rules that govern relations between states. The concept behind it can be traced back thousands of years; quite possibly the best face-saving offramp to reengage with ideological and strategic rivals despite all differences. Engaging in this manner won't align different positions overnight but may evade stalemates based on nonnegotiable values.

Fareed Zakaria, CNN host of *GPS (The Global Public Square)* stated on his show and wrote in his piece for *The Washington Post*: "As former British foreign secretary David Miliband said to me: 'A division based on the rules-based order is much more inclusive than one based on democracies versus autocracies.'"[16] The takeaway is clear: the stakes are too high when values-based divisions block inter-state dialogue. Breaking such a logjam can be achieved by working harder to align the formal diction and choice of words among all involved parties. It's an essential step in shifting the focus to fundamental norms of the international order that will then make it easier to keep the conversation going and at the same time facilitate real and lasting outcomes.

Here is one example: America's image suffered severely during the 17 years of war in Vietnam (1956–1973), especially in Asia, but also in many parts of Europe. Nevertheless, US diplomacy moved on to publicly acknowledge shortcomings rather than deny them, and it also engaged in resolving war legacies. The year 2020 marked the 25th anniversary of the normalization of diplomatic relations between the two former enemies. In 2013, a comprehensive partnership agreement was signed, followed in 2019 by a MOU to form a comprehensive energy cooperation partnership. Given the shared perceptions of Chinese coercion, Vietnam even supported the Quadrilateral Security Dialogue (Quad); the strategic partnership between the United States, Australia, India and Japan. In conclusion, even though Vietnam is not going to ally itself with the United States against China, progress can be made when there is an agreement on international norms. Unsurprisingly, this is what domestic and global audiences want to see. Yet as stated before, as soon as principles are asserted only through words but not action, the usual perception is akin to "their influence has declined" – the exact opposite of the intended message. A better approach is to set clear goals, explain them, deliver within a set timeframe and then talk about it.

What Soft Power Is Really About

Soft power has existed for ages but did not get much attention until Harvard Professor Joseph Nye coined the term in the late 1980s. He later elaborated on it in his book *Soft Power: The Means to Success in World Politics*.[17] Since then, soft power has risen to become a popular topic in diplomacy and the most valuable means of achieving global standing and leadership based on cultural and social prowess. It delivered in the traditional space and is as powerful in the digital world. But maintaining soft power requires additional work, as perceptions remain positive over time only if they cover a wider range of qualities. The list includes the efficiency of political systems and perceived strength of economies, the prioritization of innovation and education, and the preparedness to stand up for core beliefs and principles. Still, some say it is insignificant and that its effects are at best long term. As Robert Kaplan wrote, "One Singaporean after another told me: Soft power is only relevant after you have developed hard power."[18]

Of course, it won't replace hard power or define the whole of foreign policy. But that was never the primary purpose anyway. Soft power helps to persuade other nations and rally the world behind one's goals and views, which gives it a high level of influence. In addition, virtuality implies that each statement, tweet or communiqué is going to be noticed by a much larger international audience; a contemporary reality with direct consequences for diplomacy, trade and investment, talent attraction and discourse power. Together, all this elevates soft power to something closer to real discourse power.

Some political actors and business leaders have already gone on board with that and are reaping the benefits from paying more attention to balancing public and self-interest in all actions and interaction while adjusting all content and delivery techniques. But more shifts are in the making that will take time to settle down. For example, as the adoption of the metaverse moves on, Non-Fungible Tokens

(NFTs) are advancing the ability to create soft power through building culture and community online. But because this is about changing mindsets rooted in experience from a bygone era, it is still far from being commonly embraced.

I asked Joseph Nye at the 2021 Brand Finance Global Soft Power Summit 2021 what bigger nations, even superpowers, can learn from smaller ones like Singapore that lack hard power but thrive on diversity, good governance and the power of attraction. His response was unambiguous. He stressed that with fewer than five million people, Singapore indeed developed a good deal of attraction and soft power by setting examples in the region. He also brought up Norway, another small nation with fewer than five million people: "Having a well ordered society, giving one percent of their gross domestic product in overseas development assistance and taking a lead on peace processes has meant that Norway punches well above its weight in soft power."[19]

As mentioned before, the UAE has been named the world's 11th-strongest nation brand in 2021, ranking above the likes of the United States and the United Kingdom. As *Arabian Business* put it, the UAE is "punching above its weight" as it breaks the Western monopoly on soft power.[20] "Punching above one's weight" might just become the term that explains soft power to the world.

Cultural Soft Power

With destinies of nations inseparably linked and the race for discourse power afoot, no country can afford to relinquish soft power – not in Asia, not in the West, not anywhere. It is an ancient concept that just happens to draw more attention these days and won't vanish. The relationships between countries generally revolve around business, security, public health and nowadays also climate change. But that's not the entire story. The past few decades have seen an uptick in states tapping into the potential of their long history, natural wonders and richness of their architecture, education and traditional arts as well as pop culture. Human beings share many things, among them the quest for fulfillment, joy and happiness as well as a sense of hope and belonging. Cultural soft power has shown to be one of the most efficient tools to unite people from different backgrounds by creating stronger and more emotional ties based on a better understanding of these commonalities. It's a perfect way to bypass the adversity of values, which are more prejudiced.

The diversity of Indigenous cultures around the world is an actual gold mine. But it is also something that faces serious threats. Roughly 7,000 languages are currently spoken worldwide, more than half of them by Indigenous people. Yet according to the United Nations, up to 95 percent of all languages might become extinct or seriously endangered by 2100, most being Indigenous languages. That's why the UN declared 2022 the start of the International Decade of Indigenous Languages (IDIL 2022–2032).[21] For Asia, home to around 70 percent of the roughly 500 million Indigenous people in 90 countries, this should make the promotion of cultural diversity even more important. As a matter of fact, Asia has been very successful at that for ages. Interestingly, though, it wasn't just traditional culture but also Asian pop culture that pulled in a vast global audience over the past decades. In the West, much credit goes to record labels such as ECM and Peter

Gabriel's Real World Studios as well as world music festivals such as WOMAD, which promoted a variety of artists from all over the world to a predominantly Western audience. Let's take a deeper look at all that.

J-Pop, K-Pop, T-Pop, Chinese Pop and Lata

One cannot talk about the global influence of Asian pop culture without bringing up the name Anggun. In 1997, the Jakarta-born French singer-songwriter earned international acclaim with her album *La Neige au Sahara* (*Snow in the Sahara*), the best-selling album by any Asian artist outside Asia at the time.

Japanese pop music (J-Pop) has a global fan base in the millions and stretches far beyond the pop music charts as the best songs also appear in movies, TV series, anime and video games. In 1978, Haruomi Hosono, Yukihiro Takahashi and Ryuichi Sakamoto founded the Yellow Magic Orchestra in Tokyo. More than 40 years later, the band still enjoys an almost cult-like global status. Ryuichi Sakamoto also happens to be the composer of award-winning film scores like *The Last Emperor* (1987) and *The Revenant* (2015). Other Japanese pop giants include names like Arashi, Namie Amuro, Tomohisa Yamashita, Ayumi Hamasaki and Hikaru Utada, to name but a few.

South Korea, though, seems to have taken the top spot with ease. With brands like Samsung and Hyundai, the country has built its soft power over decades. Its movie industry is churning out blockbusters like *Train to Busan* (2016) and Oscar winners like *Parasite* (2019); the first foreign-language film to win the Academy Award for best picture. *Squid Game* has been the top rated TV show on Netflix. Korean beauty products are being hailed all over the world. And with immensely popular boy-groups like BTS and girl-groups like Blackpink, K-Pop has become a truly global phenomenon. Many believe it all started with PSY's "Gangnam Style," but K-Pop was already hugely popular when Seo Tai Ji & Boys hit the charts with "Yo! Taiji!" in the 1990s. In a latest development, South Korean food companies and restaurant chains are now tapping the soaring popularity of TV drama series, movies and pop music to endorse "K-Food" all over the world.

The Korean Culture and Information Service (Kocis) deserves much credit for its role in promoting South Korea for 50 years to the outside world.[22] Much to North Korea's chagrin, the success of South Korean cultural exports seems really unstoppable. The *Oxford English Dictionary* acknowledged this by adding 26 Korean words, including "Hallyu" (Korean Wave); a phrase that describes the country's relentlessly growing pop culture soft power.

And there is still more. In 2022, Thai teenage rapper Danupha "Milli" Khanatheerakul was the first T-Pop artist to perform at Coachella, California's legendary Music and Arts Festival. Meanwhile, SB19 were the first Filipino and Southeast Asian band to be nominated in the Billboard Music Awards.

Chinese pop music is also very popular, but most followers are based in mainland China, Hong Kong and Macau, Taiwan, Malaysia and Singapore as well as Chinese-speaking communities in the rest of the world. The term "C-Pop" is therefore not as widely used as J-Pop and K-Pop.

Despite drops in both the Anholt-Ipsos Nation Brands Index and the Brand Finance Global Soft Power Index 2022, India's pop culture appeal also remains high. The subcontinent's linguistic diversity, music and dance have become some of its strongest diplomatic tools. Lata Mangeshkar, the famous Indian singer who passed away in 2022, was not only one of India's greatest cultural icons but also a uniting force across all of South Asia and the global Indian and Pakistani diaspora. Her career spanned eight decades and her songs, many of which were lip-synched by actresses in countless Bollywood movies, brought people together from all walks of life. Even though her political views were not shared by everyone, tributes rolled in from political leaders in Pakistan, Nepal, Bangladesh, Sri Lanka and others.

Asian Movies and Movies Set in Asia

Most people in the West think of Hollywood as the world's undisputed leader of the movie industry. The most prolific film industry, however, happens to be Asian. Every year some 1,000 films are released in India alone. While Bollywood, the Hindi-language sector, is best-known across the world, the Indian film industry churns out movies in a variety of languages. Bengali films, for example, are known to come out of Tollywood. Other sectors focus on the Telugu and Tamil communities in South India. In a latest move, India now aims to boost its industry by offering financial incentives for shooting foreign films and foreign co-productions with India.

Bruce Lee, the Hong Kong American actor, director and martial artist, rose to fame in the 1970s. In 1999, *Time* magazine named him one of the 100 most influential people of the 20th century.[23] Actors such as Jackie Chan and Michelle Yeoh also gained global popularity that lasts till today.

Thailand's tourism industry received a major boost after the release of *The Man with the Golden Gun* (1974), which was partially filmed in Bangkok and in Phang Nga Bay in southern Thailand. It's an iconic location still widely referred to as "James Bond Island" almost 50 years later. In 1993, *The Joy Luck Club* was among the first Hollywood movies to feature a majority cast of Asian descent and still has a 7.7 IMDb rating. *Lara Croft: Tomb Raider* hit the cinemas in 2001 and introduced the wider world to the stunningly beautiful Khmer temples of Angkor Wat in Cambodia. Last but not least, Jon M. Chu's *Crazy Rich Asians* (2018) has been a hugely popular movie, despite the acknowledgment by its director of portraying Southeast Asian characters in a somewhat stereotypical manner.

From Cultural Soft Power to Cultural Diplomacy

The popularity of Asian culture in the West and beyond is seeing results that far exceed the enthusiasm of fan communities. In the UK, for example, interest in learning Asian languages has seen a constant rise for years, in particular Japanese and Korean. The concept of soft power is also drawing more attention among Southeast Asian governments where the phenomenal rise of South Korea's global influence has not gone unnoticed, either. In Thailand, the number of students choosing Korean as a second language has surpassed that of those who picked Japanese.[24] It's a clear result of the popularity of K-Pop and Anime and its impact on Thai youth culture. This signals that cultural soft power does indeed pay off in many ways.

When asking Simon Anholt which country stands out in cultural diplomacy, he made it clear that he does not measure cultural diplomacy per se, since there is no very precise definition of it. But he did state that some countries do transcend others: "I've seen very good work done by the UK (the British Council), South Korea, Poland and others. The British Council's concept of mutuality remains, in my opinion, the yardstick against which all cultural relations should be judged."[25]

To recap, the UK dropped from 2nd to 5th in the 2021 Anholt-Ipsos Nation Brands Index (NBI) but still salvaged its positive reputation. In the Brand Finance Global Soft Power Index (GSPI), the UK jumped from 3rd to 2nd place. Making it to the top five in both surveys speaks volumes about the UK's global standing. If there was any doubt, for much of the world the passing of Queen Elizabeth II served as a reminder of the UK's soft power. The endless queues of mourners in London and places like Hong Kong signaled the high respect Her Majesty had gathered during her 70 years as the UK's monarch.

Altogether, these are examples of how the public view of any place, region or country is influenced by perceptions of cultural soft power that "meets them where they are." Unsurprisingly, this has also led to a renewed push for cultural diplomacy; a real asset in the strategic toolkit of any nation that helps reshaping narratives ingrained in national identity, values and history. The motivation is patent: if the goal is to be heard and to gain influence, any investment in crafting enduring ties of affection will come with real rewards.

In Malaysia, former Foreign Minister Datuk Saifuddin Abdullah spearheaded cultural diplomacy as part of Malaysia's brand new Foreign Policy Framework, jointly promoted by Wisma Putra (the Ministry of Foreign Affairs), the Ministry of Tourism and Culture, and the Ministry of Communications and Multimedia. The initiative by the three ministries started with small-scale film and documentary festivals to promote Malaysian culture on the international stage. The nation's global visibility also increased significantly thanks to Malaysia's hugely popular zero carbon pavilion at Expo 2020. The country bagged a Gold Award at the BIE Day Awards Ceremony in recognition of the effectiveness of communicating its efforts in addressing the challenges connected to Expo's sub-themes 'Sustainability', 'Mobility' and 'Opportunity'. And its rainforest display and daily cultural performances continued to lure big crowds.

Cambodia's pavilion looked like the temples of Angkor Wat; like a film set designed for the next sequel of *Tomb Raider*. The Philippines created an IMAX-sized 3D rendering of their natural habitat. Smaller countries such as Papua New Guinea, the Solomon Islands, Timor-Leste, Laos and Bhutan took every visitor on a tour of local arts, fashion, cuisine and natural beauty in a clear move to increase knowledge of their tourism potential. Each approach created strong emotional bonds while raising genuine interest in learning more about the countries and their future outlook. Vietnam sees sustainable development closely linked to cultural soft power and therefore aims to use its cultural resources to tap into that potential. Hanoi also stated that it is committed to uphold the quality and efficiency of cultural activities, including the preservation and promotion of the cultural identities of 54 ethnic groups.[26]

A number of embassies are organizing Cultural Days to promote what is increasingly perceived as the shortest route to soft power. One of the more curious trends in recent years has been the emergence of ambassadors as de facto entertainers. Aimed at local audiences, their performances may not gain as much attention globally but can make a huge impact in bolstering ties with local communities. Daniel Kritenbrink is a US career diplomat with assignments in China, Japan and Kuwait. When he was the US Ambassador to Vietnam, he released a rap song called "Your Boy in Hanoi."[27] His play on public diplomacy worked in both his host country and at home. A few months later, Kritenbrink – a former Trump appointee – was named Assistant Secretary of State for East Asian and Pacific Affairs by the Biden administration, a role that includes the task of reinforcing partnerships with ASEAN states and demonstrating America's commitment to the most dynamic societies in the region.

South Korea's Ambassador to Egypt Hong Jin-Wook gained much praise for performing Egyptian songs on a saxophone. The Embassy even produced a video clip titled "Love for Egypt: Saxophone by the Korean Ambassador – 3Daqat and National Anthem of Egypt."[28] Relations between both countries have seen an enormous spike in recent times and the promotion of cultural exchange played a major role.

Entertaining local publics is also beginning to get entrenched in inter-Asian affairs. A good example is the silat performance by Malaysia's Ambassador to Cambodia Eldeen Husaini Mohd Hashim in front of a group of Cambodian teachers and students. Silat, the Malay term for self-defense or martial art, is considered one of Malaysia's most lasting cultural heritage treasures.[29]

Indonesia on the other hand has greatly benefited from its promotion of literature and arts. Ubud is Bali's cultural hub and one of my favorite places since first visiting it in 1990. Every year it hosts the Ubud Writers and Readers Festival (UWRF). Founded by Janet DeNeefe in 2004, the event invites domestic and international authors and readers to days of close interaction and is now the biggest literature festival in all of Southeast Asia.

Capitalizing on Soft Power's Real Potential

Public Diplomacy of course is no alternative way of communicating foreign policy narratives. Its purpose is to open new doorways to connect with global audiences based on its general appeal that includes a greater focus on enthusiasm, positivity and emotions. In an ideal world, PD will supplement foreign policy objectives but can also serve additional purposes such as countering propaganda and asserting truth. This can work particularly well when inter-state relations have not fully proliferated due to complications related to geopolitics. What we are witnessing is the breakdown of PD into its various subcategories; the best way to harvest their full potential. All are power tools in their own spheres of influence but can be leveraged even more once deployed under a unified strategy. That's how packing a punch really works.

When cultural diplomacy and soft power become more coordinated and performance-based, they are going to foster positive views, encourage dialogue among cultures and support the bigger goals of sustainable development and economic growth. Let's call it nation branding on steroids. It's an outcome that should be desired by all nations. But that does not seem to be the case. Yan Xuetong, Dean of the Institute of International Relations at Tsinghua University in Beijing and a prominent academic on US affairs, warned about the high level of nationalism and overconfidence by China's younger generations in the country's power and condescending views of other countries.[30] Other Asian nations have chosen an alternative path.

In 2021, BTS was appointed as Korea's "Special Presidential Envoy" at the 76th UN General Assembly – the equivalent of a brand ambassador in corporate and consumer communications but a previously unthinkable move of using soft power in the United Nations' main policymaking organ. Soon after, the band snagged the Artist of the Year (the top prize) at the American Music Awards and became a Grammy nominee. Former President Moon Jae-in praised BTS on his social media accounts, saying the AMA win could help Korean people increase their pride and confidence in Korean culture while boosting the nation's status globally. He then expanded on that by reaffirming that "South Korea's soft power matches its economic achievements." Months later BTS appeared at a White House press briefing in which they addressed their concerns over the surge in hate crimes against Asian Americans. US presidents have long leveraged music artists for political messaging. But never before had an Asian pop group been invited. It was an unprecedented move based on the group's status – and in particular that of the band's leader "RM" or Kim Namjoon – as true Youth Ambassador.

Global connectivity has been a boost to this nation's already extraordinary soft power. The world is now interested in learning even more about South Korea, which is no longer just the place where Samsung came from. Smaller nations with a rich and globally appealing culture are likely to follow suit and leverage not just the soft edge but what amounts to the approximation of hard power through cultural and activism power. To be clear, this is not about promoting a disguised form of "sharp power," and certainly not about censorship or propaganda. On the contrary, the objective is to capitalize on the clout unleashed by an already tuned-in global audience that doubles as some kind of protective shield against aggressive conduct such as economic coercion. What it takes is policy action designed to respond to any attempts at intimidation by galvanizing public protests, boycotts and social media debates that break the aggressor's global standing. It's about fortifying PD through the resolve to use the diplomatic muscle and start "punching" – not just "above one's weight" but also in full self-awareness of one's actual weight. In view of that, soft power may be considerably less soft than the term suggests.

While the idiom "punching above one's weight" may sound like a badly worded call for counter-aggression, the actual rationale is to leverage influence based on public consciousness and willingness to voice their opinion. This may take some time, as Simon Anholt told me. To him, soft power still derives from a conception of governance that privileges competition over collaboration: "It is still framed very much as a contest, a cheap way for countries to achieve ascendancy over each other, and in that context it hardly matters whether you're hitting people with art or hitting them with bombs." This would leave just one reasonable course for the future. In Anholt's words: "We need to get to the stage where the culture of governance is collaboration with a little competition sprinkled over the top, not the reverse."[31]

Cultural diplomacy might just be the most promising way to achieve that objective, as it carries a lot of appeal. The potential is virtually limitless even though pushing soft power is often perceived as naïve and detached from reality. This appears to have motivated Joseph Nye to clarify its function in the international system in a piece for *Project Syndicate*. In it he argues that countries fall back on coercion, intimidation and payoffs to advance their interests, but that does not spell the end of soft power. "It matters, and governments ignore its potential at their peril."[32]

In conclusion, global public opinion is what it is, global. The impact is that it minimizes the odds of being seen as driven by any single party. What's more, positive views like reputations cannot be enforced. As cannot be stated often enough, they have to be earned. Optimism plus open borders and an emphasis on people-to-people exchange and engagement are crucial. And since understanding is at the core of it all, strategic communications is one of the chief mitigating factors, provided it expands its role. Still, getting the desired returns within a reasonable timeframe depends on continuity in the management and decision-making of foreign policy and the actual conceptualization and maneuverability of these advanced strategies. No less important is how they are being communicated and how prepared spokespersons are to respond to feedback and any new developments in real time.

Conveniently, the same applies to corporate communications, where narratives and personal experiences are meant to influence public opinion and encourage third-party advocacy. The more convincing the efforts to prioritize pull, not push, the higher the chances of avoiding unsustainable competition in global markets. It all hinges on the people, or, to put in another way, on human capital.

References

1. Bernstein, William J. *Masters of the Word: How Media Shaped History*. 1st ed. (stated), First Printing, New York, Grove Press, 2013.
2. McFaul, Michael. *From Cold War to Hot Peace: An American Ambassador in Putin's Russia*. Reprint, New York, Mariner Books, 2019.
3. Lao Tzu Quotes. (n.d.). *BrainyQuote*. https://brainyquote.com/quotes/lao_tzu_144170
4. Anholt, Simon. Conversation with author. April 2022.
5. Larres, Klaus. *Uncertain Allies: Nixon, Kissinger, and the Threat of a United Europe*. New Haven, CT, Yale University Press, 2021.
6. Larres, Klaus. Conversation with author. April 2022.
7. Larres, Klaus. Conversation with author. April 2022.
8. Ullah, Mati. "Ministry of Foreign Affairs Organizes Training Session on Digital Diplomacy." *Dispatch News Desk*, 17 Feb. 2022, https://dnd.com.pk/ministry-of-foreign-affairs-organizes-training-session-on-digital-diplomacy/263936
9. "Public Diplomacy 3.0: Mapping the Next Stages of Tech Disruption." *USC Center on Public Diplomacy*, 3 Feb. 2022, https://uscpublicdiplomacy.org/event/public-diplomacy-30-mapping-next-stages-tech-disruption

10. Totilo, Stephen. "Saudi Arabia to Invest $37 Billion in Gaming." *Axios*, 29 Sep. 2022, https://axios.com/2022/09/29/saudi-arabia-invest-37-billion-gaming
11. Chen, Stella. "Gaming for the China Story." *China Media Project*, 25 Jan. 2022, https://chinamediaproject.org/2022/01/25/gaming-for-the-china-story
12. Chaudhury, Dipanjan Roy. "Communication Was Integral During India-China Clashes: EAM S Jaishankar." *The Economic Times*, 11 Oct. 2022, https://economictimes.indiatimes.com/news/defence/communication-was-integral-during-india-china-clashes-eam-s-jaishankar/articleshow/94795786.cms
13. *Confucius Quotes*. (n.d.). *BrainyQuote*. https://brainyquote.com/quotes/confucius_101814
14. Sara. "The Amarna Letters." *Rough Diplomacy*, 21 Sep. 2018, https://roughdiplomacy.com/the-amarna-letters
15. *How to Revive Multilateralism in a Multipolar World? | EEAS Website*. https://eeas.europa.eu/eeas/how-revive-multilateralism-multipolar-world_en
16. Zakaria, Fareed. "Why Are So Many Democracies Unwilling to Condemn Russia?" *The Washington Post*, 28 Apr. 2022, https://washingtonpost.com/opinions/2022/04/28/united-states-should-practice-the-rules-based-order-it-preaches
17. Nye, Joseph. *Soft Power: The Means to Success in World Politics*. Illustrated. New York, PublicAffairs, 2005.
18. Kaplan, Robert. *Asia's Cauldron: The South China Sea and the End of a Stable Pacific*. New York, Random House, 2014.
19. "Global Soft Power Summit 2021." *Brand Finance*, 25 Feb. 2021, https://livegroup.s3-eu-west-1.amazonaws.com/SoftPower/5.+SoftPower+Summit+21+-+Panel+Session+2-+The+Future+of+Soft+Power.mp4 (51:08).
20. "UAE 'Punching above Its Weight' as It Breaks Western Monopoly on Soft Power." *ArabianBusiness.com*, 19 Oct. 2021, www.arabianbusiness.com/latest-news/469924-uae-punching-above-its-weight-as-it-breaks-western-monopoly-on-soft-power
21. "Indigenous Languages Decade." *UNESCO*, 23 Mar. 2022, https://en.unesco.org/idil2022-2032
22. "After a Stellar 2021, the Future Looks Bright for Korea's Soft Power." *Korea JoongAng Daily*, 7 Jan. 2022, https://koreajoongangdaily.joins.com/2022/01/07/culture/features/park-jongyoul-kocis-korean-culture/20220107155302578.html
23. "TIME 100 Persons of the Century." *TIME.com*, 6 Jun. 1999, https://content.time.com/time/magazine/article/0,9171,26473,00.html
24. Seiya, Sukegawa. "Can Thailand Replicate South Korean Soft Power?" *The Diplomat*, 1 Jun. 2022, https://thediplomat.com/2022/06/can-thailand-replicate-south-korean-soft-power
25. Anholt, Simon. Conversation with author. April 2022.
26. "Cultural Resources to Be Turned into National 'Soft Power.'" *Vietnam+*, 24 Nov. 2021, https://en.vietnamplus.vn/cultural-resources-to-be-turned-into-national-soft-power/215784.vnp
27. Hutton, Alice. "'A Boy in Hanoi': US Ambassador Releases Rap Video to 'Connect with Vietnam People.'" *The Independent*, 10 Feb. 2021, https://independent.co.uk/news/world/americas/us-politics/us-ambassador-rap-vietnam-b1800463.html
28. El-Adawi, Reham. "Korean Ambassador Performs Egyptians Songs on Saxophone." *Ahram Online*, 13 Jul. 2021, https://english.ahram.org.eg/NewsContent/5/1188/417135/Arts--Culture/City-Lights/Korean-ambassador-performs-Egyptians-songs-on-saxo.aspx
29. "Malaysian Envoy Promotes Silat in Cambodia." *Malaymail*, 26 Dec. 2021, https://malaymail.com/news/life/2021/12/26/malaysian-envoy-promotes-silat-in-cambodia/2031226

30. Mai, Jun. "China's Gen Z Overconfident and Thinks West Is 'Evil,' Top Academic Says." *South China Morning Post*, 14 Jan. 2022, https://scmp.com/news/china/diplomacy/article/3163476/chinas-gen-z-overconfident-and-thinks-west-evil-top-academic
31. Anholt, Simon. Conversation with author. April 2022.
32. Nye, Joseph S., Jr. "Whatever Happened to Soft Power?" *Project Syndicate*, 13 Jan. 2022, https://project-syndicate.org/commentary/whatever-happened-to-soft-power-by-joseph-s-nye-2022-01?barrier=accesspaylog

7 Human Capital

Winning with New Talent Strategies

It has been widely reported that the financial outlook for the PR industry appears more than promising. In 2021, the global PR market was worth around $92 billion. By 2026 its total value might reach $149 billion. Growth in PR is a consistent trend, but as Robert Phillips explained in his previously cited book, it does not imply an advancement of the practice as such. He was definitely not alone with that opinion. Nonetheless, a projected 61 percent increase in market valuation over five years does send a clear message: despite or because of all uncertainty in these volatile times, communications is going to be in high demand. All this is reassuring but not a blank check for executive inaction with regards to future readiness. When assessing the impact of today's fast-changing environment, none of the time-honored practices or long-established views should be exempt from further scrutiny. Not dealing with that reality might cause financial and reputational losses, while expansion is almost certainly secured by competitors (usually independent and small to medium-sized agencies) that have invested in a safe and sustainable future.

In any people business such as PR or communications, talent management should always rank at the top of the list. Being in the midst of a global talent war, an all-inclusive review of long-established talent strategies is even more critical. All-inclusive means that leaders must also check out their own HR teams – the ones in charge of securing a future-ready workforce. Consensus about what the future is going to hold is essential, including what it means for specific operating environments and how to express all that in ways that resonate with the right applicants. HR should always ensure a highly satisfying candidate journey to win over the best of the best, including location independent "corporate nomads."

Attracting Millennials and Gen Zers

In communications as in other disciplines, the first choice is to attract those at the early stage of their careers. Roughly two decades ago, HR executives in communications began to broaden their talent pool by seizing not only the top graduates in journalism and mass communications, but also those from law schools and medical universities. The rationale was evident: getting those with the most highly

DOI: 10.4324/9781003385622-8

prized skills and placing them in the corporate and healthcare practices to utilize their deep knowledge helps to outperform the competition's generalists. Adapting this practice to meet today's requirements creates more diverse teams, including some broadly skilled and genuinely tech-savvy candidates who are not only familiar with office software, mobile apps and videoconferencing. The competitive advantage lies with talent familiar with the use of tech for managing the growing surge of information and the advantages it brings for strategic planning. This might include educators and commentators and even young entrepreneurs and start-up owners with backgrounds in coding and app development. Consequently, tech also needs to take center stage inside HR.

Abdul-Rahman Risilia, Founder and CEO of Dubai-based ARC Talent, an outsourced talent partner for enterprise, start-ups and multinationals, does not think we are there yet: "The demand in tech is at an all-time high and creative new methods to grow your teams are crucial," he said. "But companies haven't figured out how to implement this strategy without it impacting the performance of tech."[1] Likewise, placing an emphasis on team diversity may be the subject of a lot of talk, but according to Risilia, not many have this at the forefront of their business as they try to scale and grow.

Grooming young and diverse talent that is capable of gathering and analyzing data is vital to get a hold on perceptions, how people engage and what trends are going to shape the immediate future of any business or organization. And if these new hires are unified by advanced, shared goals and able to make significant contributions based on their familiarity with cloud and connectivity via AI and big data, the stage is set for succeeding by beating the other side's generalists. The majority of this cohort would be from Millennials and Gen Z (aka Zoomers). It is important to understand their frame of mind, values and preferences. They have witnessed a rise in social injustice, environmental crises, geopolitical tensions and the breakout of wars in countries including Afghanistan, Armenia and Azerbaijan, Ethiopia, Georgia, Libya, Myanmar, Syria, Yemen and Ukraine. On top of that, they lived through extended Covid19 lockdowns. All of it played a big part in shaping their opinions and reactions. Being connected as they are and therefore always aware of other work environments, these two generations won't tolerate poor leadership or a lack of opportunities for personal growth. Showing a true allegiance to regular and even personalized training schedules adds testimony to claims of caring about employees.

According to the Deloitte Global 2022 Gen Z and Millennial Survey,[2] the two age groups are striving for balance and advocating for change. Their empathy for truth, social justice and activism is another key factor as Gen Z is getting involved in politics in ways not seen before. When young people deeply care about any social issues, the chances of those soon covering other subject matters too are quite high. In his book *Fight* (2022),[3] John Della Volpe looks at the concerns Zoomers care most about and how they channel fear and passion to tackle America's unsolved issues, all with a unique willingness to disrupt the status quo. This is echoed by young activists in other parts of the world, namely Sweden's environmentalist Greta Thunberg, Hong Kong's pro-democracy fighter Nathan Law and Pakistan's advocate for girls' education Malala Yousafzai.

Candidates from both generations also expect their leaders to show a serious commitment to organizational ethics and purpose-driven values that go beyond making a profit. However, simply backsliding to past accomplishments won't work. Potential new hires, especially from overseas, will do their own research, looking for reputable companies with a known employer brand and leadership with a clear vision. That's the way to earn their trust and loyalty. Proof of that can be delivered in various forms, for example by clearly stating the organization's values and planned expansion over the next decade. One way to demonstrate that is to showcase a track record of adapting and adjusting to new developments. It gives candidates a sense of job safety and career opportunities, even when the world around them keeps changing. Of course, it is also necessary to listen and always reassure employees and candidates that their voice is being heard. After all, they are supposed to cooperate with a keen eye on present and future opportunities and will be most committed when getting a sense of appreciation and ownership for their own ideas and contributions.

When people move on to new (or their first) jobs, there is always a degree of uncertainty about their expectations, actual ability and preparedness to adapt to any specific work culture. One way to address this would be to exhibit that their contribution matters; that there will be a serious commitment to offer guidance and no uncertainty about what is expected of them. It's a way to reduce doubt about what their future in that organization might look like. Together, this serves as a reminder that Purpose and Shared Values are once again at the center of future readiness.

How Covid19 Changed Talent Strategies

Globalization, climate change and sustainability: all define our destinies. The biggest short-term impact, however, stems from the Coronavirus pandemic. It affected not only our social life but also the work environment. The disruptions caused by office space lockdowns are only matched by the invention of the internet. Whether Covid19 eventually disappears like SARS (the virus that emerged in Asia in 2002 and was contained in 2003) or becomes endemic, businesses must develop and implement winning strategies undeterred by further disruptions, delays in growth and geopolitical challenges. The question is how to lead high-performing remote teams. When physical presence in offices was reduced to a few days per week or even outright banned, everything changed and people began to weigh their options. As a result, access to a skilled workforce has become a matter of priority. The good news is that more global talent is available now than before the pandemic.

Labeled as the "Great Resignation," some 40 to 41 percent of all employees worldwide were planning to leave their jobs at the peak of the pandemic. According to surveys by Mercer, Microsoft and the World Economic Forum,[4] this included more than half of the 18- to 25-year-olds. The number of first job seekers with a university degree is also rising and expected to reach a record 260 million in the coming ten years. For HR, this may sound like good news but does not make the task at hand easier. Job applicants in a "seller's market" will always compare their actual experience with private and public declarations about how much a company values its staff. If the established corporate culture and perceived employer value match all key objectives and expectations, the chances of winning over the best are increasing. But who exactly are these rock stars? The time has come to check whether HR has a good answer.

After years of first being forced and then getting used to remote work, the opportunity to work from home – at least partially – has become a critical factor in talent acquisition. However, it also makes it harder to closely observe their progress and facilitate remote interactions. Besides, there are limits of virtual collaboration. It is important to strike a balance between written and verbal communication and to avoid a drop in trust in the employer's interest or attention in guiding jobholders in their career advancement. Some people, on the other hand, have been missing the vibe of the workplace and are longing for a return to the office where they can meet their colleagues and socialize with friends at the watercooler. Getting feedback from bosses and talking to HR on matters related to career development or other issues is also best done in person.

How can organizations balance the needs of remote and physical teams? Both remote and on-site work must be accommodated with a view on collaboration and reassurances that employees feel connected, valued and excited about their jobs and workplaces. The upside is obvious. When people are encouraged to team up with others, both physically and online, they don't just deliver what earns them their monthly paychecks. By jointly solving problems and creating value, they get a sense of belonging that keeps them from looking out for other jobs.

Another arguably groundbreaking move would be a review of the traditional workweek. This may sound odd to some senior executives, but in order to compete in the global war for talent, a shift to a four-day workweek might be much easier to implement than having to increase pay. According to Global Talent Trends 2022, work–life balance trumps even bank balance and colleagues and culture for job seekers.

One future-oriented state has already made this the new national law. In January 2022, the UAE introduced a four-and-a-half-day workweek, which follows the Western world's Monday-through-Friday model. Friday, the traditional prayer day in the Islamic world, is now a half-workday. That's a shift to a two-and-a-half-day weekend; a clear move to attract young talent. Belgium was the first European nation to give workers the right to request a four-day week from employers. Japan and Iceland are following a similar path. Other countries, such as Portugal and Spain, are either considering or already beginning trials of a four-day workweek. The largest trial with 100 percent pay began in the UK in summer 2022. Pilot programs were also underway in the United States, Canada, Ireland, Australia and New Zealand and have probably been enacted as of this writing.

Leading with Multiculturalism and Diversity

Whether it's the four-day workweek, certain values, new corporate policies or all combined, building more diverse teams should become a top priority. While traditional selection criteria such as language skills, solid industry knowledge and digital prowess are as valid as ever in communications, the ideal candidates are those who also exhibit open-mindedness to work in multicultural environments. While it may be first and foremost a lifestyle choice for them, it also signals some real curiosity about other cultures and values, which hints at a promising future of performance. It is therefore no surprise that many small and large businesses leaders are looking to build more cosmopolitan teams. Adapting to ethnic and cultural diversity without bias is precisely what gives communications a competitive edge. And the benefits don't end there, as the subject is also gaining traction across the media. According to the Advancing News Diversity in Asia (ANDA) report by the Asian American Journalists Association (AAJA),[5] 90 percent of journalists agree that diversity improves the quality of news. And 83 percent said more diverse reporting attracts audiences. Having comms teams in place that match DEI (diversity, equity and inclusion) programs and policies can be a real competitive advantage. Hence, leaders and HR managers should take this as a primary reason to be more empathetic and inclusive in their recruitment process and even revolve around the positive impact of DEI workplace initiatives.

Hiring foreign talent that can work from anywhere also allows both sides to see how all goes before committing to a physical and long-term appointment. As most international travel restrictions are being removed, global talent mobility is also seeing the beginning of a return to where it was before the pandemic. Multinationals are once again on the lookout for locally based foreign talent, as on-the-ground presence is still a must wherever they run their operations. Several nations support this trend by introducing special legislative frameworks to make it easy to hire and relocate global talent.

In late 2021 Dubai announced it would grant golden visas to 100,000 entrepreneurs, owners of enterprises, and start-ups specialized in coding. It's a strategic move preceded by the appointment in 2017 of Omar Bin Sultan Al Olama as the UAE's (and the world's first) Minister of State for Artificial Intelligence. At the Diplomacy Lab Dialogue hosted by Fatima Bint Mohamed Bin Zayed Initiative and Anwar Gargash Diplomatic Academy in April 2022, the Minister laid out the UAE's vision. He also kindly spoke with me afterwards, making clear that attracting ever more young people to create a smart and innovative future has become a top priority. He emphasized that online learning is a great opportunity to become a top coder and gain skills in vital sectors. And he added that the UAE's mission is to create the highest-ranked coders, who have the best abilities, qualities and attributes in the country. This aligns with the UAE's declared objective to lead the world in AI by 2031. The UAE also launched a "Talent Pass" aimed at attracting global talent and professionals in the fields of media, education, technology, art, marketing and consultancy. In short, diversity writ large.

Japan, which has no record of showing any devotion to win over foreign talent, now offers a visa class aimed chiefly but not only at tech talent. And South Korea introduced the Hallyu visa to draw global cultural talents eager to learn about the Korean culture and entertainment industry. A similar pattern is emerging in the Western world. Two of the better-known exceptions are China and the United States. Due to its border shutdown from spring 2020 until December 2022, China lost enormous numbers of expatriates. In January 2022, Beijing announced new tax laws aimed at foreigners, which abolished the option of deducting housing rent and schooling expenses from personal taxable income. Beijing and Shanghai combined were said to have fewer non-Chinese residents than Luxembourg, one of the world's smallest countries. The Biden administration initially struggled to redesign Trump's immigration policy but in late 2022 examined recommendations by a Presidential Commission to reduce the decision-making and processing time for Green Card applications, which could help hundreds of thousands of immigrants.

With connectivity being fundamental to the architecture of a multilateral world, welcoming foreign talent is more than just a smart move. It is the accelerator of enhanced international relations, stronger trade ties and even a driver of soft power. What matters, though, is to always tap into the sentiments and perceptions of those informal "national brand ambassadors." Overseas stints are great career accelerators that can boost job performance. Any time spent living, studying or working abroad also widens people's sense of self, especially when seeking purpose in their careers. One would assume that identifying talent receptive to such opportunities should be quite easy. Interestingly, though, the way younger people view multicultural experience was not always crystal clear. According to a study quoted by *Time* magazine back in 2014,[6] Millennials at that time believed they are doing just fine by gaining international experience through social media, personal networks and technology. Their upbringing happened to coincide with the emergence of the internet, which made them more tech-dependent. However, with innovation cycles getting ever shorter and expanding into new areas, a certain degree of unease and a longing for stability should be expected.

Considering virtual foreign work experience as having equal career value as physical multicultural experience would obviously not bode well for multinationals. When planning an expansion of their market share in the developing world, what matters the most is teams with professional qualifications and cultural know-how, all for the purpose of building confidence among local partners, customers or other stakeholders. In communications that would include assembling teams experienced in crafting the right narratives and strategizing any outreach for the sake of adding to one's international influence. The same applies to political actors in quest of achieving foreign policy goals in countries with differing values.

In any case, while the desire for stability exists, there are observable differences between various parts of the world. The aforementioned study revealed that the numbers of those who prefer real international experience over global social connections were lower in the developed world. Millennials in nations such as India, China and Brazil, on the other hand, were more open for overseas assignments; a trend that fueled the rapid development of several Asian states over the past decades. The majority of Asians, especially younger demographics, welcomes disruptive change as the precursor of a better future. Parag Khanna explained why: "Mobile phones come before landlines, digital banking before ATMs, cloud computing before desktops, electronic road payments before toll booths, and solar and wind power instead of oil and gas."[7] Many parts of Africa are on a similar path. The continent never had many fixed-line phone subscribers but has seen a dramatic growth in mobile phone users.

It's plain and simple: growing up in rapidly modernizing places affects the way of thinking and removes negative perceptions from disruption, more likely seen as a path to opportunity and real-life improvements. That makes Asia the go-to place to find young, flexible and tech-savvy talent. Plus, the Millennials of 2014 are obviously well out of college, and many are more than ready for leadership roles, both domestically and overseas.

How Connected Is the Most Connected Workforce?

The advantages of a well-articulated envisioned future for all stakeholders are self-evident. In any professional setting, gaining persuasive power relies as much on the content of the argument made as on those who express it and their preparedness to adjust to audience needs. Since convincing third parties relies on authentic commitment and dialogue, the main question should be where and how to obtain that level of knowledge and insight into the "Lebenswelt" (life world) of others. This is even more critical when the audience is global, as their life worlds obviously diverge. This is where big tech comes into play.

Due to mandated stay-at-home orders and face-to-face interactions being off the table, video conferencing software quickly rose to become the new standard in 2020 and 2021. The implications seem to be fully known, but there is more to assimilate. Unbeknown to most, the technology had been around for decades. Its modern version was first introduced at the 1968 World's Fair in New York but made no real impact because of its high cost, limited accessibility and enduring technical challenges. Two decades later, IBM and PictureTel released a commercial video conferencing solution that enabled larger corporations to offer telehealth and higher education distance learning. Yet only when laptops and mobile phones began being equipped with better cameras did the use of this technology surge among consumers.

In the mid-2000s, Skype pioneered video calls and gained enormous global popularity that turned the brand into a verb and gave global connectedness an added meaning. "Let's skype" even preceded "Just google it" by a few years. Years later, though, the app saw user ratings drop due to a less popular change in functionality and design features. Zoom's Founder Eric Yuan, for his part, deserves credit for alleviating the global pandemic by connecting people through video, voice, chat and content sharing. The free-to-use app had existed since 2012 but experienced a pivotal moment when no physical meetings could be held. In a short time, video conferencing became as normal as landline telephone calls in the 20th century. Zoom calls quickly turned into the closest thing to actually delivering happiness in these challenging times. "Let's zoom" is the new "Let's skype." Other providers also saw download numbers for their apps going up; including (but not limited to) Microsoft Teams and Cisco WebEx, Eric Yuan's former company, which developed one of the first videoconference tools.

Despite that, participants who spent months on webinars began to have second thoughts about the efficiency and ROI of virtual connections. The public debate about webinar fatigue was constructive, as it addressed a real concern. When online meetings were marketed for distance learning but turned into endless lectures without any real audience involvement, the time invested appeared much less valuable. Zoom responded by adding plenty of new features such as auto-generated captions, whiteboards and a whole range of apps for collaboration, note taking, gaming and more. Some large organizations, including think tanks, NGOs and educational institutions, realized that drawback too and began to introduce virtual conferences that placed an emphasis on user mobilization and participation. For instance, the virtual Paris Peace Forum brought together heads of state, international organizations and representatives from the private sector, civil society, philanthropy, academia and other stakeholders to discuss ways to build a more sustainable world. It is just one high-profile example of expert panels and actual networking on a single platform. Other online gatherings expanded on that by offering private interactive sessions with top experts.

While some events are limited to the C-Suite, plenty of others provide opportunities for younger generations to get virtually (no pun intended) unlimited access to market intelligence or academic insights that would be hard to acquire via any other means. Research institutes and think tanks in particular provide not only facts but also profound expert opinions. Much of the research output by universities and think tanks is easily accessible for anyone with a credible professional profile and evidence of genuine interest. Regardless of these advantages, very few communicators tap into these resources. The absence of PR pros on webinar panels or among delegates says a lot. Of course, this is different when the subject itself is related to communications. That, however, amounts to PR pros catching up with PR pros at PR events. It makes for some good networking but should not be the only step toward broadening knowledge and achieving future readiness.

The verdict is still out on how lasting these professional digital relationships are. Nevertheless, virtual meetings are the future and a test of everyone's ability to extract real value from the core content presented in an online setting. When engaging with the best scholars and diplomats, the chances for young talent to propel their careers can increase right away. And not only that: getting to know more experts than one could possibly meet in person is a reliable method of attaining knowledge similar to traditional research and study, in particular when there is also some genuine engagement via the Q&A tab or chatbox.

Change may be within reach once the industry settles on the expansion of knowledge at all levels as the defining elements of "The Future of the Agency" or "The Agency of the Future." Seeking to base counsel on constant learning about any area of interest and its cultural, economic and geopolitical context is best achieved by taking advantage of in-depth analysis provided by real experts outside one's own area of expertise.

How Millennials and Gen Zers Need to Adapt

Being digital natives is a good thing. But even when connectivity is being recognized as a key factor in securing that dream job, it certainly is not a one-way road. Millennials and Gen Zers need to adapt, too. According to LinkedIn, Zoomers emerged as its fastest-growing audience that is much more active on its platform than Millennials.[8] That aligns with the core belief of Gen Z that anyone can break though the social media clutter and become a de facto broadcaster or newsmaker. The influence of user-generated content is undeniable and shapes ever more opinions worldwide. It would be hard to dismiss, though, that spending hours on social media shortens the attention span and does not usually lead to deeper insight. It may advance the discovery of useful content sources, but it still demands a commitment to dig deeper. Hence, a publicly shared fondness for reading books would be a good sign, as this is where arguments are laid out in chapters, not just posts and tweets with a 280-character cap.

This relates to a similar argument made by Telum Media's Michael Webster who referred to the comments of a speaker at one of his company's media events. As he told me,

> PRs also need to consume media as part of their job. Whether it be reading, watching, listening, it's only by consuming the media and building relationships with journalists that PRs understand what makes a story and how their client might fit into a news cycle, and in a crisis situation, what particular risks there are of engaging media in a certain way and how to craft messages that resonate with an audience.

He also pointed out that this can be both internal as well as external. "In short, understanding how the media works provides the foundation for many other communication skills PRs require today."[9]

Most business leaders also expect employees to pick up new skills. Apart from seeking job candidates with an understanding of the wider impact of tech in any work environment, employers are looking for those with an evident capacity to think critically, communicate clearly and be able to adapt and work well with others. In view of that, foreign language skills have always been a big plus. Being prepared to work in a multilingual environment is important even though companies replace their native language with English to meet the requirements of global teams. But connecting in the local language can make a huge difference. Once being bilingual has been accomplished, the next thing is the readiness to relocate to other offices. To comply with that and work in different geographic and virtual environments is a real career accelerator. If that view is not echoed, perhaps the candidate that looked like a perfect fit for that vacant position is anything but. Yet if it is adopted, such proactive thinking and acting might become the hallmark of two generations that change the current relationship between employers and employees.

Considering its people focus, the communications industry should be better equipped than others to adapt quickly to all these new requirements. Millennials who feel comfortable about solely fulfilling the conventional criteria they are familiar with must realize that this might no longer be enough. By no means does that imply that everyone in communications now needs to have a PhD. What makes the difference is the pledge to broaden one's skills and knowledge and where possible seek connections with other experts in fields of personal and professional interest. Pursuing professional growth beyond the shared job description is what advances the chance of securing that dream job.

Job seekers who understand that the early stage of any search is about the identification of future leaders – including outside talent – who are not just prepared for change but actually desire it may choose to accentuate their preparedness and proactive mindset. What would make sense to call attention to is laying out thoughts about how to settle in new workplaces, beat the competition with new thinking and demonstrate readiness to adapt. In addition, they might emphasize looking out for strategic advantages while always avoiding reputational risks that could undo any corporate accomplishments. The people they are going to work with are from Gen Z, who adopted the digital-first lifestyle and are quick to share experiences with each other in real time. With at least two generations of tech-dependent young people with a strong sense of social justice and representing the majority of available human resources, the pulling power is going to hinge more and more on the ability to provide something appealing to those who grew up with a bigger sense of purpose.

HR's Role in Preparing Senior Leaders

As I have often noticed, even some senior communications leaders remain risk-averse and comfortable working in a somewhat shielded space without having to accept responsibility. At the same time, those who are conscious of the need for change may find themselves unprepared to operate in fast-moving and sometimes chaotic surroundings. For multinational companies, this portends a need to beat the competition by identifying or training senior staff open to change, including a more committed engagement with the younger generations.

As Abdul-Rahman Risilia of ARC Talent explained to me, the general progression of HR is still at a very early stage, even in future-oriented societies.

> When I compare HR departments here (in the Gulf States) to the ones in more mature markets, I still feel there is a huge gap. The gaps are in leadership, strategy, structures and execution. To their defense, I don't believe they're as empowered to have an impact as they should be.[10]

Leaders should demonstrate a level of emotional intelligence and empathy and always take into account the human element in business. To Risilia, nowhere near enough training and development is done with leaders in the region:

> They still believe supervisors or high performers are automatically leaders, when that couldn't be further from the truth. Too many companies have the wrong people involved in the recruitment process or they drag it out to four to five stages over the course of four to eight weeks.[11]

Sooner or later the consequences will become impossible to evade. As he added,

> In a competitive market like it is now, time and the overall candidate experience have a huge impact on successfully attracting the best talent for your business. I keep bringing this back to the "why" … do businesses understand why they are hiring and what impact it has if they don't?[12]

Since the days of the old top-down leadership model are numbered, trying to better understand the preferences and values of younger generations makes perfect sense. This involves removing any bias and adapting to their thinking while transitioning to a more inclusive and participatory employment model based on a new Leadership KPI (Key Performance Indicator): Keeping People Inspired. "Meeting them where they are" sets the stage for early success. HR departments might therefore change their concept of investing in future capacity building.

In order to attract top ranking talent, leaders might also consider some new ways to reach the target audience. Spotify is the world's largest music streaming platform, with over half of all users under the age of 25. A majority of free listeners say they pay more attention to ads there than they do to ads on traditional radio; an open invitation to place audio job ads. It may not work for all, as the digital platform also contains podcasts that have raised ethical concerns over the spread of Covid19 and vaccine misinformation. This led to a surge of boycotts by lots of artists and users. It's up to HR to assess such instances on a case-by-case basis. The main task is to ensure that senior executives who favor handshakes (or fist bumps) over Zoom calls won't unravel the progress to be made such as the rollout of technology.

For executive search firms, the future is with those who spearhead the integration of recruiting software tools and human capital management software. The technology is available, including talent intelligence systems, testing and assessment tools as well as interviewing tools – anything needed to score applicants against hiring criteria. As Risilia said: "Digitizing the process by using these tools will only make us more efficient and successful in our jobs."[13] His views stand out in an industry that has long relied on the assumed advantage of having exclusive access to the best talent. Now the focus must be on placing the best talent inside HR departments. Some top recruiters keep publishing "latest marketing jobs in public relations, corporate communications." It's a mash-up of terms that does not meet the needs of an industry in the midst of evolving from classic marcom to a more comprehensive service offer. Beyond all that, headhunters must also adhere to the highest ethical principles.

Some years ago a consultancy contacted me, as they wanted to secure one of the market's biggest and most prestigious accounts. Their leader knew I had previously developed the Middle East content for a global proposal that had won on technical terms but lost due to budgetary restrictions. The new and smaller agency wanted me to lead their effort and even run the team once the account was secured. When I asked for the proposed team structure, I was told: "We don't have a team. I have asked [recruiter name] to provide some CVs." That would have been unacceptable not only for the prospective client, but also for all staffers. I replied, and the MD went silent. Of course, such tactics should have been stopped in their tracks by the executive search firm they had contacted. But that did not happen, either. It was unethical, and not helpful in building a respectable name brand for that newly formed agency. Not to mention that the junior and mid-level team members they planned to assemble only after the account was won were likely to resign once they realized what went on there.

As said, Millennials and Zoomers treasure compassionate leadership, culture, values and social causes. They are perfectly right to demand the best, as organizations also demand the best from them. It is the job of the heads of departments and agencies as well as practice leaders and HR to foresee these developments and improve their candidate experience. No part of the recruitment process is exempt; whether it is the employer branding or the first contact, the onboarding or mentorship for the newly appointed cohorts.

The essence of how to strategize communications in the Asian Century will be addressed in Chapter 9. It's a mix of ostensibly irreconcilable methods and approaches, but that just underscores the uniqueness of this age. Progress is close at hand once certain preconditions are met. And when human capital is seen as valuable as capital, the opportunities are limitless. And when the best people come up with ways to enhance strategies based on structured assessments and feedback mechanisms that utilize solid data analysis and real measurement, a stable and predictable progression of any business and continuity in diplomatic outreach strategies is literally guaranteed.

References

1. Risilia, Abdul-Rahman. Conversation with author. March 2022.
2. "The Deloitte Global 2022 Gen Z and Millennial Survey." *Deloitte*, https://deloitte.com/global/en/pages/about-deloitte/articles/genzmillennialsurvey.html
3. Volpe, John Della, and David Hogg. *Fight: How Gen Z Is Channeling Their Fear and Passion to Save America*. New York, St. Martin's Press, 2022.
4. "Survey: 40% of Employees Are Thinking of Quitting Their Jobs." *World Economic Forum*, 2 Jun. 2021, https://weforum.org/agenda/2021/06/remote-workers-burnout-Covid19-microsoft-survey
5. *AAJA-Asia Launches News Diversity Research Report*. 6 Apr. 2022, https://aaja-asia.org/andareport
6. "The Huge Mistake Millennials Are Making Now." *Time*, Mar. 2014, https://time.com/16103/the-huge-mistake-Millennials-are-making-now
7. Khanna, Parag. *The Future Is Asian: Global Order in the Twenty-First Century*. London, W&N, 2019.
8. Southern, Matt. "LinkedIn: Gen Z Is Our Fastest Growing Audience." *Search Engine Journal*, 24 Nov. 2021, https://searchenginejournal.com/linkedin-gen-z-is-our-fastest-growing-audience/428187/#close
9. Webster, Michael. Conversation with author, November 2022.
10. Risilia, Abdul-Rahman. Conversation with author. March 2022.
11. Risilia, Abdul-Rahman. Conversation with author. March 2022.
12. Risilia, Abdul-Rahman. Conversation with author. March 2022.
13. Risilia, Abdul-Rahman. Conversation with author. March 2022.

8 AI and Big Data
Enrolling Technocracy in Communications

Introduced in 2015 by Klaus Schwab, founder of the World Economic Forum (WEF), the term "Fourth Industrial Revolution" (4IR) captures a future shaped by an unprecedented progression of the industrial value chain. The previous three industrial revolutions stood for the gradual advancement of technology from mechanization to electrification and the emergence of computers and the internet. 4IR, on the other hand, marks the moment where technology became an enabler of new forms of interaction within and between machines, societies and even the human body – a real breakthrough moment for mankind.

Among all innovation-led development, two transformations stand out: blockchain and AI. The total value contribution of AI to the global economy alone is estimated at around $15.7 trillion by 2030 while boosting GDP by up to 26 percent.[1] Much of the world's top AI talent hails from China, but only one-tenth actually works there. Most R&D is happening in labs in the United States and Europe. Yet we are already witnessing an accelerated rollout all over the world, and in particular in the emerging markets of Asia and the Middle East.

To appreciate the journey that got us here, it is useful to recall the history of smartphones and mobile apps. Ordinary cell phones became a mainstay only in the early and mid-1990s when everyone was craving a Nokia, Motorola or Ericsson phone. A short time later, another technology emerged: "Personal Digital Assistants," or PDAs. The best known of these gadgets was the Palm Pilot. For a while, people carried two devices. But then developers began to merge PDAs with mobile phones; the origin of smartphones. The first one designed for the consumer market was the Simon Personal Communicator, released by IBM in 1994. The price, however, was high. In 2000 Ericsson launched the R380; the first mass-market smartphone. Blackberry rose to fame around the same time and shortly became the device most professionals chose because it gave them access to their email. In 2007 Steve Jobs released the world's first iPhone, which instantly became the most popular device. Things changed again in 2008 when Apple launched the iOS App Store. It was the moment that marked the beginning of the "app economy." Back then, just about 500 apps were available for download, a stark contrast to the roughly 3.4 million apps that are accessible today. At the same time, Google introduced Android Market, rebranded in 2012 as Google Play. Today, Android users can pick from about 2.7 million apps that can either be purchased or downloaded for free. From that point forward, mobile applications

DOI: 10.4324/9781003385622-9

have seamlessly integrated their way into our daily lives. The total number of mobile phone users stands at roughly 5.3 billion, equating to 67 percent of the global population.[2]

Social media and messaging apps not only changed how we access news, share images and videos or play games; they also revised the ways we learn languages, interact with one another and even make friends. Just like videoconferencing, apps played a particularly critical role during the Covid19 pandemic, allowing for at least some degree of mobility and connectivity by helping to smooth the process of social distancing and contact tracing. It is also worth noting that not all are Western inventions. Some of the world's most famed apps have in fact been developed in Asia or by Asians. They include WeChat and AliPay, both of which are a mainstay of China's society; the previously mentioned Zoom, and of course, TikTok. The number of mobile app downloads worldwide has reached a record 255 billion in 2022. And this is just the beginning, as more administrations and corporate entities are making the use of apps mandatory to access vital government or corporate services. The added value that smartphones and apps brought to everyone's life is staggering.

Much of the growth in tech did in fact happen over the past ten-plus years. If the rising influence of social media during that last decade is any indicator, the upcoming changes to be brought upon by 4IR will occur at an even faster pace and be more profound and possibly more disruptive than anything we have witnessed over the past 100 years. Singapore's Foreign Minister Vivian Balakrishnan elaborated on this in his opening speech at Singapore International Foundation's Public Diplomacy in Asia 2021 conference on July 26, 2021: "Digitization brings the world together but also divides us more."[3] This makes it more important to plan ahead and consider measures to guard reputations. Standing by and watching how others comply is no option. A much safer and more sustainable strategy is to use all available tools to deepen an understanding of what is driving customers, citizens and users while also defending organizations from any damage to their political or civil rank.

Communications would be best placed to guide people-centric disciplines in this transition. To be clear, I am talking about strategic communications, not PR. Robert Phillips wrote that PR has run out of options, missed its moment to lead and is in terminal decline. "About to be overrun and overwhelmed by the age of data, PR today is to communications what analogue was to digital at the turn of the century."[4] His take would surely have caused some rethink among PR practitioners, helping the practice to adjust a bit. But the actual integration of artificial intelligence and big data into day-to-day PR operations is still met with some apprehension, even by those who publicly portray themselves as being enthusiastic about it. This is not surprising. Misperceptions about the value-add of technology are rather common in any space that is traditionally defined by human relationships and autonomy. The growing consciousness of AI imposed threats is linked to the rise of disinformation, the possibility of greater inequality and the potential to disrupt labor markets, including the PR industry. But again, that may be the view within PR, but not necessarily in strategic communications or public diplomacy. In both disciplines there appears to be consensus that this is not about replacing humans but to assist them with tools and techniques to deliver more and in less time. Relationship building, for example, is a soft skill that cannot be replaced but assisted by AI. Even so, the outlook is different for communication in general.

As Carrington Malin, the UAE-based AI expert shared with me: "Artificial intelligence will both enhance and replace human communications – and it will become increasingly hard for us to tell the difference."[5] Together with the assumed but never verified lack of proof that tech can radically change the equation in one's favor, all these mix-ups are hard to overthrow. But the upsides are abundant. Machine learning employed by AI may actually be the easiest, fastest and most efficient way to collect data and make sense of it.

Back in 2004, I founded FutureScore Communications in Hong Kong. The purpose and name choice represented my emphasis on future-proofed strategies (S) that shape better communications (CO) and lead to more resilient reputations (RE). Together: SCORE, otherwise known as a record of the accomplishments made and a true measure of progress. It is something I always considered to be essential. Clients had asked for it throughout my career but did not always get it. If I would have had access to data like we do today, that would have specified FutureScore's rationale behind "scoring": leveraging the science beneath the art of public relations. As stated by computer programmer and science-fiction writer Daniel Keys Moran: "You can have data without information, but you cannot have information without data."[6]

Of Pioneers and Followers

The shift to improved intelligence gathering and ramped-up and values-based stakeholder engagement has already led to deeper insights and better connectivity, progress in innovation and development, and the exploration of new business opportunities. Moreover, it also fueled the growth of corporate players. It's a trend that will not only continue but accelerate, changing how we interact, read the reaction of others and develop strategies that improve interactions for all participants. In a nutshell, it is one of these classic moments in time that separates the pioneers from the followers.

Martin Sorrell, the founder of S4 Capital, is perhaps the best-known global investor in that space. With a widely recognized personal name brand, the ad world's pioneer drew attention to his new enterprise and managed to ignite a much broader public debate about the importance of adtech, data analysis, content development and emerging digital media. His firm laid the foundation by merging with more than two dozen acquired companies, including MediaMonks, Mighty Hive, Firewood and TheoremOne. The result is greater awareness among practitioners and greater attention to the risks of failing to act early. And his former holding company WPP is now also incorporating more and more tech and making use of new digital marketing services.

Being named among the best digital PR companies and professionals at the first edition of the Davos Digital PR Awards, some PR firms managed to be seen at the forefront of this trend.[7] The awards recognized outstanding campaigns based primarily on the use of digital and social media. What this does not necessarily imply, however, is that they incorporated AI and data analytics. For decades, the most common form of media analysis by PR firms has been based on print media clippings that contain a set of keywords. In recent years, agencies began to include social media, but most still stayed away from advanced data analysis. According to the AI and Big Data Readiness Report by the UK's Chartered Institute of Public Relations (CIPR), the required skills are not something that many PR professionals possess.[8] In essence, the pioneers are clearly on track to lead the field, but the followers seem stuck in the old age. A good example is the Advertising Value Equivalent (AVE). This outdated and inaccurate evaluation metric compares earned column inch space with the size of paid-for ads – a strong case to finish it off. But AVEs are still alive and kicking despite several attempts to replace them. In 2010, the public relations industry agreed on a set of voluntary guidelines to measure the efficiency of PR campaigns and communications strategies. Named after the place where PR leaders met to discuss these steps, the "Barcelona Principles" made it clear that output is not the same as outcome. Beyond that, they also pledged to prioritize an improved measurement of PR campaigns, including social media, that would spell the end for the outdated AVE metrics.

The Barcelona Principles were updated in 2015 and again in 2020 with a purpose of adding digital and social measurement and broaden the range of organizations and roles to be included. But that did not ring the knell of AVEs, as they are easy to produce. According to Fares Ghneim, Partner of Dubai-based data analytics company AnaVizio, some clients keep asking for AVEs and demand that clippings be counted; even from the most obscure media outlets. But that should never dictate one's own strategy of gathering insights. Michael Webster of Telum Media is convinced that PR is all set for change:

> I am an optimist in general and about our industry. There are very talented people in communications and I am sure the industry will adapt to any changes as it has to the digital developments of recent years and more.[9]

The readiness to adapt is more common in environments where insights into the preferences, needs and abilities of Gen Zers are already prevalent. That's just one more reason to bring in tech-savvy candidates right now and to build data analytics capabilities by non-data scientists.

Resolving the Really Big Data Question

While some advisors have made good progress in getting the C-Suite's attention, even the best thinkers and doers can lose that critical audience without warning when failing to prove the ROI that comes with "intangibles" such as perception, image and reputation. The truth, of course, is that they are not intangibles at all. Reputations may be harder to pin down but can be retrieved from perception and sentiment data points. The blame is with those who have not yet invested in a comprehensive understanding of what big data entails and how to analyze and gauge its impact; two key factors in reassuring that real progress is achievable or has been made already.

The task commences with securing access to new, relevant and protected data sources and having the right toolkit and analysts in place to measure performance. This helps to predict stakeholder preferences and reactions and to extract insights into the efficiency of current and future outreach activities to target audiences. Of course, all of these change as quickly as technology evolves. But certain aspects are likely to stay for at least some time. Part of that is the division of big data into three main categories: structured, unstructured and semi-structured. All three offer valuable but vastly diverse insights and information that are different to access.

Structured data is the most customary form of data and is relatively easy to analyze, as it mostly contains statistics and numbers that are extractable from well-thought-out and systematically structured designs. The classic sources include questionnaires and survey forms where data is filled into dedicated fields or lines that are aligned with certain predetermined parameters.

Unstructured data makes for the bulk of all available data. It is like free and open-ended speech, aligned with original thinking and relationships. It is highly valuable but also harder to classify and extract in large quantities. The sources span from emails, webpage contents and customer feedback to social media conversations, which call for sophisticated text analytics. Apart from that, there is also visual content, such as posted images and video, and also audio recordings like interviews, podcasts and more.

Semi-structured data, on the other hand, represents both word-based (i.e. unstructured) and structured data from various sources that may be delivered in various formats. The system of analyzing all depends on each and every single case. For example, if the main source is "quote tweets" or emails, then certain parameters like length and word choice are comparable, whereas others such as tone of voice require additional analysis.

So, how to go about it? The most useful research starts with an evaluation of the kind of data that will have to be assessed on a regular basis, from which sources it stems, and for what purpose it is being analyzed. Multiple questions need to be addressed before such systematic research can begin. In some parts of the world, getting a full picture depends on the extension of mobile communication networks that provide access to rural areas in low- and middle-income countries.

Step two is to reach a decision on what data can be collected and manually examined by in-house analysts. Fares Ghneim of AnaVizio has not yet seen agencies hiring data scientists but is convinced that a number of the larger agencies in the Middle East will be moving in that direction: "By bringing capabilities in-house and providing services to their clients through integrated platforms they can integrate all data points and use natural language processing (NLP) and AI to mine, analyze and interpret data and connect the dots."[10] The advantage of these algorithms is that they can analyze large and complex datasets from multiple sources that no human would manage to go through in any reasonable amount of time. However, Ghneim is sure that external providers of such services won't go out of business anytime soon: "A very likely scenario, at least in the short to medium term, will be that agencies seek white-labeled solutions."[11]

Step three is about presenting the findings in the most convincing ways. That could be done via dynamic data visualization, eye-catching charts and graphs and executive summaries that make it easy for decision makers to draw actionable conclusions.

Even though the technology is still far from being perfect, it is improving fast. Software developers such as Vuelio, Blackbird.ai and Propel have released products specifically designed for public relations, public affairs and stakeholder communications. In the years ahead, the role of predictive data analytics is likely to become ever more entrenched across public and private sectors, especially in organizations with a sense of foresight. In communications and public diplomacy, investing in this future is indispensable. Those who commit to data and analytics functions now will reap the rewards many times over when making reliable predictions about the public perception of corporate strategies and foreign policy, and having a foundation to base their strategies on. It is equally significant to also factor in that the application of some technologies and platforms is not so popular – at least not for everyone, or not yet – and needs to be constantly improved. In the meantime, it helps to surround oneself with empathetic teams who understand tech's impact on those who are less passionate about it.

Managing the Great Disruption Caused by Digitization

Looking at the role technology plays in our lives, even Klaus Schwab raised concerns about the possibility of tech diminishing compassion and cooperation.[12] It's a valid point, as emotion shapes human communication in ways that are not easily automated. It also corresponds to the process of decision making. The increased efficiency of tech in various spaces matters a lot, but the transition to a more tech-enabled world has to be managed carefully, as much of the world has not yet entirely caught up. Many of the emerging issues are linked to speed. Expecting people to adjust to "digital first" is alright, but pushing digital transformation too quickly and with zero redundancy in customer service may ultimately lead to a credibility gap.

The advancement of tech must be delivered via a seamless, safe and protected user experience. While younger generations might be more compliant with today's CX Tech tools, they may fail to realize that many are still far from being optimized. With data breaches being on the rise, retaining or in some instances even regaining public trust in digitization is of utmost importance. Full compliance with data privacy and keeping a spotlight on cybersecurity should be self-evident. One key concern is the compulsory use of facial recognition software, a clear target for cyber threats. That calls for a review of regulatory and enforcement priorities. In early 2022, the US Internal Revenue Service (IRS) suspended the use of that technology to authenticate people. "No one should be forced to submit to facial recognition to access critical government services," a Treasury Department member commented.[13] Věra Jourová, Vice-President of the European Commission for Values and Transparency, made another important point, emphasizing that for AI technologies to thrive in the EU, people need to trust digital innovations.[14]

For Carrington Malin, cybersecurity is going to become an increasing priority for communicators as security risks accrue an increasingly higher potential to impact customers, employees and other stakeholders:

Predictably, regulation and compliance is going to be brought back under the spotlight whenever there is a big breach of security. The obvious problem in automating corporate, customer and public communications on a large scale is that data breaches, hacking and hijacking of systems can threaten your entire business. We've not yet seen hackers take over a big brand's digital systems in order to reach their customers. But as brands add more and more AI powered communications they arguably make themselves more of a target.[15]

It's a foreseeable scenario that demands some significant investment in crisis preparedness; a task best addressed via advance scenario planning. "In my view," Malin explained,

> we'll see winners and losers in the move to end-to-end marketing automation, as we do whenever there's a new wave of any new technology. However, more difficult to track and manage will be the impact of algorithms and other automation on brand perceptions, consumer rights, and ethics issues.[16]

The surge of "Intelligent Virtual Assistants" (IVA) and "Interactive Voice Response" (IVR) systems is a case in point. Many companies have jumped on conversational AI as part of their modernization of tech infrastructure. The tools, however, are still at a nascent stage and often fail to deliver on user expectations. "Many large organizations have rushed to install AI chatbots and other automated communications systems to provide better 24/7 support and to decrease call center costs", said Malin:

> The best implementers of these technologies generally invest a great deal of time blending human communications with AI-powered ones to ensure that the customer is always served. However, at the other end of the scale, many companies have replaced call centers with bots that answer a limited number of questions or requests. The customers that fall through the cracks could be lost forever.[17]

Having to navigate call menus loaded with audio ads and self-praise only to end up talking to a robot can be frustrating. The lack of personalization is counterproductive. An even larger stumbling block is the somewhat limited but unknown choice of words set by the IT department. None of that backs up the narrative, "This is to better serve the needs of our customers." On the contrary, the overarching message is "Engage with us on our terms, not yours." However, for Malin, the long-term impact on brands has still received very little attention so far:

> I believe that today, most users of chatbots, voicebots and other automated customer service have pre-existing perceptions of their favorite brands that have been validated by a human-to-human experience. So, as long as AI doesn't let them down, brands can build on those perceptions.[18]

Yet some brands have automated from the ground up. "Most Netflix customers have never spoken to a Netflix representative," Malin said. He continued:

A customer's perception of the brand may therefore be built purely on automated interactions. It may prove to be a different matter for companies who have built their brands around their human touch points. Fully automated customer service requires different thinking and different approaches.[19]

As Malin specified, the most serious dangers associated with relying on AI-powered communications will be a result of inadequate corporate governance and regulation. What makes this such a challenge for AI is that the more seamless we make AI-powered experiences, the more complexity is going to be hidden. This could be because of black box algorithms that are not visible to corporate and government users, or it could be hidden simply because it's no one's job to check all that hidden detail is ethical, responsible and compliant.

Moreover, having to connect via social media or a small-scale chat box to report a technical glitch, request some detailed information or provide in-depth feedback can also be rather irritating. Besides, it is much harder to keep a record of these conversations. Online chats don't usually come with ticket or reference numbers and tend to get lost swiftly. The effect is that following up on unresolved issues becomes much harder.

Removing customer support email IDs from websites and the surge of online message boxes can be another drawback, particularly on sites that come with a host of conditions that must be met before one can hit the send button. The mandatory use of third-party messaging apps is one more worrying trend. While it speeds up some common customer service processes, insisting that these platforms are also safer than email ignores the well-documented breaks in safety protocols by various apps. Considering this, the support of end-to-end encrypted email should prevail, as they have proven to be 100 percent safe.

In essence, future-orientation shall never limit options to connect. The rise of "no-reply" emails as a response disregards the fact that people try to reach out for help when the new platforms don't deliver. And while efficiency is the often-stated official goal, at this juncture it's almost always about cost-cutting. Even when managing to get a human on the phone and he or she turns out to be yet another self-proclaimed "Happiness Officer," the reaction might be the opposite of what was intended. As is often the case, that agent quickly asks for a five-star rating in the customer satisfaction survey at the end of the call. The message this sends is undisguised: "We are very keen to collect positive feedback based on the courtesy of our agents." It is another transparent attempt to swerve public opinion before addressing the actual issue that prompted the customer to reach out in the first place. That brings us back to a previously made point, which also applies in this context: "Happiness is an outcome, not a message."

When organizations adopt new technologies, some kind of disruption is always to be expected, especially during 4IR. But when people-to-people connectivity becomes a target of cost-cutting measures while the benefits are not yet fully accessible, the perceived discrepancy between words and action can be very damaging. A better choice would be to ramp up traditional channels until the untested tech solutions are debugged and widely accepted. Everything else hints at future-orientation and keenness to be at the forefront of the tech deployment across all operating areas, while the mindset of those in charge is stuck in the pre-4IR age; a time where the customer response did not matter as much as there was no option to make their voices heard like they can today. The outcomes are predictable: a rise of unfavorable reviews on iOS App Store, Play Store, Trustpilot, Mopinion and other feedback channels.

Email is a good example about how to handle this. While available for some elites since the early 1970s, email services were rolled out en masse only in the 1990s when the current internet suite of SMTP, POP3 and IMAP email protocols became the standard. People were not suddenly forced to abandon sending letters via postal services. Instead, they were given an additional way to connect. The same principles should apply today. The smart choice is to offer a wide range of communications channels and tools and make it easy to connect via any channel that users prefer, especially the ones that are self-owned. Offering social media as one of the additional ways to engage can be useful, but it's too early to make it the only option.

Some players are now acknowledging the deficits that come with chatbots. One of them is Cascade, a leading online strategy execution platform that vows to provide "support that goes beyond a chatbox." Another example is SimpleTexting: "Hey you, yes I'm a bot, but not the boring kind. I can even prove it… Want to see something cool?"[20] The user is then given three choices: "Let's do it," "Awkwardly ignore me" and "Bring me to your human." It's evidence of thinking like customers and makes for a good start. In late 2022 the global debate about the future of AI in communications took another turn when OpenAI launched ChatGPT, a highly advanced NLP model that resembles human conversation. It has already recast discussions about future readiness of the PR industry and even came up in several talks at the World Economic Forum 2023 in Davos. Its rapid rise and influence in business and politics comes with huge opportunities but also raises questions about potential risks related to compliance with industry or company policies and user safety. The progression of AI will undoubtedly improve communications. But it sure makes sense to reverse the policy of "on our terms, not yours." That applies not just to corporate communications and customer service but also to diplomacy, where it serves some nations as an excuse to pay no heed to international law, norms and standards. Once implemented, that's a way to claim legitimacy based on genuineness in all actions and interactions.

How Technocracy Reshapes Communications

As already stated, the changes brought upon by 4IR and the convergence of AI, hyper-connectedness and data analytics represent a quantum leap in a whole range of areas. The impact will be faster, more profound and perhaps more disruptive than any comparable event in modern history.

Social media has already shown its effectiveness in shifting democratic dialogue, manipulating political debates and in some cases fueling extremism by influencing the outcome of elections and also national referendums like the UK's Brexit vote. AI and robotic devices are altering jobs and redefining productivity. Big data can protect but also disclose people's private information. And as the Internet of

Things (IoT) becomes more closely integrated in everyday life, it draws attention to the need for cybersecurity. More change is to come across nanotechnology, biotechnology, cloud and quantum computing. And even Augmented Reality (AR), blockchain, 3D printing and autonomous vehicles can disrupt lives in ways never seen before.

With everything changing at lightning speed, communications should be at the forefront of adjusting. Many businesses and governments are now finding themselves in uncharted territory – a make-or-break moment for some in leadership positions. Ignoring that may still work for a short while, but complacency is no reliable path to follow, even when pushing the line that constant transformation is the new normal and people must get used to it. AI and big data can in fact provide exactly the kind of information and insights that can help with the formulation of strategies for the rollout of new policies, products and services based on a deep analysis of public sentiment. While that may be widely accepted in principle, assessing the implications for governance, business and social life with a predetermined set of parameters that date back decades is unlikely to deliver the desired outcomes.

The extent of the necessary adjustment goes beyond the usual adaptations such as adding social media analysis to traditional media analysis. The surge of big tech already expands the full scope of terms such as research and analysis. Whatever defined "deep insight" in the 1990s would be considered superficial today. In order to make headway in any professional field, one must be ready for a departure from conventional thoughts and practices. Likewise, it is also expedient to question the validity of deep-seated idioms and phrases that seem immutable. What is needed today are free thinking and a systematic review and challenge of some presumptions. In 1919 William H. Smyth, a California engineer, coined the term "technocracy." It was his way of explaining the concept of management of society by technical experts. While governance is at the center of his reflection, "management of society" hints at the possibility of a wider interpretation. This does not mean that all its manifestations, especially complete technocracy, are supreme. But one of its forms comes with numerous upsides: meritocracy.

To followers, the idea of introducing technocracy to communications may sound as outlandish as using AI and data analytics to improve connectivity and relationship building. In some quarters, the term itself also has some negative connotations directly linked to perceived overconfidence and inefficiency. But that should be relatively easy to overcome. As mentioned before, most communications pros are generalists, while some specialize in areas such as corporate and financial, consumer, health, public affairs and so forth. Yet this traditional segmentation into long-established practices does not meet all criteria of technocracy or meritocracy in communications.

The pioneers who see an opening here might avow its practical use and move on quickly to embrace both in communications as a way to bring in people with specialized knowledge and qualifications beyond editorial proficiency and general people skills. Hill+Knowlton Strategies, for example, appointed a head of behavioral science and a behavioral science consultant. India's top agency Adfactors PR teamed up with the Indian Institute of Management (IIM) Calcutta to organize an advanced management development program covering fintech and blockchain for its teams. What makes the difference is new thinking, added know-how in analytics, a familiarity with tech providers and their solutions. That plus cultural and emotional intelligence and local insight, all underscored by a proven track record of successful intercultural engagement. Together, this enhances the potential of unlocking emerging and developed markets. Adjusting with that purpose surely amounts to a big reset of long-standing processes. But that's what PR needs now.

As in the case of 4IR, the progression of communications in the Asian Century won't happen without a rethink of the definitions and ways of doing things that shaped the practice for years if not decades. AI is going to reshape more than just media monitoring and putting an end to AVEs. It reaches as far as the optimization of content, digital and social media, multimedia and creative, and digital listening, to name just a few. Mastering all this will sooner or later be the standard course of action. As APCO's Imad Lahad said: "As early as 2018, APCO Worldwide unveiled its Digital Lab, a first-of-its-kind innovation center, which deploys AI-driven solutions to build and protect the reputations of major global brands, governments and organizations."[21] Picking Dubai as the hub for APCO's AI-Powered Comms Lab was no coincidence. Mamoon Sbeih, APCO's President for the Middle East and North Africa (MENA), explained what drove this decision:

> APCO chose Dubai, which is integrated into other offices throughout the firm's global network, because it's a natural pairing – the city of the future has become the test bed for the futuristic technologies and innovations that shape the way we communicate with multiple stakeholders.[22]

For his company, being based in Dubai relays a clear message to the world: "An innovation-led practice has no better home than a place that is driven by innovation."

Fares Ghneim of AnaVizio believes that the one key issue that will crack open the use of AI for PR in the Middle East will be Arabic text analytics: "The moment this happens will be a watershed that opens a realm of possibilities and opportunities. There are many projects to develop Arabic NLP across the region and every so often word spreads that someone has succeeded."[23] However, Ghneim is conscious that nobody has built a strong reliable Arabic NLP engine thus far. Lahad has no doubt that in the next two years alone, we will see predictive insights and scenario planning technologies emerge that can be harvested for insights that keep clients and brands ahead of the curve:

> From the swathe of data that will emerge in the coming years, we can create even more effective adaptive audience and stakeholder mapping dashboards and platforms. We will see more scientific sentiment analysis in Arabic covering different dialects, which has until now been a market that is yet to be fully developed. We will also see voice and audio technologies shape and refine search engine optimization (SEO) in ever greater detail.[24]

For Sbeih, AI's evolution in government and corporate communications is the natural next step:

In the Middle East, where governments practice what would usually be considered more G2C (Government to Citizens) style communications than in other parts of the world, I see conversational AI in Arabic dialects being mainstream and shaping how citizens and residents interact with, and access their public services and providers.[25]

It is all about envisioning ways of engaging with an increasingly more tech-savvy public: "As governments seek new ways to engage their people, harnessing the full potential of audio technologies will not be optional, but essential to stay relevant in the digital age," Sbeih said.

And it's not just the Middle East. As in much of the West, Asia as a whole is adopting big data and analytics platforms across industry sectors for various purposes, including strategy planning and operational efficiency. Spotting progress in tech and incorporating it before others do is giving in-house communicators the much needed buy-in from the board. Once secured, this can help rewrite the content of job specs, reshape the questions raised in job interviews and redefine KPIs for the next cohort of employees in the consulting line of business – another step toward future preparedness.

When empowering those with added technical and scientific skills determines the choice of future-oriented policy decisions, things are likely to move faster and in the right direction. Technical and practice-related qualifications are the added value, but awareness of the historical, economic and political trends that impact strategies are equally important. And by maintaining an element of oversight by elected officials (as in democratic technocracies) or experienced operators (as in corporate communications), those who champion this will find it easier to project executive power and full accountability – two critical factors in any setting where speed is as critical as human connections. It also serves as a lifesaver for consultancies and might eventually secure that revered "Fifth Seat at the Boardroom Table." It's a frequently used figure of speech among independents in PR; those who are nonaligned with big networks or management strategists. This is exactly where strategic communications should be: in a position of exercising managerial authority where building and protecting hard-won reputations is essential.

Two decades into the 20th century, the advantages of modern technocracy and meritocracy in government are self-evident. The pivot to systems with innovation-led governance, industrial expansion, wealth generation and an emphasis on the efficient handling of Covid19 has clearly paid off. Likewise, once reputation management taps into the automated analysis of published content, speeches (including language patterns and tone), presentations, media appearances and overall public sentiment, things can move faster and yield the desired results, while data points help adapting strategies more easily. Applying this approach comes down to gathering some kind of a digital sixth sense, the foundation for delivering innovation and future outcomes in real time. While the technology is still not flawless, corporate reputation and communications professionals are better off adjusting to the idea now. "Doing nothing until you can claim there's nothing you can do" is like taking a dead-end road; a high risk of becoming the target of internal and external distrust. In the Asian Century, time waits for no one. It may look like complicating matters even further, but there are ways around it.

References

1. Holmes, Frank. "AI Will Add $15 Trillion to the World Economy by 2030." *Forbes*, 25 Feb. 2019, https://forbes.com/sites/greatspeculations/2019/02/25/ai-will-add-15-trillion-to-the-world-economy-by-2030
2. "Digital Around the World." *DataReportal*, Apr. 2022, https://datareportal.com/global-digital-overview
3. Singapore International Foundation. "SIF to Mark 30th Anniversary with Inaugural Conference on Public Diplomacy in Asia." *Singapore International Foundation*, https://sif.org.sg/Latest/Newsroom/Data/Newsroom/SIF-to-Mark-30th-Anniversary-with-Inaugural-Conference-on-Public-Diplomacy-in-Asia
4. Phillips, Robert. *Trust Me, PR Is Dead*. London, UK, Unbound, 2015.
5. Malin, Carrington. Conversation with author. May 2022.
6. *Daniel Keys Moran Quotes*. (n.d.). *BrainyQuote*. https://brainyquote.com/quotes/daniel_keys_moran_230911
7. World Communications Forum Association. "2021 Best Digital PR Companies and Professionals Revealed at Davos Digital Awards." *PR Newswire*, 12 Jan. 2022, https://prnewswire.com/news-releases/2021-best-digital-pr-companies-and-professionals-revealed-at-davos-digital-awards-301459409.html
8. Harrington, John. "PR Pros Lack Technical Knowledge on AI and Big Data." *PRWeek*, 23 Nov. 2021, https://prweek.com/article/1733851/pr-pros-lack-technical-knowledge-ai-big-data-says-wake-up-call-report
9. Webster, Michael. Conversation with author. November 2022.
10. Ghneim, Fares. Conversation with author. April 2022.
11. Ghneim, Fares. Conversation with author. April 2022.
12. Schwab, Klaus. "The Fourth Industrial Revolution: What It Means and How to Respond." *World Economic Forum*, 14 Jan. 2016, https://weforum.org/agenda/2016/01/the-fourth-industrial-revolution-what-it-means-and-how-to-respond and *Klaus Schwab Quotes*. (14Jan. 2016). BrainyQuote. https://brainyquote.com/quotes/klaus_schwab_745768
13. "IRS to End Use of Facial Recognition to Identify Taxpayers." *AP NEWS*, 7 Feb. 2022, https://apnews.com/article/technology-business-data-privacy-ron-wyden-f955f9f3ad074f0263018ef2ae38ea01
14. European Commission. *"New Liability Rules on Products and AI to Protect Consumers and Foster Innovation."* 28 Sep. 2022, https://ec.europa.eu/commission/presscorner/detail/en/ip_22_5807
15. Malin, Carrington. Conversation with author. May 2022.
16. Malin, Carrington. Conversation with author. May 2022.
17. Malin, Carrington. Conversation with author. May 2022.
18. Malin, Carrington. Conversation with author. May 2022.
19. Malin, Carrington. Conversation with author. May 2022.
20. https://simpletexting.com/
21. Lahad, Imad. Interview with author. April 2022.
22. Sbeih, Mamoon. Conversation with author. April 2022.
23. Ghneim, Fares. Conversation with author. April 2022.
24. Lahad, Imad. Conversation with author. April 2022.
25. Sbeih, Mamoon. Conversation with author. April 2022.

9 Shenzhen Speed and Dubai Spirit

Engineering the Asianization of Communications

Winning with multicultural campaigns is never an easy task, even under the best of circumstances. And when speed in delivery determines the public perception of success, then the job can get even harder. But that's no excuse to abandon any commitment to adjust. Zoom Founder Eric Yuan made it crystal clear: "In business, speed is everything."[1]

Asia's perceivable and rapid transformation is more than just an imaginary blueprint for future readiness. In business as in government, it might be the turning point for anyone who has been pondering the idea of reviewing tactical and strategic approaches but then got stuck in endless internal procedures. The same applies to communications. The process often gets slowed down by executives who fear disruption and argue that speed and strategy are observably incompatible. Some communicators also find it hard to comprehend what differentiates emerging markets from other economies.

In business, speed is indeed everything. Likewise, as stated by Piyush Goyal, India's Minister of Commerce and Industry: "The speed of decision making is the essence of good governance."[2] In both cases, "resting on your laurels" is simply off the table; particularly in a highly connected world. What matters the most is securing real outcomes in less time. And getting ahead of the curve is never achieved by waiting until the last doubters are on board. Afshin Molavi is very clear about that:

> Companies that succeed in global markets must be agile, flexible, nimble, resilient, and highly attuned to local tastes and mores. The same is true of communications professionals. There will never be a one-size-fits-all communications strategy, or even an "emerging markets" strategy. After all, the world looks a lot different from Chile to China, but there is a common thread across the emerging world, a theme that runs through societies from Buenos Aires to Beijing and from Cape Town to Calcutta. That theme is Aspiration with a capital "A."[3]

As laid out before, aspiration works in all environments and can even become part of the "great unifier." Molavi made a similar point: "All across the emerging world, people are aspiring meaningfully to achieve a better life, in the expectation that

DOI: 10.4324/9781003385622-10

through hard work or education or migration or entrepreneurial flourish, a better life beckons." This is not just an opinion but a fact-based stance: "The numbers don't lie. With middle classes rising from Africa to Asia to the Americas and more people achieving higher education, this powerful force multiplier of aspiration will change the world." Communications professionals should keep this in mind whenever they operate in the East: "It has been unleashed, and it is literally changing the face of Asia."[4]

By the same token, the Asianization of Asia should never be seen as being unrelated to the rest of the world. In fact, it has reached an advanced stage that stretches across many divergent cultures and operating environments. The obvious questions, then, are: who is leading it all; whom to follow; and what comes next? In communications the answers are linked to an adjustment in future strategies based on "Gaining ACCESS." It's an inspirational model laid out in Chapter 10.

Speed and Strategy

"So, tell me, of all the places in China, Southeast Asia and the Middle East you've lived in, which one did impress you the most?" This question comes up frequently in conversations about my work and life in the East. For many years, the response was pretty easy: "It's actually two cities, Shanghai and Dubai." Both stood out for the breathtaking pace at which they had turned into an international showcase for national development and regional hubs for professional services, finance, trade and logistics, arts and culture. They also pursued the same strategy in achieving these crowning accomplishments; one that is best described as "Building landmarks, not just tall towers."

Years ago in Shanghai, I had a chat with David Ignatius, then executive editor of the *International Herald Tribune*. Our talk soon turned to the city's startling transformation since the 1980s. We quickly agreed on a slightly dated but still fitting catchphrase about the futuristic look of this urban sprawl: "It's like 'The Jetsons' are back." Soon after, that same line appeared in his feature for the *New York Times*.[5]

What comes to mind each time I visit Dubai Creek Harbour is the mind-boggling pace at which this once humble fishing and pearl diving town has evolved into one of the most cosmopolitan and innovative cities in the world. The view of Dubai's cityscape is more than stunning. A skyline of super high-rises in breathtaking shapes and forms emerges from the waters of a wide inlet creek. And the sunset and subsequent light show creates a dramatic visual impression that resembles a modern movie set.

The remarkable progress of the UAE and most of all Dubai started after gaining independence from the British in 1971. The former "Trucial States" managed to create a globally recognized master plan for national expansion. While all countries have their own preferences and priorities, most neighboring Gulf States that initially viewed Dubai as glitz and glamour have since embarked on a similar journey. What unites them are the same towering ambitions, central leadership, market dynamics, great designs for high-profile projects of all kinds, and last but not least, a sense of "now or never."

Skeptics who question the rationale behind all this may want to go back to the early 1930s when New York was constructing the Empire State Building. It was an unfailing and inspiring way to signal the city's (and the nation's) arrival on the world stage. For cities that rapidly grow while skyscrapers rise in very little time, the set of rules is just different. In New York City, this triggered the line: "In a New York Minute" – a reference to the fact that things happen much faster there than anywhere else. It later became the title of a book, a song, and a film. And it's the perfect equivalent of Shenzhen Speed and Dubai Spirit, isn't it?

Wait, Shenzhen? Shouldn't it be Shanghai? True, but to me it's Shenzhen now. I revised my choice a few years ago. Dubai kept its spot as the Middle East's "Alpha City," but Shenzhen became China's most modern city; a true metropolis with over ten million inhabitants. Similar to Dubai, this once small town with a population of just 30,000 became a special economic zone and quickly developed into China's new global center for tech, R&D, manufacturing, finance and transportation. The Chinese people recognize that by framing its growth rate as "Shēnzhèn sùdù" (Shenzhen Speed).

In boom times it's all about pace. No case for strategic communications, then? Not really. "Shenzhen Speed and Dubai Spirit" is about vision and "can-do" spirit. It's a modus operandi that comes with a guaranteed ROI. That should make it attractive enough for others to adapt. While the speed at which all this is happening may not always be associated with Western standards, those who conform to it are in a good position to lead the field. None of that is supposed to be seen as being merely theoretical. Neither should it be watered down just to make it acceptable across the board. Speed, of course, is irrelevant when moving in the wrong direction. Some Western-trained communicators use that as an excuse for refusing to "act without a plan." Their claim is that such fixed terms for research, creativity and strategic planning in high-pressure environments are simply not up to scratch. It exposes them as rookies who just haven't yet figured out how things work in developing markets and other dynamic and fast-moving places. Western experience is certainly useful, but a lack of on-the-ground experience, reliable information sources and knowledge about history and culture can make it all the more testing. The same goes for an understanding of political systems, social priorities and, in some places, the extent of (self-) censorship.

A key insight from working in Asia is that once decisions are made at the top level in business as in government, advisors are often presented with partial briefs but are expected to come back with strategic plans, not just tactical ones. The implementation is expected to start immediately and deliver results without delay. Making real progress is therefore best secured by the aforesaid advance scenario planning; not just in fast-moving markets, but in any place where speed and strategy are entrenched in national development plans and business strategies.

Tactical communications still has its space, but trying to build and protect the reputation of a multibillion-dollar company with global operations, or a government with global ambitions, without a clear and adaptable master plan and some investment in crisis preparedness is bound to fail. This is just more proof that the window for traditional public relations is closing. Classic PR has certainly evolved over the decades but for the most part remains tied to a sender–receiver model that prioritizes push over pull. As younger leaders are taking over from generations of CEOs who grew up in the pre-digital age, things are going to change, and the time to plan ahead has come.

Of course none of that is easy; not even with a supportive board or cabinet and a full grasp of the cultural, political and economic realities. Relationship building and strategic planning both take time, a precious commodity in any fast-moving environment. That's precisely where the misunderstandings begin. How much time is too much for proper research and planning? How long is too long until progress can be demonstrated? How to keep internal stakeholders engaged and supportive? And what price is too high or too low to meet the set objectives? The answers vary depending on where these questions are being asked and by whom, leading to the ever-present confusion over tactical vs. strategic measures.

When working in multicultural settings and with diverse teams, business partners and/or customers, one has to stop comparing all the time. When truly settled in a place, there's no point in over-rationalizing and constantly seeking answers to the many "Why's." This is what consultants do who parachute in. Things are what they are. You're free to focus on getting stuff done in exactly the way stuff gets done in these places. There is even an advantage here: ambiguity of the brief can be used as an opening to add structure, purpose and direction based on international best practice. This validates all assessments and makes the judgment sounder; a significant advantage in any competitive setting and a strong argument for seeking diversity in HR.

Importing Western business models looks smart but still requires modification. What is the alternative? Taking an "Eastern" (i.e. non-Western) approach? What would that be? It would obviously not mean the abandoning of internationally established best practice; far from it. Parts of the Middle East and Asia are more "Westernized" when it comes to doing business than outsiders might think. Many of the corporate and government actors eagerly appoint Harvard or Wharton graduates to run their operations or departments. In an interconnected world, this makes perfect sense. The point is that in order to function, Western economic concepts – if and when they are considered applicable – must be adapted in view of the cultural and economic background. The key to success is seeking flexibility and greater nuance.

A Lesson from the Past

The outcome-focused model that prioritizes speed without downplaying or even undercutting the value of deep insight and analytics has delivered results for years. Even in the pre-social media age, it made all the difference. Here is one older case study that still stands out for all cited reasons.

In early July 1997, Thailand allowed its currency, the baht, to float against the US dollar. The move marked the beginning of the Asian financial crisis that soon hit much of East and Southeast Asia including the so-called Asian Tigers: Hong Kong, Singapore, South Korea and Taiwan. Months later, Malaysia was struggling with an increasing amount of nonperforming loans (NPLs). As a result, banks refrained from lending fresh capital to even viable businesses, and the country's economy kept deteriorating. In June 1998 the Malaysian Ministry of Finance (MoF) decided to establish a National Asset Management Company (AMC) to ease the burden on Malaysian banks. The AMC was based on similar models introduced in the United States, Sweden and South Korea. The objective was to help the ailing banking sector and to reassure the business community that Malaysia was in control of things and primed to take the right measures.

The MoF promised to present details of the AMC within two weeks from the initial proclamation. After rushing through a ten-day selection process, business consultant Arthur Andersen (AA) and investment house J.P. Morgan were confirmed as external advisors for project management and fundraising. My agency, Shandwick (Weber Shandwick today), was introduced to the MoF by AA. At that time I was Malaysia Country Manager. One Sunday night I received a call from colleagues in Thailand who had assisted AA and the Thai government in its crisis response: "Oliver, you were just invited to advise the Malaysian government. But you've got to be at AA's offices right now. They are setting up legal, HR, strategy and comms as we speak." That was four days before the scheduled second press briefing. At this stage, the AMC was neither incorporated nor operational; it was just a vision shared by a handful of people out to help the Malaysian economy to recover. The specific challenge was to quickly get an overview, prioritize tasks, and to formulate an ad-hoc media strategy for this highly sensitive and technical enterprise – all without any written brief or having the time for in-depth studies.

Shandwick took a decidedly proactive stance. Since this effort was of highest national interest and success had to be proved, we concluded that public relations needed to change gear. Keeping the deadline was a must, and the only way to deliver was to immediately set up a core team of senior financial PR and crisis comms specialists from within the region. This was critical for safeguarding on-the-spot judgment and decision-making and to ensure senior strategic counsel was constantly available. The mixed Singaporean and Malaysian team commenced work with the formulation of basic communications guidelines and directions for the client and its advisors.

Over the next days, we developed a media strategy, emphasizing the need for full transparency at any stage of AMC's implementation. Transparency was to be constantly shown by addressing operative details such as the timeframe, funding, valuation methods, independence from political interference, and necessary changes to the legislation. Strategy meetings were held to identify communications pitfalls and followed by media skills training with AMC management. An international media monitoring program was installed, providing the client and its advisors with valuable information on Malaysia's financial and economic performance as seen by opinion leaders from both domestic and foreign press. The team also created a comprehensive press kit for the official announcement of the AMC, now named Danaharta, and prepared internal presentation material to brief the Deputy PM/Minister of Finance Dato' Seri Anwar Ibrahim on the progress made. In addition, a speech was drafted for the Minister. A Danaharta press office was set up to furnish media enquiries and regularly distribute statements and background information to all media. Q&A documents were updated on a regular basis, taking into account the published opinion from international and domestic media. Using additional resources from the local Shandwick office, the team then developed animated presentations, press releases, CVs, background papers and press graphs, and coordinated the translation and production of all materials.

Within four days of working literally around the clock, the strategic positioning for Danaharta was accomplished. The spokesperson was trained on every aspect of it, and backup material and collaterals for a truly professional appearance were being produced. The strategy was to position this AMC as a duly qualified organization that meets its set objectives, and to demonstrate stability, consistency and an understanding of tasks, integrity and professionalism. Shandwick recommended defining what success means for Danaharta and communicating the completion of tasks. Another piece of advice was to address all target groups in order to secure grassroots support.

Attended by roughly 80 journalists representing global print and broadcast media, the press conference by Anwar Ibrahim delivered on setting out the objectives and operating modalities of Danaharta, using much of the terminology created by Shandwick that was incorporated in the press material. The briefing was followed by a presentation created by our team. A subsequent Q&A session with the world media reinforced the perception of its management being very capable of meeting the tasks. All questions were already covered by our Q&A briefing document, thus allowing the client to deliver his own answers in the most convincing and effective way.

The announcement of Danaharta was met with great interest from domestic and international media; most of whom showed confidence about Malaysia's pre-emptive measure, praising the establishment of an AMC as a right, timely and meaningful step that may prevent the country from what had hit other Asian markets. While some concerns remained over the long-term impact and ability to raise around 25 billion Malaysian Ringgit of funds, the consensus was that Malaysia had taken action before it was too late. Initial concerns like "bailout," expressed before the actual announcement, did not come up again. Danaharta was seen as being in control of its public perception. Despite the capital controls imposed by the government to ease the crunch on NPLs, reporting on Danaharta remained overall positive and supportive. Four weeks later, banks began to announce that they considered selling NPLs to Danaharta. The strategy of transparency had paid off.

It was a decisive moment for Malaysia, as Danaharta helped to steer the country through the financial crisis and Malaysia got out of it relatively unscathed. Shandwick also gained from it, winning the Asian PR Award for Best Financial Campaign, and soon after was appointed to advise the new AMC during the entire process of becoming fully functional. The necessary milestones to achieve this were the announcement of the Board of Directors, the "Danaharta Bill" (changes to the legislative framework) passing the Parliament, and achieving royal assent. Shandwick then advised the newly founded AMC on the selection of graphic artists and designers to create a corporate identity for the company, and staffed the judging panel of three.

Speed and Strategy Are Compatible

This case study kept its significance until today, as it shines a light on how to manage the process of developing a winning strategy in a situation where lengthy research and planning are simply no option. What worked well in this instance was the early assessment of what would be the only agreeable result: a positive global reaction. It mandated a well laid-out course of action to overcome the crisis and validated all steps taken, especially the appointment of a senior team with agency. The accumulated experience and managerial authority to prospectively assess all options and then move on with quick and critical decisions was instrumental in meeting all set goals. Full accountability came with unrestrained access to senior executives, opening the path to obtain all available insights and evaluate them in view of the broader situational context. Together this was crucial for delivering the best outcome in the shortest period of time while staying focused on building trust, an indispensable asset when so much is at stake. The Danaharta project ticked all the boxes and proved that speed has become an intrinsic element of future-ready strategies. Both are not just compatible, but two decisive factors in any dynamic environment, even when the conceptualization of strategies takes longer than four days.

The publicity that came with Danaharta's success quickly led to more high-profile assignments for Shandwick, including a reputation research and management project for Bank Negara (Malaysia's Central Bank). As I prepared to deliver on those, I was fortunate enough to tap into the groundbreaking work by Shandwick International's CEO Scott Meyer and Charles Fombrun, Professor at Stern School of Business of New York University, who together pioneered the concept of Reputation Management (RM).

RM was not an attempt to rebrand communications or come up with another management consulting solution *du jour*, nor was it a new name for brand management. "Driving reputation from the inside out" stood for an approach that aligned the way an organization deals with its stakeholders around its core values, producing measurable financial and cultural success. It was a true breakthrough moment for public relations, based on realistic assessments such as PR having worked too long without research, process, measurement and management support. As Scott Meyer said:

> The advent of Reputation Management communication can allow us to identify what is best and true about an organization; help instill these values deep into the organization, transform and help it achieve its best, raise its reputation and differentiating it by making these values transparent to the outside world.[6]

Research played a crucial role as judging reputations needed agreements on standard terminology, a defensible measurement and clarity about the process behind it. Further action included academic and business literature reviews and focus groups and surveys with stakeholders. The First Reputation Quotient (RQ) was developed by Harris Online and Charles Fombrun, sponsored by the *Wall Street Journal* and underwritten by the Reputation Institute. It was done online and augmented by telephone interviews, generating 20 attributes surrounding stakeholder relations.

To make it work in Asian markets required some adaptations. This was already factored in by Meyer and Fombrun, who had affirmed that "Managing through rules doesn't allow for creative and cultural differences."[7] By placing a greater emphasis on in-person meetings and personal interviews, the ground was laid for creating deeper relationships and delivering quick results. Within months, that model had become a personal template for all future work on strategy development in fast-paced but stability-craving environments. What made the difference was to get out of the office and engage board members via a series of management interviews and workshops that revealed unleveraged strengths as well as narrative gaps and inconsistencies while validating all internal and external research and analysis. The early involvement of top decision makers reduced the odds of misunderstandings about the available time window and expected results. It also heralded a higher degree of longevity of the strategies, as the buy-in from senior management translates to a high degree of risk insurance – a secure and fast way to achieve the desired outcomes while sustaining competitive advantage. Without knowing it back then, this decision represented what accounts for "Technocracy in Communications" today. It was a fact-based and outcome-oriented model that instrumentalized deep research and the adaptation of technical and other skills while prioritizing speed and people-to-people connectivity; the best model to gather insights that would shape strategies with a campaign approach rather than roadmaps loaded with standalone activities and events.

Scott Meyer, who today serves as an Instructor at Hubbard School of Journalism and Mass Communication at University of Minnesota, said this while looking back at the launch of RM more than two decades ago:

> Over the past 20 years, reputation management has moved to the forefront in boosting sales, improving brand visibility, building brand image, and growing trust and credibility. Simply stated, reputation management has proven to have the power to ignite business growth. Importantly, today, reputation management is taught at the collegiate level to ensure we will have many professional practitioners in the years ahead.[8]

The lessons learned in Malaysia paid off over many years and in places all over Asia. I was once invited to join Fudan University in conducting a reputation management seminar with members of Shanghai Municipality on behalf of the Shanghai Pudong Development Council. It was a great opportunity to combine academic insight with my own take as a practitioner. The purpose was to create an understanding of the benefits of coming up with a vigorous and defensible narrative that supported Pudong's future readiness as China's financial hub. Centered on deep research on existing perceptions, the event swiftly changed the views of community leaders and led to a commitment to embrace the process. Today the approach would include the incorporation of new content, channels and digital platforms as well as media intelligence and data analysis that meet the requirements of a fully digitalized world. And one more thing must be considered to ensure the long-term success of speed and strategy.

Managing the Reputational Risk of Speed and Strategy

"Wēijī is Chinese for crisis and composed of two characters: danger and opportunity." It's one of the favorite presentation openers by Western consultants; an acknowledgment of the situation and a motivating call to action – and not entirely accurate. "Wēijī" translates to "danger at a point of juncture."

Despite its proven record of delivering the goods, the original Danaharta model of technocracy, speed and strategy obviously needs to be adapted to work in today's rapidly changing environment. But that is more about technicalities than the general thinking behind it. Deploying data analytics would always provide the kind of deep insights needed to predict domestic, regional or global reactions to any fast developed strategy. Another step is to anticipate external and internal threats to its resoluteness and prolonged existence. Losing the competitive advantage because of some overconfidence or lack of concern would be devastating.

As can be expected, the nature of these risks changes as fast as the entire operating environment. The chapters on mis- and disinformation, human capital and AI and big data already addressed this point. The proper response is what has emerged as the biggest catchphrase in the compliance industry: risk management. Embracing that is the actual point of juncture. Companies use risk assessment and management as a means to identify potential vulnerability and related harms, determine the right course of action and limit financial exposure. But although traditional advisors such as legal counsel, management consultants, accountants and investment bankers can provide the objective metric to help the decision-making process, they are not always addressing the potential risk and reward associated with corporate or even diplomatic reputation. In the Asian Century, this marks a shortfall in any risk mitigation strategy. Today's publics demand the highest standards for corporate citizenship and value corporate reputation higher than ever. As comms leaders stress: reputation isn't a popularity contest; it's money in the bank. That makes sense, as attracting new clients and customers can cost much more than retaining existing ones. That aligns perfectly with an older study by Prophet, a strategic brand and marketing consultancy, which revealed that consumers are two times more likely to purchase, four times more likely to pay more for, and close to 15 times more likely to recommend products and services from a company with a leading reputation.[9] A similar outcome of newer studies ties consumer preferences to purpose-driven companies.

The traditional approach to risk management overlooks the power of the public voice, and that does not serve the concept of championing purpose. What is needed is not just remote assistance in navigating complex operating environments, but experience in reputation management and brand stewardship that helps corporations capitalize on opportunities in periods of rapid change and turbulence. If the public holds the key to failure or success, then companies need to come up with ways to analyze and fully leverage the power of the public voice while investing in their own reputational advantage. Strategic comms pros have been saying this for years: if you run a fairly large and successful business without consulting your communications advisors on a regular basis, you are gambling. Better to get that Paul Newman– the architect, strategist and trusted advisor with a seat at the boardroom table who will watch over your corporate reputations and exercise veto power if needed.

Maintaining a competitive reputational advantage requires an evidence-based understanding of those who determine the fortunes of a business, including the public at large. The better advisors, though, go one step further. Understanding that effective communications models and reputation management require an integrated, channel-neutral and multidisciplinary approach, they will take a closer look at all touch points across the various audiences and channels that are being used in the process; all while keeping an eye on real sentiment and shifts in opinion. These are the insights that can now be extracted from data points.

The relationship among operations, strategy, reputation, communications and value is complex, but research proves a real correlation between them and the reputation equity that is reflected in a company's premium and latent value, both of which shape public perceptions. Premium value corresponds to anything that surpasses the book value or equity value as reported in balance sheets. This includes global presence, brands, intellectual property and the expertise and experience of its senior executives and general workforce. Also included is reputation. Latent value, on the other hand, represents the intangible or "hidden" value of assets that are accessible but not yet seen, found or being utilized. Among them are less known or less popular brands, innovation that lacks patents, and an unenthusiastic workforce in doubt of the organization's future.

High premium values indicate investors have confidence in the company's future performance. Managing to build a name brand for delivering growth, attracting top talent and avoiding ethical mishaps can account for much of the 30–70 percent gap between the book value of most companies and their market capitalizations. Companies with higher reputation equity have proven more resilient to business threats and recover from crises more efficiently. That alone should suffice to make the case for an investment in a pragmatic and effective way of handling risk management that includes a distinct strategy to protect a company's reputation. Whatever its final shape or form may be, it must be rooted in practicality and based on real insights. Facing and understanding the entirety of the operating environment is the way to build corporate resilience and protect all accomplishments from being undermined by unexpected events or missteps.

What cannot be ignored in that context is the company we keep. Globally operating or sourcing companies need to revisit their web of contracts and relationships and ensure best practice compliance. Companies that accept bad business practices of their associates are as culpable as their partners – either legally or "just" in the court of public opinion. This brings us back to the West's fascination with "wéijī" as the supposed Chinese way of seeing upsides in any crisis. Semantics aside, speed and strategy are indeed everything you may wish to read into "wéijī." It's that point of juncture that represents a potential risk if rolled out without any preparation and a real opportunity for those who have invested in advance scenario planning and risk management. The bottom line is that risk and corporate responsibility cannot be outsourced. The good news is that the tools for assessing and influencing corporate strategy from a reputational point of view do exist, and corporate reputation can be a strong driver and motivator to remedy what's wrong.

Giving advisors access to the inner circle and solidifying their claim to a seat in the C-Suite might just prove to be the best strategic move.

Preparing for the Asianization of Communications

With Asian markets representing billions of future revenues for industry players with the right expertise, it certainly makes sense for Westerners to place smart operators on the ground; those with a great deal of "wasta" (Arabic for "personal connections"), "guanxi" (Chinese for "personal and professional contacts and relationships") and similar culture-related skills. The same applies to Asians that operate outside their cultural sphere. But that's not all. In fact, the Asianization of communications is more about taking a technocratic approach to planning and implementing comms strategies, irrespective of time and place. That includes the acceptance of new business models based on speed and strategy.

The ideal scenario is one where planners share the same vision and adhere to a farsighted and imaginative way of tackling challenges and exploring opportunities that are not yet seen by others. The strategies that address all of the above are long term and go beyond the mere tendering and operational delivery process. The difference is twofold: (a) aligning all tactics and dealing with the situation on the ground, including influencers, competition, decision-makers and those who are directly affected; and (b) anticipating and preparing for setbacks and obstacles of all kind while helping to leverage competitive advantage.

It all starts with the resolve to overcome the apparent contradiction of having to act fast yet without cutting corners. As shown, speed and the need for deep planning and real outcomes can be reconciled; perhaps not instantly but with some practice and – as should be obvious by now – a willingness to invest in using tracking and sensor technologies for integrated decision making.

A range of factors such as geopolitical, funding or operational hazards might still impact how far one is willing to go and how much to spend on future preparedness in the near and mid-term. But if recent history is any indicator, things will continue to move down the right path. All stakeholders, including investors, governments, project owners, engineering and construction companies, and MNCs need to prepare for the best while hedging against any adverse events.

The road to success is always hit by various roadblocks. But when communications strategists learn how to circumvent speed limits and guide the progression from sheer repair and maintenance to upgrading roads to highways, then speed and strategy are suddenly within reach. Time to recall a simple truth: "No one was ever lost on a straight road" (Indian proverb), certainly not when staying focused on efficient road networking and traffic management. That's why having a shared vision and an associated communications strategy and rollout plan are essential.

References

1. "Eric Yuan Quotes." *BrainyQuote*, https://brainyquote.com/quotes/eric_yuan_1127881
2. "Piyush Goyal Quotes." *BrainyQuote*, https://brainyquote.com/quotes/piyush_goyal_846703
3. Molavi, Afshin. Conversation with author. May 2022.

4. Molavi, Afshin. Conversation with author. May 2022.
5. Ignatius, David. "The Last Boomtown: Shanghai's Festival of Exuberance." *New York Times*, 29 Jun. 2002, https://nytimes.com/2002/06/29/opinion/IHT-the-last-boomtown-shanghais-festival-of-exuberance.html
6. Meyer, Scott. Conversation with author. April 2022.
7. Meyer, Scott. Conversation with author. April2022.
8. Meyer, Scott. Conversation with author. April 2022.
9. Sachs, Mary Lee. "A Blended Approach to Comms and Marketing." *PR Say*, 2011, https://prsay.prsa.org/2011/07/07/a-blended-approach-to-comms-and-marketing

10 ACCESS and BEAT

Two Ways to Develop Future-Proof Strategies

A vision without a long-term strategy is tantamount to a daydream that lingers on. It sure looks beautiful and inspiring, but it quickly loses its magnetism when the world moves on and there is no action plan that can be adjusted. Staying on top of the game is contingent on accepting the vastly dynamic operating environment of the Asian Century and mastering it with a robust and well-laid-out strategic plan based on real insight and flexibility.

Lawyers know how the sausage gets made. Here is what they say when preparing for cross-examinations of witnesses: "Never ask a question unless you know the answer." What applies to courtroom proceedings is also true for communicators who must look at their strategies from various angles in order to predict the kind of response they will draw from the variety of stakeholders. Just how can we ensure that all works out as planned?

Creating strategies that stack the dominoes end-to-end may look like a preventive measure and way to secure the much-cited advance scenario planning. But the truth is, there is no room for error. Things are fine as long as everything goes as planned. But if one piece tips over, they all fall down. Advance scenario planning is about addressing multiple scenarios, an openness to constantly assess and adjust while never slowing things down. In toeing the line of Speed and Strategy, this final chapter is about fast moves without knocking over the dominoes. When adapting the lessons from Asia's rapid modernization in ways that work across geographies, the ultimate goals of mutual understanding, support and advocacy can be accomplished. It's for this reason that the next steps are being charted in two ways, not one. Both are crafted to predict desired outcomes. But depending on cultural backgrounds and personal as well as professional preferences, one model might work better than the other in drafting the individual course of action. That said both can definitely be combined. In fact, that may just be the best formula to achieve all set goals.

ACCESS – The Inspirational Model

When entering the planning stage of strategy development, it is all about getting the creative juices flowing and to come up with original ideas while staying focused on both the originators and recipients of all communications efforts. It's what I call the process of prioritizing 'ACCESS': Agility, Can-do, Creativity, Entrepreneurship, Strategy, and Staff.[1] Each of these factors has the capacity to make a lasting difference

DOI: 10.4324/9781003385622-11

ACCESS 1: Agility

Expanding into new markets can be a daring task as the landscape is marked by diverse cultures, political systems, languages and different value systems. Besides, there are varying levels of economic development, access to technology and new media and, of course, the much-cited geopolitical challenges. Along with a lack of reliable case studies this makes for a big amount of obstacles to overcome. The upsides, however, are obvious: almost boundless economic opportunities. But that comes with enormous pressure, especially since speed matters.

In the Asian Century, everything can change overnight: consumer preferences, the competition and market conditions. Plans change all the time, yet everyone expects the highest quality. Nothing is ever carved in stone, but it often looks as if it were. The way to deal with this and to reach the full potential is to untie communications from all organizational bias and to make agility a core part of the managerial setup. One has to be quick, anticipate events and develop strategies and processes to keep up with the high volatility of stakeholder demands, technological shifts and changing societal conditions.

And there is more. The fact that results are expected at the earliest possible time is no excuse for pushing tactical measures while pretending they are strategic. It's an opportunity to leverage multicultural expertise to promote innovation in strategic communications and combine it with purely outcome-oriented plans.

On top of that is the need to put in place systems that accelerate the process of analyzing data, identifying options, spotting trends and putting ideas through a testing process to probe for their downside weaknesses. And of course, one must ensure that strategy and execution don't diverge. That trait is closely linked to the next one: Can-do.

ACCESS 2: Can-do

Page one of the Asian Century communications playbook has "Strategy plus Can-do" on top. Creatives in the Middle East know what I am talking about: "They've only briefed us today and now they ask for the video by tomorrow!" A realistic demand? Certainly not. But using that as an excuse to walk away won't help. The better option is to get on with it. The correct answer is the least expected one: "Consider it done."

"Can-do spirit" is a quintessential part of the Asian way of doing things and will sooner or later be adapted all over the place. Being resourceful enough to absorb any blow from unexpected events is crucial. "No" is rarely the right answer, under any circumstances. You've either internalized "Can-do" already or will have to embrace it very fast. All operators are expected to deliver quickly, and the best way to go about it is to observe and learn how it's been done.

There are those who will always claim that this runs counter to the old maxim, "Don't act without a plan." But audiences in the East may see it differently. To them, speed and efficiency are synonymous with progress and being future-oriented. Of course there needs to be a plan, but business continues while you're drafting it. As mentioned before, the trick is to use ambiguity of the brief as an opening to add structure, purpose and direction based on experience in handling similar situations, all while managing expectations by under-promising and always over-delivering. It just requires some creative thinking.

ACCESS 3: *Creativity*

Ideation and problem solving are closely interlinked. As argued earlier, plans will change — they always do — but expectations don't. The best way to prevent bad things from happening is to appoint tech-savvy and creative thinkers and doers who can double as problem-solvers.

Thinking of any business as a brand can help. Once accepted, it becomes more common to look for shortcuts to the hearts and minds of all stakeholders, including clients, customers and constituents. While this applies anywhere in the world, it is even more significant for Asia's young and brand-conscious consumers. That's not to say that all prefer Western or global brands. In fact, many more buy Asian, either as a matter of trust, national pride or price. Young Asians are social media savvy and well informed while also looking for guidance. Brands that take a social stance inspire and can score big time.

The linkage between all is Purpose and Shared Values. When looking for an equivalent from within that same line of work, here are some. It's the difference between selling a mattress and "a good night's rest" or an iPod and "a device carrying 1,000 songs in your pocket." And taking a clue from the previously stated example of successful nation branding, it is about "building landmarks, not just tall towers." This focus on action plus action words is a proven way to supercharge narratives that helps to excite, motivate and accelerate. This has worked phenomenally well with audiences and should also become a blueprint for attracting the right kind of talent, those who continue to look out for the same. The good news is that the world now boasts of creative talent. It makes a lot of sense to appoint them faster than the competition. If you're with me on that, you probably agree on the next one as well: entrepreneurship.

ACCESS 4: *Entrepreneurship*

In the Asian Century, no one can merely cherry-pick where, when and how change shall affect the operating conditions. The better option is to pay attention to one's own mindset; the most critical asset for any leader. For Peter Diamandis, the book author, international pioneer in the field of innovation and curator and mentor at Abundance360, the most successful entrepreneurs have four of them: a moonshot mindset, an abundance mindset, an exponential mindset, and a longevity mindset.[2] For anyone who grew up in Bengaluru, Chongqing, Doha, Dubai, Ghaziabad, Kuala Lumpur, Shanghai, Shenzhen, Singapore, Seoul or Surat over the past 20 years, all this is normal or at least desirable, as it creates the conditions for entrepreneurs, many of whom are Asia's new role models.

Big tankers obviously need time to change course, while smaller ones are more agile. With that in mind, emulating Asian-style entrepreneurism is a choice businesses can make, and it's a strategic one. Turning vision into a master plan that aims for leadership by acting as quickly and flexible as start-ups is a way to handle it.

ACCESS 5: *Strategy*

Strategy is the art and science of managing options. In communications, it is also a measure of rhetorical preparation and therefore key to survival. The options are linked to outcomes and the effects on short- and long-term perceptions and reputations. It requires the much-cited analytical and creative thinking and a deep understanding of the place and cultural context in which communications takes place. Hint: the cookie-cutter approach won't work. Successful communications is the result of searching for and identifying the uniqueness in each and every business, brand, cause or foreign policy. The goal is to understand what worked and what didn't and to articulate one's own future in any industry or space and society or the global community — long before the actual storytelling starts. That always works.

The increasingly more complex and fast-moving environments make strategic planning a priority, under conditions that can be challenging. But what's the alternative? Ancient Chinese military strategist and philosopher Sun Tzu wrote, "Strategy without tactics is the slowest route to victory. Tactics without strategy is the noise before defeat." Likewise, if you sacrifice strategy for speed, you're running fast but without a compass. And if you sacrifice speed for strategy (i.e. never leave the planning stage) your competition will eat your lunch. The bottom line: you'll need both while not failing to carry out risk assessment and advance scenario planning. It starts with the resolve to overcome the apparent contradiction of having to act fast, yet without skipping steps. The easier road would be to stay tactical. But that's a fool's errand.

It can all be done. The best choice is to hire people who think like you on that.

ACCESS 6: *Staff*

Companies and organizations are as agile, can-do oriented, creative, entrepreneurial and strategic as their people. It is therefore fair enough to assemble a team that thinks and functions along these lines. Business partners will trust them because they are positive, thrive in high-pressure and high-reward environments where the focus is less on procedure than outcomes, and will respond quickly and efficiently in all scenarios.

Since Millennials are looking for purpose-driven organizations with stated missions, there is a clear upside in bringing in talent with the right skills as well as openly expressed values. This does not mean one has to concur with all their personal beliefs. What matters is their will to spare no effort to properly analyze any situation and make their point. This can be a distinguishing factor in any professional setting.

At the COP26 climate summit in Glasgow, climate activist Greta Thunberg publicly denounced world leaders for their inaction in addressing the climate emergency, dismissing it as "blah, blah, blah." This appeared to have drawn more global attention than the official statements and declarations at the World Leaders Summit. In his book *Freedom: How We Lose It and How We Fight Back*,[3] activist Nathan Law warned world leaders of the dangers of authoritarianism and urged them to protect democracy and freedom now or face losing them forever. His calls were echoed on international broadcast, traditional and social media. These are just two examples of young leaders standing up for what they believe in: real action, fairness and equity, a perfectly reasonable stance. Imagine having these two on your team. Of course, they stand out, but common sense and bravery seem sensible in any setting.

The move from storytellers to thinkers, doers and strategists is the most consequential one in the process of preparing for the future. By staying focused on the long-term goals, providing evidence of the progress made, and displaying readiness to constantly adjust, communicators become change agents or change accelerators. It elevates them to the level of decision makers with broader authority. Another aspect is the diversity of the team lineup. As argued in Chapter 7 about human capital, being engaged with the world requires talent that are not just willing to relocate but also pretty "gung-ho" (Chinese for eager or enthusiastic) to work in a multicultural environment. However, it's not all done by sending your own people overseas. You also need to hire local, encourage a culture of collaboration between empowered, self-organizing teams with flat hierarchies. Plus, diverse local teams can communicate in multiple languages, creating stronger bonds with audiences that add to that sense of belonging. A commitment to provide training – still a rare commodity and real game changer in many organizations – and decent compensation is another way to build loyalty.

In summary, pursuing ACCESS is the path to engage audiences and those in charge; whether it is senior board members, government leaders or diplomats. They are more likely to listen to strategic counsel and advice when you can prove you've got your own house in order. Speaking of which, gaining access (and ACCESS) obviously requires a key. But who holds it? Can it be shared? And what if someone replaces the locks? The answer is simple: autonomy. The more empowered a team is to take decisions and act swiftly, the higher its value contribution. Such level of authority is what eventually leads to trustworthiness. It is the master key that opens all doors.

BEAT – The Aspirational Approach

The chapter structure of this book was conceived as an accumulation of all factors that define the unique surroundings for communicators in the Asian Century. As comms pros would have noticed, it is also to some extent aligned with the actual process of strategy development. That process includes a comprehensive situation analysis, tapping into academic research and addressing the need to identify the general path forward. All this while identifying opportunities, challenges and obstacles, and picking the right team and tools needed to broaden the understanding of existing perceptions and sentiments. That is no coincidence.

The logic behind this concurrence is straightforward: the more insights and facts we gather by investing in research and listening to our audiences, the better we understand the sociocultural, economic and political realities of those we engage with. Learning to cope with separate points of view helps with 'BEAT': Building and Earning Authority and Trust; the two key conditions for getting things done. Since each scenario is unique, the openness to change begins as early as the planning stage. This is where an aspirational and systematic approach comes into play.

Stage 1: External Intelligence Gathering (Assessment #1)

For those actively engaged with Asia and for Asians strongly associated with organizations in the West, the distinguishing feature is having a solid grasp on the historical and sociocultural context and global connectivity. Seen through the lens of history, geography, economics and culture, certain attitudes, views and responses suddenly begin to ring true. This is also a way to come up with sensible conclusions and to clarify motivations and rationales; all of which translate to better communications and competitive advantage. Here are the steps to follow.

1.1 Initiation

- Requesting and analyzing a written brief plus existing research and market analysis

1.2 Desk Research

- Corporate history and outlook, including current and future products and services
- Assessment of existing communications infrastructure, e.g. team structure, website, branding, suppliers, measurement, etc.
- Competitive landscape (real and perceived) and societal trends in key markets
- Assessment of business objectives as they relate to communications
- Traditional and social media analysis (including academic journals, policy publications)
- Review of industry, company and competitor reports; policy papers, product data, etc.
- Initial review of challenges, priority audiences, role of public and influencers, and advance scenario plans

1.3 Data Analytics, Surveys and External Interviews

- AI-based media monitoring, digital listening and analysis
- Polling, quantitative marketing research (omnibus surveys), audience and issues matrix
- Interviews with key stakeholders, elite panels, media, analysts, researchers and influencers to understand their perceptions as well as the role of public opinion

1.4 Ongoing Strategic Counsel and Advice

- Determination of the level of client involvement in the process, e.g. upcoming additional interviews, positioning and messaging workshops

Stage 2: Internal Intelligence Gathering (Assessment #2)

Once the external research has been completed, the insights gathered can be used to structure all internal research and to begin listening to management, staff and other stakeholders in order to understand their viewpoints, values and objectives. It is important not to share the findings from external research at that point, as it might distort responses while making it harder to unearth hidden facts. Listening is central to connect the dots and steer the discussion with the goal of drafting a list of challenges and setting realistic objectives and expectations.

2.1 Internal Interviews

- Face-to-face interviews and digital surveys with internal stakeholders, including senior executives and staff to define ambitions, challenges and objectives, and realistic outcomes
- Stakeholder and constituents mapping (including needs, priorities and attitudes)
- Stakeholder segmentation (e.g. top clients, institutional investors, competitors, regulators, key opinion leaders and influencers, etc.)

2.2 Ongoing Strategic Counsel and Advice

- Review session and alignment with senior management
- Communicating the approach to the client journey plus the range of expected outcomes

2.3 Additional Tasks

- Moving on from a transactional relationship to a trust-based, sustainable one
- Displaying full commitment to problem co-ownership and reputation custodianship
- Taking full responsibility for all proposed actions

Stage 3: Positioning and Messaging (Strategy #1)

After completing both external and internal research, all findings need to be consolidated and analyzed with a look at business risks, perception and narrative gaps, and opportunities for future-ready communications. That includes an assessment of Purpose and Shared Values, which might reduce the impact of sociocultural and political differences. Then the next step is to conduct a client workshop to jointly develop the "conceptual space" of the organization: the positioning it aims to occupy in the mind of its key stakeholders. Alfred Schütz's progression from "because" to "in-order-to" motives might stimulate some new thinking, as it is based on competitive advantage and literally purpose-made to form the basis of all messaging and narrative development.

3.1 Preparation

- Consolidating all research outcomes in one document
- Highlighting business risks and opportunities and internal and external perceptions

- Forming initial view of communications priorities
- Speed Summit 1 (review and discussion of all findings from research phases 1 and 2)
- Collecting feedback and framing the client's business priorities
- Preparation of a half-day positioning and messaging workshop

3.2 Workshop

- Short recap of research conclusions and communications challenges
- SWOT Analysis (Strengths, Weaknesses, Opportunities and Threats)
- Positioning framework
  - Clarification of Purpose and Shared Values (incl. the "In-order-to" motives)
  - Forcefield Analysis (Worst Perception, Rational and Emotional Drivers, Current Perception, Barriers, Best Perception)
- Messaging architecture and message house (including a link between action and action words)

3.3 Validation and Follow-Up

- Finalization of draft message house
- Drawing up and refining the master narrative
- Internal message testing
- Speed Summit 2 (internal validation of messaging and narrative)
- Goal setting and measurement: develop first outline of measurable success
- Putting people first: achieving internal agreement to put the needs, voices and rights of stakeholders and audiences at the center of each strategy
- Obtaining the commitment to be accessible, open and accountable, transparent, ethical, fair and objective

Stage 4: The New Engagement Game Plan (Strategy #2)

As stated, the new imperative of strategic communications is influence, not control. Corporate communications can capitalize on insights gathered from industry pioneers and begin to use digital platforms to broaden and intensify stakeholder engagement. Data analytics helps to collect the proof points for strategies, for example by analyzing user sentiment on social media toward certain topics, brands and causes.

4.1 Preparation and Strategy Formulation

- Leveraging master data to build more complete profiles of stakeholder needs, wants and preferences
- Creative internal brainstorm on audience focus, geographic priorities, communications channels, thought leadership criteria, digital emphasis and campaign theme

- Developing a domestic and international stakeholder engagement strategy aimed at supporting the long-term strategic objectives and striking the right balance between symmetry and complementarity (Watzlawick), while building trust to reduce complexity (Luhmann)
- Adding greater value by thinking up thought leadership and creative concepts
- Conceptualizing visual, conversion-focused campaigns
- Defining the Standing Operating Procedure (SOP) to outline the implementation of concepts, communications tactics and procedure for all stakeholder engagement in a transparent and objective manner
- Laying out a detailed campaign plan timetable and roadmap rollout

4.2 Content Development and Optimization

- Formulating a master plan that aligns the main components of all messages with narratives that connect with publics in various localities (including local viability and suitability checks)
- Optimizing existing digital and social media, multimedia and creative tools
- Developing gaming strategies (where applicable)
- Refining the narrative, tactics, activities and concepts that deliver the desired outcomes
- Content and collaterals development (photo shoot, press kit, website, briefings and itineraries, infographics, animations)
- Interactive content, including chatbots, podcasting, interactive audio, and social media platforms
- Crisis and issues planning: develop scenario matrix to prepare for foreseeable and unforeseeable events
- Integrating all in one budget plan

4.3 Staffing

- Resource estimation, capability development and local, regional and international team assignment
- Hiring and onboarding
- Development of personalized training schedules

4.4 Additional Deliverables

- Advancing the cause of leaders by guiding them how to engage audiences with a thought leadership approach and influence perceptions with convincing and verifiable narratives and stories
- Optimizing strategic relationships
- Portraying the ability and confidence in taking intelligent risks
- Brand activism reality check
- Defining KPIs and benchmarking objectives plus monitoring

Stage 5: Campaign Rollout and Implementation

When strategies are based on solid internal and external intelligence gathering and a process of orchestrating senior management buy-in along all steps of positioning, messaging and content development, the foundation is laid for a well-coordinated campaign approach that is almost guaranteed to succeed.

5.1 Rollout

- Team introduction and clarification of individual responsibilities
- Implementation of communications plan against agreed deliverables and KPIs
- Documentation of progress (work reports with strategic and tactical feedback)
- Setting up a virtual press office and distributing content
- Integrating automatically updated real-time dashboards to analyze, track and report on an entity's live data with the help of interactive data visualizations
- Rolling out viral and interactive storytelling
- Advance scenario and crisis response planning
- Optional: Launch of digital engagement tools such as gaming, responsive and dynamic audio products, and live video (a more authentic way to share a story)

5.2 Ongoing Strategic Counsel and Advice

- Helping clients to set up infrastructure to capture data
- Continuous guidance for senior management in delivering on all objectives (including presentation, public speaking and media skills training)
- Supervision of all communications activities with a focus on audience reaction, digital emphasis, staffing and other resource requirements
- Public consultations, advisory and focus groups, one-to-one meetings
- Regular review meetings with senior management

5.3 Measurement against Pre-Agreed Criteria and Methods

- Analyzing data related to media coverage and social media engagement levels
- Conducting stakeholder surveys and digital research to measure behavioral change among stakeholders including investors, opinion leaders and influencers, and media
- Continuously monitoring reputation

Integrated Communications Has Branched Out

ACCESS and BEAT are two approaches to inspire and structure future-proof communications strategies that work in all operating environments, both geographically and business-wise. What remains critical for long-term success is to secure top-level support, as comms can no longer function in isolation. Making a compelling internal case warrants some clarification about the changing scope and scale of integrated communications. Leaders must realize that the concept has expanded and now relates to two forms of cooperation that affect the operational setup.

The integration of creative disciplines has long been a core service offered by most advertising holding companies. It remains as important as ever but needs to be reviewed because, as mentioned before, the number of companies that are bringing the creative and strategic functions inhouse is going up. That's why integrating services "under one roof" is expected to be tied to a new value proposition. In view of that, agencies must assess all individual contributions and also challenge that old model of "brand guardianship." Coordinating PR, advertising, branding, digital, events, sponsorship and marketing with the purpose of aligning all cross-functional objectives requires a unified approach and strategy. Such a strategy is best managed by experienced but discipline-neutral advisors, as handing it to PR or advertising can lead to biased proposals.

The other concept of integrated communications is linked to the objective of achieving active participation of senior executives in charge of various business functions. As exemplified in the "BEAT" section of this chapter, their input is needed at literally every stage of the planning process as well as the campaign rollout. Besides, they are the ones to approve the acquisition and use of the new AI toolkit, a smart move that gives everyone a better understanding of perceptions and improved ways of connecting with audiences. Last but not least, they must be convinced to place a greater emphasis on renewed talent strategies and Purpose and Shared Values.

Without senior buy-in and endorsement, building and protecting reputations is going to be much harder to accomplish. Again, that leaves organizations with just one sensible option: to scale up communications with leaders that speak their language and are committed to deliver tangible outcomes based on a more holistic and inclusive approach. As the designated C-Suite leader for purpose or sustainability, your own Paul Newman will always do what is right and when it's right – not just when the lawyers finally ring and give the green light to some watered-down version. With a strong background in politics, economics and international relations, one's own "architect" can assist in adding clarity and opening channels of dialogue for those with diverging points of view.

It's like signing up to some new kind of insurance policy and a more far-reaching business strategy. Once the board is "on board," the process of adjusting long-established practices can begin and the concept of Speed and Strategy will be on track to become the new normal in communications in the Asian Century. As stated, it's a complex task, but when reflecting upon future-ready communications (and public diplomacy), nothing shall ever be considered unchangeable. It can all be done. To make a long story short: "If the future is Asian, the future of communications is Asian, too."[4]

References

1. Stelling, Oliver. "Asia Is More Connected Than Ever. But Have You Got ACCESS?" *LinkedIn*, 25Mar.2019, https://linkedin.com/pulse/asia-more-connected-than-ever-have-you-got-access-oliver-stelling

2. Corcoran, John. "Peter Diamandis | Exponential Thinking, Moonshots, and Abundance Mindset." *Smart Business Revolution*, https://smartbusinessrevolution.com/peter-diamandis-exponential-thinking-moonshots-and-abundance-mindset
3. Law, Nathan, and Evan Fowler. *Freedom: How We Lose It and How We Fight Back*. New York, The Experiment, 2021.
4. "Homepage." *oliverstelling.com*, www.oliverstelling.com

Epilogue

Given the intensifying geopolitical tensions, the trade and industry disruptions caused by the Covid19 pandemic, and the prospect of more economic decoupling, some observers seem to be convinced that Asia's rise has peaked. But that is ignoring the economic and demographic facts on the ground. The Asian Century has arrived and is here to stay. The reason why this is not yet universally acknowledged has less to do with facts than with deep-rooted traditions and sentiments, most of which emanated from the European and American centuries. The 21st century, however, marks the arrival of globalization's next phase and is co-owned by the global community.

Regardless of location or line of business, anyone who is engaged with both the East and the West should revisit long-held beliefs and assumptions and adapt to the new realities. That applies to Western business leaders and communicators as well as Asian leaders and entities with vested interests overseas. Being open to listen to other views and accepting different takes remains critical. Likewise, there is a huge upside in swiftly embracing Shenzhen Speed and Dubai Spirit and to prepare for all possible scenarios before the pressure becomes overwhelming. The task at hand is strategic, but that's no excuse for delays. There is no doubt that the impressive changes across the Indo-Pacific and Asia's progress in industrial development, trade, science and tech will continue to draw the world's attention in the decades to come. A number of Asian technocracies are setting the pace and direction of global development. One cannot ignore that, as this is what shapes our collective future. Public perceptions are the ultimate reputational front line.

Back in 2014 I attended a conference in Delhi on the future of communications. On my way home I did what I always enjoy the most: having a chat with the driver. Sitting in the back of that beautiful oldtimer Ambassador taxi, we spoke about Narendra Modi, India's newly elected Prime Minister. I was keen to know what he expected from him. "A lot," he said with conviction. "But he's got no time. Look around you (he was pointing at the traffic), it's the same thing every day. How long to clean up this mess? He hasn't got the time." My driver then changed his plan, took another road and got me to the airport sooner than I had even anticipated.

If one needs a simple yet proper analogy to describe what awaits communications in the Asian Century, here it is: the road ahead is known, the obstacles too, the pressure to deliver real and people-centric outcomes is ramping up, and time could be running out soon. Having agency means one can always keep going and remain flexible to adapt to new developments. The chances are that everything sorts itself out. The right course is to take quick decisions followed by real action. In that same spirit, communicators have to hold themselves to the highest standards, always take an ethical yet pragmatic approach and adapt to fast-moving and often commoditized environments – all while continuously staying outcome-focused.

The App That Gets the Final Word

Live Transcribe is a mobile app developed by Google in partnership with Gallaudet University. It creates real-time captions of spoken language and, with over 500 million downloads on Google Play, ranks among the most popular apps. The functionality is superb, especially in view of the different pronunciations of words by millions of speakers. And even when detecting words it does not recognize, it won't shut down. Instead, it churns out whatever comes closest. That's how things continue without disruption. When my name appears in a webinar or interview, Live Transcribe usually displays it as "all of us telling" – a funny but perfect fit with *CommunicAsian* and the growing influence of tech and the public voice. This is what defines the future of communications – not just storytelling, which emanates from one source or synchronized community of storytellers, but "all of us telling."

Bibliography

Anholt, Simon. *The Good Country Equation: How We Can Repair the World in One Generation*. Berrett-Koehler Publishers, Inc, Oakland, US, 2020.

Aronczyk, Melissa. *Branding the Nation: The Global Business of National Identity*. Oxford University Press, New York, US, 2013.

Batey, Ian. *Asian Branding: A Great Way to Fly*. Prentice Hall, Upper Saddle River, US, 2002.

Bernays, Edward, and Stefano Di Lorenzo. *Propaganda: With a New Foreword*. Independently published, 2022.

Bernstein, William J. *Masters of the Word: How Media Shaped History*. 1st ed. (stated), First Printing, Grove Press, New York, US, 2013.

Beveridge, Ivana. *Intercultural Marketing: Theory and Practice*. 1st ed., Routledge, New York, US, 2020.

Bhutto, Fatima. *New Kings of the World: Dispatches from Bollywood, Dizi, and K-Pop*. Columbia Global Reports, New York, US, 2019.

Bühler, Karl. *The Theory of Language: The Representational Function of Language (Sprachtheorie)*. Donald Fraser Goodwin, John Benjamin's Publishing Company, Amsterdam, NL, 1990.

Cave, Tamasin, and Andy Rowell. *A Quiet Word: Lobbying, Crony Capitalism and Broken Politics in Britain*. The Random House Group, London, UK, 2014.

Chan, John. *China Streetsmart: What You Must Know to Be Effective and Profitable in China (13 Sep. 2004) Paperback*. 1st ed., Pearson Ed Asia, HK, 2004.

Duhigg, Charles. *The Power of Habit: Why We Do What We Do, and How to Change*. Random House Books, London, UK, 2013.

Eberl, Ulrich. *How We Invent the Future Today*. Beltz & Gelberg, Weinheim, DE, 2011.

Fombrun, Charles, and Cees van Riel. *Fame and Fortune: How Successful Companies Build Winning Reputations*. FT Prentice Hall, Upper Saddle River, US, 2004.

Frankopan, Peter. *The Silk Roads: A New History of the World*. Bloomsbury, London, UK, 2015.

Gernet, Jacques. *Die Chinesische Welt: Die Geschichte Chinas Von Den Anfängen Bis Zur Jetztzeit*. Suhrkamp, Frankfurt, DE, 1988.

Gladwell, Malcolm. *The Tipping Point: How Little Things Can Make a Difference*. Back Bay Books, New York, US, 2002.

Habermas, Juergen, and Thomas McCarthy. *The Theory of Communicative Action: Volume 1*. Beacon Press, Boston, US, 1985.

Harris, Thomas. *Value-Added Public Relations: The Secret Weapon of Integrated Marketing*. NTC Business Books, Chicago, US, 1998

Hillman, Jonathan. *The Digital Silk Road: China's Quest to Wire the World and Win the Future*. Harper Business, New York, US, 2021.

Irwin, Harry. *Communicating with Asia: Understanding People and Customs*. (1st ed. 1996)., Routledge, New York, US, 2020.
Isikoff, Michael, and David Corn. *Russian Roulette: The Inside Story of Putin's War on America and the Election of Donald Trump*. 1st ed., Twelve/Hachette Book Group, New York, US, 2018.
Juchem, Johann G. *Kommunikationssemantik*. Nodus Publikationen, Münster, DE, 1998.
Kant, Immanuel, et al. *Critique of Pure Reason (the Cambridge Edition of the Works of Immanuel Kant)*. Cambridge UP, Cambridge, UK, 1999.
Kaplan, Robert. *Asia's Cauldron: The South China Sea and the End of a Stable Pacific*. Random House, New York, US, 2014.
Keay, John. *Mad About the Mekong: Exploration and Empire in South East Asia*. Harper Perennial, London, UK, 2006.
Khanna, Parag. *Connectography*. Weidenfeld and Nicolson, London, UK, 2016.
Khanna, Parag. *The Future Is Asian: Global Order in the Twenty-First Century*. Weidenfeld and Nicolson, London, UK, 2019.
Krane, Jim. *Dubai: The Story of the World's Fastest City*. Atlantic Books, London, UK, 2009.
Larres, Klaus. *Uncertain Allies: Nixon, Kissinger, and the Threat of a United Europe*. Yale UP, New Haven, US, 2022.
Law, Nathan, and Evan Fowler. *Freedom: How We Lose It and How We Fight Back*. The Experiment, New York, US, 2021.
Leitner, Gerhard, et al. *Communicating with Asia: The Future of English as a Global Language*. Cambridge UP, Cambridge, UK, 2016.
Leonnig, Carol, and Philip Rucker. *I Alone Can Fix It: Donald J. Trump's Catastrophic Final Year*. 1st ed., Penguin Press, New York, US, 2021.
Lindstrom, Martin. *Brandwashed: Tricks Companies Use to Manipulate Our Minds and Persuade Us (1 Jan. 2012)*. Crown Publishing Group, New York, US, 2011.
Littlejohn, Stephen W., and Karen A. Foss. *Encyclopedia of Communication Theory*. SAGE Publications, Los Angeles, US, 2009.
Lu, Zhouxiang, and Peter Herrmann. *Conflict and Communication: A Changing Asia in a Globalizing World – Social and Political Perspectives (Asian Studies)*. UK ed., Nova Science Pub Inc., Hauppauge, US, 2016.
Luhmann, Niklas, and Peter Fuchs. *Reden und Schweigen*. Suhrkamp Verlag, Frankfurt, DE, 1989.
Maktoum, Rashid Mohammed Al. *Flashes of Thought*. Motivate Publishing Ltd., Dubai, AE, 2013.
Marshall, Tim. *Prisoners of Geography: Ten Maps That Tell You Everything You Need to Know About Global Politics*. Scribner/Simon & Schuster, New York, US, 2015.
McFaul, Michael. *From Cold War to Hot Peace: An American Ambassador in Putin's Russia*. Reprint, Mariner Books, Boston, US, 2019.
Mooij, De Marieke. *Human and Mediated Communication around the World: A Comprehensive Review and Analysis*. Softcover reprint of the original 1st ed. (2014), Springer, Cham, CH, 2016.
Moore, Geoffrey A. *Crossing the Chasm*. Revised ed., Harper Business, New York, US, 1999.
Nisbett, Richard. *The Geography of Thought: How Asians and Westerners Think Differently … and Why*. Reprint, Free Press (imprint of Simon and Schuster), New York, US, 2004.
Nye, Joseph. *Soft Power: The Means to Success in World Politics*. Illustrated, Public Affairs, New York, US, 2005.
Orwell, George. *Politics and the English Language (1946)*. Reprint by Penguin Books, London, UK, 2013.

O'Sullivan, Edmund. *The New Gulf – How Modern Arabia Is Changing the World for Good.* Motivate Publishing, Dubai, AE, 2008.

Patten, Chris. *East and West.* Abridged, Macmillan, London, UK, 1998.

Phillips, Robert. *Trust Me, PR Is Dead.* Unbound, London, UK, 2015.

Pisani, Elizabeth. *Indonesia, etc.: Exploring the Improbable Nation.* W. W. Norton and Company, New York, US, 2014.

Prestowitz, Clyde V. *Rogue Nation: American Unilateralism and the Failure of Good Intentions.* Basic Books, Perseus Books Group, New York, US, 2003.

Rogan, Eugene. *The Arabs: A History.* Revised, Basic Books, New York, US, 2017.

Schütz, Alfred. *The Phenomenology of the Social World.* Heinemann Educational, Portsmouth, US, 1972.

Schweitzer, Sharon, et al. *Access to Asia: Your Multicultural Guide to Building Trust, Inspiring Respect, and Creating Long-Lasting Business Relationships.* 1st ed., Wiley, Hoboken, US, 2015.

Simpson, Glenn, and Peter Fritsch. *Crime in Progress: Inside the Steele Dossier and the Fusion GPS Investigation of Donald Trump.* 1st ed., Random House, New York, US, 2019.

Stiglitz, Joseph, and Thorsten Schmidt. *Die Chancen Der Globalisierung* (German ed.). Siedler Verlag, Random House, Munich, DE, 2006.

The Towering Inferno. Motion Picture. Directed by John Guillermin; produced by Irwin Allen; performances by Paul Newman, Steve McQueen, Fred Astaire et al., Warner Bros. & Twentieth Century-Fox, Los Angeles, US, 1974.

Volpe, John Della, and David Hogg. *Fight: How Gen Z Is Channeling Their Fear and Passion to Save America.* St. Martin's Press, New York, US, 2022.

Watzlawick, Paul. *Pragmatics of Human Communication.* W. W. Norton and Company, New York, US, 1967.

Williams, Jeremy. *Don't They Know It's Friday? Cross-Cultural Considerations for Business and Life in the Gulf.* Motivate Publishing, Dubai, AE, 1999.

Willnat, Lars, and Annette Aw. *Political Communication in Asia (Routledge Communication Series).* 1st ed., Routledge, New York, US, 2009.

Wimberly, Cory. *How Propaganda Became Public Relations (Routledge Studies in Contemporary Philosophy).* 1st ed., Routledge, New York, US, 2020.

Winchester, Simon. *The Map That Changed the World: William Smith and the Birth of Modern Geology.* Penguin Books, London, UK, 2002.

Winchester, Simon. *Outposts: Journeys to the Surviving Relics of the British Empire.* Revised ed., Penguin Books, London, UK, 2003.

Winchester, Simon. *The River at the Center of the World: A Journey up the Yangtze, and Back in Chinese Time.* Revised 2nd ed., Picador, New York, US, 2004.

Winchester, Simon. *Pacific: The Ocean of the Future.*, William Collins, London, UK, 2015.

WIPO. *Global Innovation Index 2021 and 2022: Tracking Innovation Through the COVID-19 Crisis.* World Intellectual Property Organization, Geneva, CH, 2021, 2022.

Wolf, Guido. *Der Business Discourse: Effizienz Und Effektivität Der Unternehmensinternen Kommunikation.* German ed., Gabler Verlag, Wiesbaden, DE, 2010.

Wolf, Guido. *VUCA. SINN. AGILITÄT: Navigationshilfen Zur Lösung Alltäglicher Und Nicht Alltäglicher Aufgaben in Unternehmen – 3 (German Edition).* Cleevesmedia, Meckenheim, DE, 2018.

Index

Abdullah, Saifuddin 85
Abu Dhabi 8, 9, 45, 54
Adfactors PR 112
Advance scenario planning 32, 109, 118, 125, 128, 131
Advertising Value Equivalent (AVE) 106, 113
Africa 8, 15, 46–47, 55, 63, 96, 117
African Continental Free Trade Area (AfCFTA) 12
AI & Big Data 92, 103, 106, 112, 124
AI chatbots 75, 109, 111, 136
AliPay 104
al-Iraqiya List 39
Allawi, Ayad 38–39
Amarna letters (of Egypt) 79
"American Century" 5
Amman 39
Amnesty International 62
AnaVizio 106, 107, 113
Angkor Wat 84, 85
Anholt, Simon 45, 73, 85, 87
Anholt-Ipsos Nation Brands Index 13, 84, 85
Anwar Gargash Diplomatic Academy 95
APCO Worldwide 41, 60, 113
"app economy" 103
Apple 59, 103
Arabian Business 82
Arabic NLP 113
Arabic text analytics 113
Arthur Andersen (AA) 120
Artificial Intelligence (AI) 52, 103–112; Asian investment in 6, 11, 95; connectivity via 92; economic and societal impact of 60, 68; human communications and 105, 108, 111, 114; technologies powered by 60
ASEAN 6–8, 16, 86

Asia 26, 46–49, 67, 75, 104, 123, 133; emerging markets in 11, 12, 53, 54, 103; rapid modernization of 6, 56, 128; rise of 1, 10–12, 15, 16, 40, 55, 140
Asian American Journalists Association (AAJA) 95
Asian Century 4, 11, 48, 80, 130; arrival of 5, 10, 140; core idea of 11, 13, 15–17, 115; dynamic operating environment of 128, 129; progression of communications in 28, 102, 113, 132, 138; Public Diplomacy in 73; risk mitigation in 124
Asian Development Bank (ADB) 7
Asian discourse power 15, 16
Asian diversity 10, 40
Asianization: of Asia 117; of Communications 1, 116, 126
Asian markets, trajectory of 7
Asian Movies, and movies set in Asia 84
Asian pop culture 83, 84
Asian talent 97
Asian technocracies 1, 10, 140
Asian Tigers 119
Asia-Pacific Communication Monitor (APCM) 37
Asia Society 51
Aspiration to Inspiration, From 44, 45, 47, 48, 55, 56
Association of Southeast Asian Nations *see* ASEAN
Augmented Reality (AR) 112
Austin, Lloyd 77
Australia 15, 51, 81

Baghdad 39
Bain & Company 38
Balakrishnan, Vivian 104
Bangkok 84

146 *Index*

Bank Negara (Malaysia's Central Bank) 7, 122
Barcelona Principles 106
Basilinna 41
Because-motives 23, 27
Beijing 15, 55; "ethnic unity" and Chinese culture as viewed by 11; non-Chinese residents in Shanghai and 95, 96; Washington and 73, 74, 78
Bell-Pottinger 37
Belt and Road Initiative (BRI): Lessons from 46–48; shifting opinions about 47; strategy behind 50–52; path forward for 48–52
Berkshire Hathaway 59
Berlin Brandenburg Airport (BER) 7
Bernays, Edward 69
Bernstein, William J. 72
Bhutan 85
Biden, Joe 7, 12, 77, 86, 96
big tech 59, 97, 112
Bjola, Corneliu 75, 76
Blackberry 103
Blackbird.ai 108
Blackrock 1
Blinken, Anthony 77
blockchain 8, 103, 112, 113
Bollywood 84
Borrell, Josep 48, 80
Boston Consulting Group (BCG) 38
Brand Finance Global Soft Power Summit 14, 82, 84, 85
brand stewardship 124
Brennan, John 42
Brexit 12, 69, 111
Britain 5; *see also* United Kingdom (UK)
British Council 85
Brown, Gordon 13
Brunswick Group 41
Bühler, Karl 22
Bureau International des Expositions (BIE) 9

Calcutta 112
Cambodia 84–86
Cambridge Analytica (CA) 62
Campaign In-Housing Summit 36
Canada 14, 15, 61
"Can-do" spirit 118
Cascade (strategy execution platform) 111
Central Asia 6
Chartered Institute of Public Relations (CIPR) 106
ChatGPT 111

China, People's Republic of (PRC): Africa's trade with 15; AI, tech, apps and games in 75, 103, 104; EU and 47, 48; India's stance on 78; Middle East North Africa relations with 5; Olympics in 48, 49; rise of 6, 12, 17, 50; Taiwan relations with 15, 77; 20th National Congress of CPC 47; universal values as seen by 10; US and 4, 11, 15, 41, 48, 73, 74, 77; Western relations with 13, 51
China Media Project 76
China's "Community of Shared Future" 10, 48
China's discourse power 50
China's perception 11, 14, 15, 46–49
China's wolf warrior diplomacy 77
China's Zero Covid Strategy 50
Choong, William 16
Chu, Jon M. 84
Cisco Webex 97
climate change 4, 10, 28, 49, 82, 93
climate talks 77
cloud computing 112
CNN 9, 41, 68, 80; *Connect the World by* 9; *GPS (The Global Public Square)* by 80
co-creation across civilizations 50
Common Economic Partnership Agreements (CEPAs) 54, 55
Communication: cross-cultural 17, 20, 25, 30; global crisis of 60; openness and transparency in 51, 77; politics and 72, 77; truthfulness and ethics in 28, 29; understanding Asia's rise through better 15; verbal, paraverbal and nonverbal 20, 33, 76, 94; vs. communications and/or PR 26–28, 35; *see also* communication theory
Communication theory 2, 18, 20–29, 79; Eastern/Asian 24, 25; Western 20, 22–24
Communications: competitive edge in 95; crisis preparedness in 32, 34, 40, 109, 118; future of 1, 2, 5, 22, 138, 140, 141; future-readiness in 37, 44, 55, 125, 131, 134, 137, 138; innovation-led 3, 53, 56, 113, 129; pursuit of broader authority in 1, 122, 132, 133; real engagement in 17, 25, 39; results-driven 10; Speed and Strategy in 116, 117–119, 122–126, 128, 138; talent management in 91; technocracy or meritocracy in 103, 111–113, 123; *see also* strategic communications

Comprehensive and Progressive Agreement for Trans-Pacific Partnership (CPTPP) 12
Conex Institute 21, 44
Confucius (Kong Fuzi) 78
Connectivity 1, 4, 15, 17, 29, 49, 56, 104, 133; in digital and AI 48, 92, 105, 112; people-to-people 25, 110, 123; Public Diplomacy and 74; soft power and 87; talent and 96, 98
content marketing 34; *see also* marketing
COP26 climate summit 131
Corporate Social Responsibility (CSR) 38
Correctiv 67
Covid-19 2, 4, 6, 7, 9, 14, 54, 92, 101; Diplomacy during 75; efficient handling of 114; global and Asian trade shifts during 12; nations brand, reputations and global soft power hit by 13, 14; role of apps during 104; talent strategies affected by 93, 94; trade and industry disruptions caused by 140
Cowen, Glenn 73
Cox, Chris 63
C-Pop 83
Crazy Rich Asians (motion picture) 84
Crisis response 32, 120, 137
Critical Thinking 66
The Cube on Euronews 68
Cultural Diplomacy 84–88
cultural diversity 82, 95
Cultural Soft Power 82, 84
Cybersecurity 76, 108, 112

The Daily Beast 68
Danaharta 120–124
Data analytics 38, 106–108, 111, 112, 124, 133, 135
Davis, Julia 68
Davos 63, 111; Digital PR Awards in 105
"debt-trap diplomacy" 47
Defterios, John 31
DEI (diversity, equity and inclusion) 95
Delhi 51, 140
"Delivering Happiness", spike of 33
Della Volpe, John 92
Deloitte Global 2022 Gen Z and Millennial Survey 92
democratic technocracies 15, 56, 114
DeNeefe, Janet 86
Deng Xiaoping 51
Denial and Deflection 64
Diamandis, Peter 130
digital communications 60
digital marketing 34, 105; *see also* marketing

Digital sixth sense 2, 114
Digitization 104, 108
Diplomacy 72, 73, 76; communications in 75, 76, 78, 79; fragmentation of 72, 74; social media in 74–78, 87
discourse power 29, 65, 69, 77, 78, 81, 82; by Asia 9, 15, 16, 50; by West 55
disinformation 57, 59, 60–67, 104, 124; learning to live with mis- and 29, 41
Dispatch Fact Check 67
Djalal, Dino Patti 16
Doublethink Lab 67
Dubai 52, 55, 56, 95, 113, 117, 118; future-readiness of 8; hosting Expo 2020 8, 9, 14, 45; soft power rise during 14
Dubai Spirit 116, 118, 140
Dyer, Wayne D. 30

East Coast Rail Link (ECRL) 47
East-West relations 40
Economic decoupling 4, 50, 140
Edelman 41
Egypt 5, 6, 86
Einstein, Albert 20
Eisenhower, Dwight D. 7
emerging markets 4, 5, 8, 41; AI rollout in 103, 114; aspiration and communications in 116; rise of 17
environmental sustainability 47
ESG, Environmental, Social, and (Corporate) Governance 37
Europe 10, 12, 55, 81, 103; fighting disinformation in 67; strategic competition managed by 51; trajectory of Asian markets vs 7
Europe and China: Comprehensive Agreement on Investment (CAI) by 48
"European Century" 5
European Commission for Values and Transparency 108
European Parliament's "Special Committee on Foreign Interference in all Democratic Processes in the EU, including Disinformation" (INGE 2) 67
EU Chamber of Commerce in China 48, 49
EUvsDisinfo 67
Expo 2020: trade deals at 9; legacy program of 9; *see also* Dubai

Facebook 59, 62, 63, 74
fake news 37, 38, 59, 60–62, 66, 68
Fatima Bint Mohamed Bin Zayed Initiative 95

Fink, Larry 1
Firewood 105
Flooding the Zone 65
Fombrun, Charles 122, 123
Forcefield Analysis 135
Foreign Affairs 78
Foreign Policy 78
Foreign Policy Institute (FPI) 4
Foreign policy, strategies that shape 72, 76, 78, 81, 86, 96, 108, 131
Foss, Karen A. 24
four-day workweek 94
Fourth Industrial Revolution (4IR) 103, 104, 110, 111, 113
Frankfurt School 24
Frankopan, Peter 5
Friedman, Milton 38
Fuchs, Peter 23
Fudan University 123
Future-Readiness, The Art of Stage-Managing 2, 52, 53

Gabriel, Peter 82–83
Gallaudet University 141
Gallup 14, 15
Gandhi, Mahatma 64
Gaslighting 65
GCC (Gulf Cooperation Council) states 6; *see also* specific countries
Generative AI 60
Gen Z (aka Zoomers) 38, 74, 91, 92, 98, 100
geoeconomics 2
Geopolitics 1, 16, 17, 47, 55, 72, 86
George Washington University 66
Germany 7, 14, 61
Ghneim, Fares 106, 107, 113
Ghobash, Omar 45
Global Communication and Disinformation Crisis 59–61
global energy crisis 4
Global Financial Centres Index (GFCI 32) 6
"Global Gateway" initiative 47
Global Innovation Index by WIPO 14, 54
global PR market value 91
Global South 11, 47
Global Talent Trends 91, 94
global talent war 91
"Global Village" 2
Globalization 2, 4, 17, 93
Good Country Index 45, 73
Google 26, 59, 97, 103, 141
Google Play 103, 141
Goyal, Piyush Vedprakash 116

Great Information War 61
"Great Resignation" 93
The Great Translation Movement 68
"great unifier" 45, 47, 61, 116
Greco-Roman culture 5
"Greenwashing" 37
G7 48, 77; Partnership for Global Infrastructure and Investment (PGII) by 48
G20 12, 77
"guanxi" (Chinese for personal and professional contacts and relationships) 126
Gunaratne, Shelton A. 24
"gung-ho" (Chinese for eager or enthusiastic) 132
Guterres, António 28

Habermas, Jürgen 23, 24; Four speech act classes; Communicativa, Constativa, Representativa and Regulativa, by 28
"Hallyu" (Korean Wave) 83, 95
"Happiness Officer", talking to 110
Harris Online 122
Hashim, Eldeen Husaini Mohd 86
Haugen, Frances 63
having agency 41, 141
Heritage Foundation: Index of Economic Freedom by 14
Hill+Knowlton Strategies 112
Hillman, Jonathan 47
History, lessons from 2, 5–7
Hive 59
Hollywood 84
Hong Jin-Wook 86
Hong Kong 6, 119
Hubbard School of Journalism and Mass Communication 123
Hu Jintao 48
human capital 88, 91–102
Human interaction 1, 2, 20, 22–24, 108; lies and "white lies" in 28; pragmatics as a way to broaden 25; real life conditions of 24
human rights 37, 48
Hussein, Saddam 38
Husserl, Edmund 23
Hymes, Dell 20
Hyundai 83

IATA 6
IBM 97, 103
Ibrahim, Anwar 11, 120, 121
Ignatius, David 117
IMD-SUTD Smart City Index (SCI) 54

India 6, 7, 11, 81; cross-border tensions between China and 78; outperforming economy of 6; pop culture by and film industry of 84; UAE and 54
Indian Institute of Management (IIM) 112
Indigenous cultures 82
"individual world theory" 20
Indonesia 7, 11, 16, 26, 86
Indo Pacific 15, 77, 140
Industrial revolution 5, 103
influencer marketing 34; *see also* marketing
"informal communication" 44
Infrastructure 7, 8, 11, 46, 49, 50, 55, 56, 133; global spending and investment in 6, 9, 15; China's investment in 46–48
innovation-led national development 2, 5, 8, 53–55, 103, 114
In-order-to motives 23, 27, 134
Instagram 59, 74
Institute for Communication Research and Phonetics (IKP) Bonn 20, 21
Institute of International Relations at Tsinghua University 87
Institute of Strategic and International Studies (ISIS) 16
Intelligent Virtual Assistants (IVA) 109
Interactive Voice Response (IVR) systems 109
intercultural dialogue 26, 27, 39
internal communication 44
International Herald Tribune 117
International Olympic Committee (IOC) 49
Internet of Things (IoT) 54, 111, 112
Interpret China 68
Intra-Asian communication 15, 16
iOS App Store 103, 111
Iraq 38, 39
Iraqi National Movement (INM) 39
ISEAS–Yusof Ishak Institute, Singapore 16
Israel 54

Jakarta 26, 83
Jakobson, Roman 22
Japan 6, 14, 15, 61, 73, 81, 83–85, 95
Jobs, Steve 103
Johns Hopkins University School of Advanced International Studies (SAIS) 4
Johnson, Lyndon B. 7
Jordan 39
Jourová, Věra 108
The Joy Luck Club (motion picture) 84
J.P. Morgan 120
J-Pop 83
Juchem, Johann G. 20, 22

Kafka, Franz 21
Kalimantan 26
Kant, Immanuel 63
Kaplan, Robert 16, 81
"Keluarga Malaysia" (Malaysian Family) 11
Keys Moran, Daniel 105
Khanna, Parag 9, 15, 16, 50, 56, 96
Kissinger, Henry 73
Kleist, Heinrich von 21, 22, 63
Korean Culture and Information Service (Kocis) 83
K-Pop 83, 85, 87
Kritenbrink, Daniel 86

Lahad, Imad 60, 113
Lamy, Pascal 41
Laos 85
Lao Tzu (Laozi) 73
Lara Croft: Tomb Raider (motion picture) 84
Larres, Klaus 73, 74
The Last Emperor (motion picture) 83
Law, Nathan 92, 132
Leadership KPI 101
"Lebenswelt" (Life-world) 23, 24
Lee Kuan Yew 55
"License to operate" 1, 33, 70
Lincoln Project 67
linguistics 20, 25
LinkedIn 59, 98
Littlejohn, Stephen W. 24
Live Transcribe 141
Luhmann, Niklas 13, 23, 29, 136

Mahathir, Mohamad 47
Mahbubani, Kishore 10
Maktoum, Sheikh Mohammed Bin Rashid Al 52
Malaysia 7, 11, 16, 47, 85, 86, 119–122
Maliki, Nouri Al 39
Malin, Carrington 60, 105, 108–110
The Man with the Golden Gun (motion picture) 84
Marketing 34–36, 38, 95, 101, 133, 138
Marx, Karl 24
Mastodon 59
McFaul, Michael 72
McKinsey & Company 38
McQueen, Steve 32
Media Literacy 66
MediaMonks 105
Mercer 93
MERICS think tank 48
Mesopotamia 5
Messaging architecture & message house 135

Meta 59, 63
metaverse 63, 81
Meyer, Scott 122, 123
Michigan State University 68
Microsoft 59, 93
Microsoft Teams 97
Middle East 14, 27, 34, 63, 101, 117, 119; accelerated rollout of AI in 103; Can-do spirit in 129; China's BRI in 46; construction boom in 6; data analysis in 107; prioritizing speedy delivery in 8; use of AI for PR in 113, 114; *see also* specific countries
Middle East North Africa (MENA) 5, 14, 113
Mighty Hive 105
Miliband, David 80
Millennials (aka Generation Y) 74, 91, 92, 96–99, 102, 131
misinformation 29, 41, 60, 61, 67–69, 79, 101
Miyamoto, Musashi 2
Mobile apps 92, 103
mobile phones 96, 97, 103
Mobius, Mark 1
Modi, Narendra 140
Mohan, C. Raja 51
Molavi, Afshin 4, 17, 55, 56, 116
Moon Jae-in 87
Moscow 77
MSNBC 68
multicultural communications 30
Multiculturalism and Diversity 94, 97
Multilateralism 11, 46, 49, 51
multipolarity 1, 12, 13, 17
Muratov, Dmitry Andreyevich 37
Musk, Elon 59
mutual understanding 2, 20, 24, 25, 29, 34, 40, 41, 44, 128
Myanmar, Rohingya in 63

National Asset Management Company (AMC), Malaysia 120, 121
National Development and Reform Commission (NDRC), China 51
nation branding 8, 87, 130
Netflix 75, 83, 109
Newman, Paul 32, 41, 124, 138
NewsGuard 68
New Silk Road Monitor 17
New Silk Roads 49
New York Times 4, 62, 117
Nick, Andreas 41
Nisbett, Richard E. 40
Nixon, Richard 73, 74

Nobel Peace Prize 37; "no limits partnership" between China and Russia 13, 47
Non-Fungible Tokens (NFTs) 81
North Atlantic Treaty Organization (NATO) 13
North Star (Polaris) 60, 61, 64
Norway 82
Nusantara 26
Nye, Joseph 81, 82, 88

Obama, Barack 60
Ohio State University 66
Olama, Omar Sultan Al 95
OpenAI 111
Organon Model 22
Orwell, George 57, 59
Oxford Dictionaries 69, 83

Pacific nations 8, 12
Pakistan 11, 47
Papua New Guinea 11, 85
Parasite (motion picture) 83
Paris Peace Forum 41, 98
Paulson Institute 41
Pelosi, Nancy 77
Pennycook, Gordon 61, 63
people-to-people communication 25–27, 65, 108
Persuasive power 5, 30, 45, 57, 97
Pew Research Center 14–15
Philippines 26, 85
Phillips, Robert 33, 39, 91, 104
Picasso, Pablo 44
PictureTel 97
Piromya, Kasit 16
Poland 85
Polaris (North Star) 60, 61, 64
Post News 59
Postman, Andrew and Neil 59
"post-truth" 69
PR 26, 35, 69, 79, 91, 98; challenges faced by 34; client scrutiny over value of 36; future of 40, 41, 111, 113, 114, 122, 138; old-school (classic) model of 34, 37, 70, 104, 118, 119; public perception of 28; *see also* Public Relations
PricewaterhouseCoopers (PwC) 55
Project Syndicate 88
Propaganda 29, 57, 59, 79; China's department of 3; conspiracy theories and 80; detecting and combating 2, 51, 61, 63, 66–69, 70, 86–87; hard and soft 64, 69; tactics of 64–66

Propel 108
Prophet, strategic brand and marketing consultancy 124
Protection from Online Falsehoods and Manipulation Act (POFMA), Singapore 67
PRovoke18 40
Public Diplomacy (PD) 1, 2, 10, 45, 72, 78, 104, 129; ambassadors using pop culture in 86; being a subset of communications 78; expansion of 80; foreign policy vs. 86; future of 76, 138; main objectives of 29; nation and place branding's ties to 79; openness to other worldviews in 70; tech and social media's impact on 74–76
public health 6, 10, 49, 82
Public Relations 27, 101, 105, 106, 108, 118, 120; industry problems in 28; purpose in 33; RM as breakthrough moment for 122; *see also* PR
Public Relations and Communications Association's (PRCA) 37
Purpose and Shared Values 38, 39, 42, 44, 69, 79, 93, 130, 134–138
Putin, Vladimir 24, 68

Qatar 9, 11
Quadrilateral Security Dialogue (Quad) 81
quantum computing 112

Rand, David 62, 63
Rastam, Mohd Isa 16
Regional Comprehensive Economic Partnership (RCEP) 12
Reid, Joy 68
The ReidOut 68
Reliable Sources 68
Reporters Without Borders (RSF) 67
Reputation 13–15, 36, 85, 106, 118, 124, 125, 134, 137; communications' 27; image vs 72; safeguarding an organization's 35
Reputation Institute 122
Reputation Management (RM) 38, 60, 114, 122–125
Reputation Quotient (RQ) 122
Reputation research and analysis 79, 122
Ressa, Maria 37
The Revenant (motion picture) 83
Risilia, Abdul-Rahman 92, 100, 101
risk management 124, 125
robotic innovation 54
Roosevelt, Franklin D. 7
Rudd, Kevin 51

Russia 51; China and 47; Ukraine's invasion by 4, 68; propaganda spread by 67, 68
Russian Media Monitor 68

Sabri Yakoob, Ismail 11
Sakamoto, Ryuichi 83
Samsung 83, 87
Sao Paulo 55
SARS 93
Saudi Arabia 6, 75
Saudi Aramco 59
Savvy Gaming Group 75
Sbeih, Mamoon 113
Schmitz, Heinrich Walter 20, 22
Schütz, Alfred 23, 27, 134
Schwab, Klaus 103, 108
Semantics 10, 20, 23, 25, 80
Semiocast 26
sender–receiver model 22, 25, 119
S4 Capital 40, 105
Shanghai 55, 96, 117, 118, 123
Shanghai Pudong Development Council 123
Sharjah 45
Shenzhen 116, 118
Shenzhen Speed 116, 118, 140
Simmel, Georg 23
SimpleTexting 111
SIF Public Diplomacy in Asia 2021 conference 104
Singapore 6, 11, 66, 67, 119; public diplomacy by 76; soft power by 82; UAE and 54–56
Singapore International Foundation (SIF) 104
S Jaishankar 78
Skype 97
Smyth, William H. 112
Social media 17, 21–28, 36, 96, 99; big tech and 61, 105–107, 110, 113; increasing influence of 28, 60–68, 104, 111; most popular platforms of 59
social sciences 20, 41
Sociology 20
Soft power 1, 13, 14, 81–83, 96; concept of cultural 84–87; Leveraging the Strong Side of 72
Solomon Islands 85
Somalia 76
Sony 75
Sorrell, Martin 40, 105
South China Sea 47
South East Asia 11, 16, 54, 86, 117; Asian financial crisis hitting 119; China's BRI in 46; gaming expansion across 75; infrastructure projects in 47

South Korea 6, 15, 83–87, 95, 119, 120
Special Economic Zones (SEZ) 5
speed and strategy 116–118, 122–126, 128, 138
Squid Game 83
Sri Lanka 24, 47
stakeholder engagement 2, 27, 35, 105, 135–136
Stanford University 60
StarLab Oasis 54
Stelter, Brian 68
Stern School of Business of New York University 122
storytellers 1, 3, 35–36, 38, 70, 132, 141
storytelling 16, 53, 75, 131, 137, 141; progression from 35–38
strategic communications 16, 20, 28, 30, 38, 79, 88, 135; investing in 36, 40–41, 106; PR's progression toward 35, 104, 114, 118, 129; public diplomacy and 88
Sun Tzu 131
Susarla, Anjana 68
Sweden 120
SWOT Analysis (Strengths, Weaknesses, Opportunities and Threats) 135

Tactical communications 118
Taiwan 6, 119; relations between China and 15, 77
talent management 2, 91
Talent Strategies, Winning with New 91
Tan Kiat How 67
Technocracy 114, 124
"techplomacy" 74
Telegram 76
Telum Media 35, 99, 106
Tencent 59, 75–76
Thailand 16, 84–85, 119
TheoremOne 105
Think tanks 10, 17, 30, 50, 78; communicators and 69; impact of research and analysis by 79, 98
Thought and speech 21, 63
3D printing 54, 112
Thunberg, Greta 92, 131
TikTok 59, 63, 75, 104
TIME Magazine 84, 96
Timor-Leste 85
Tollywood 84
The Towering Inferno (motion picture) 32, 42
T-Pop 83
Train to Busan (motion picture) 83
Transparency International: Corruption Perceptions Index (CPI) by 14

Trucial States 117
Trump, Donald 7, 12–13, 28, 59, 69
Trumpism 37
Trust: Co-Creation, Self-Restraint and Mutual 50–52, 78; communication, PR, and 1, 13, 23, 28, 30, 33, 35, 38–40, 76; discourse power and 69, 78; earning 53, 93, 133, 108; engaging as a means to build 13, 17, 53, 94, 122; in international relations 29, 72; protecting reputations based on 34, 37, 73
Truth Social 62
"twiplomacy" 74
Twitter 22, 59, 62, 67
Twitter parody accounts 68
2005 United Nations World Summit 46, 54
2008 financial crisis 5

Ubud Writers & Readers Festival (UWRF) 86
Ukraine 4, 16, 24, 48, 52, 77
UNC in Chapel Hill 73
Ungeheuer, Gerold 20, 29
United Arab Emirates (UAE) 6, 8, 9, 11, 14, 45, 82; close partnership between Singapore and 54, 56; future-readiness and leadership by 52, 53, 117; Great Narrative Meeting in 52; innovation in 54, 94, 95
United Kingdom (UK) 14, 15, 69, 82, 84, 85, 111
United Nations (UN) 28, 45–47, 54, 82, 87; Human Development Report released by 14
United Nations General Assembly (UNGA77) 28, 77
United States (US) 5, 7, 10, 12, 14, 15, 67, 68, 81, 82, 103, 120; China and 41, 48, 73, 74, 77, 78; trade war between China and 4, 11
University of Minnesota 123
University of Oxford 75
USC Center on Public Diplomacy (CPD) 10, 75

Vietnam 7, 15, 85, 86; US war with (1956-1973) 74, 81
voicebots 109
Vuelio 108

Wall Street Journal 122
Wang Wei 49
Wang Yi 77
Washington Post 80; Fact Checker by 66

"wasta" (Arabic for personal connections) 126
Watzlawick, Paul 33, 136; five axioms of communication by 22, 26
Weber, Max 23
Weber Shandwick (formerly Shandwick) 120–122
Webster, Michael 35, 99, 106
WeChat (Weixin) 59, 104
Wei Fenghe 77
Wēijī (Chinese for danger at a point of juncture) 124, 125
West: China and the 48, 50, 51; initial view of China's BRI by 46; popularity of Asian culture in 82–84; understanding of Asia by 10, 25; world history views in 5, 12
Western discourse power 55, 56
WestExec Advisors 42
WhatsApp 59, 76
Wisma Putra (Malaysia's Ministry of Foreign Affairs) 85
Wolf, Guido 21, 44
WOMAD 83
Wong, Brian 15
World Bank 6

World Economic Forum (WEF) 52, 93, 111
World Government Summit 45
World Intellectual Property Organization (WIPO) 14, 54
World Trade Organization (WTO) 12, 41
worldviews 1, 17, 20, 24, 29, 47, 69, 70, 80; Eastern vs. Western 25, 40
WPP 40, 105
Wuttke, Jörg 48

Xi Jinping 46, 47, 50, 77
Xinjiang, Uyghurs in 48

Yan Xuetong 87
Yoka Games 76
Yousafzai, Malala 92
YouTube 59
Yuan, Eric 97, 116

Zakaria, Fareed 80
Zelensky, Volodymr 77
Zhang Weiwei 50, 51
Zhuang Zedong 73
Zoom 97, 98, 101, 104, 116
Zuckerberg, Mark 63

For Product Safety Concerns and Information please contact our EU
representative GPSR@taylorandfrancis.com
Taylor & Francis Verlag GmbH, Kaufingerstraße 24, 80331 München, Germany

www.ingramcontent.com/pod-product-compliance
Lightning Source LLC
Chambersburg PA
CBHW061717300426

44115CB00014B/2724